The artist's guide to drawing people

**The Artist's Guide to Drawing People:
600 Reference Images for Body Movements,
Facial Expressions, and Hands**

Jean-Pierre Lamérand, Gilles Cours

Editor: Kelly Reed
Project manager: Lisa Brazieal
Marketing coordinator: Katie Walker
Copyeditor: Barbara Basbanes
Graphic design and layout: Cyril Terrier
Cover production: Aren Straiger

ISBN: 978-1-68198-911-2
1st Edition (1st printing, July 2022)
© 2022 Jean-Pierre Lamérand, Gilles Cours

Les Modèles du Dessinateur first published in French © Mango, 2021
www.mangoeditions.com

Rocky Nook Inc.
1010 B Street, Suite 350
San Rafael, CA 94901
USA

www.rockynook.com

Distributed in the UK and Europe by Publishers Group UK
Distributed in the U.S. and all other territories by Ingram Publisher Services

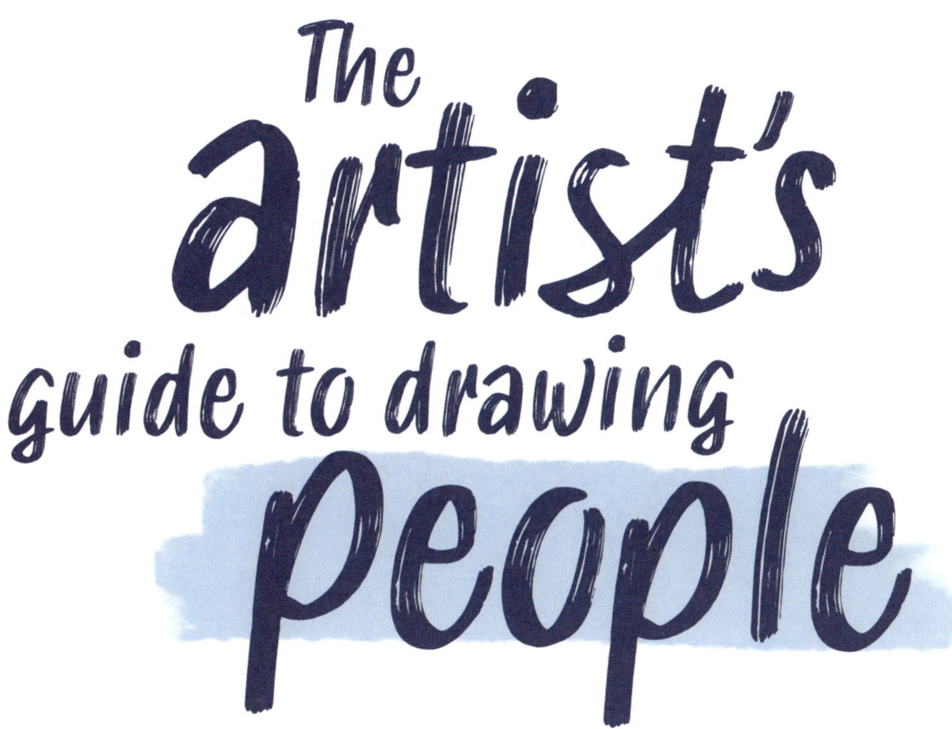

The artist's guide to drawing people

600

Reference Images for
Body Movements,
Facial Expressions, and Hands

Jean-Pierre Lamérand
and Gilles Cours

rockynook

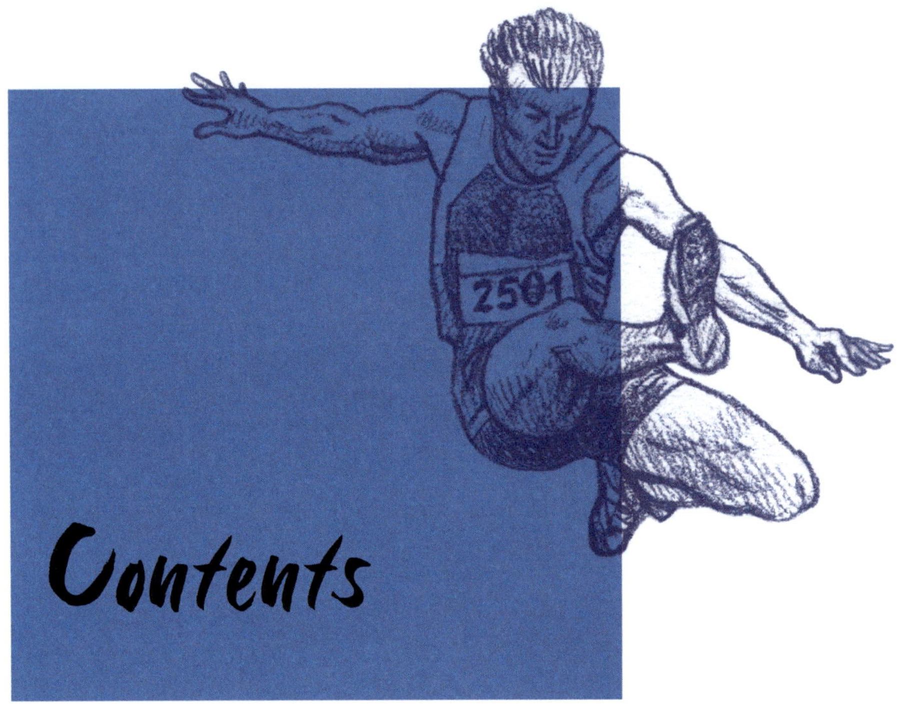

Contents

Hands

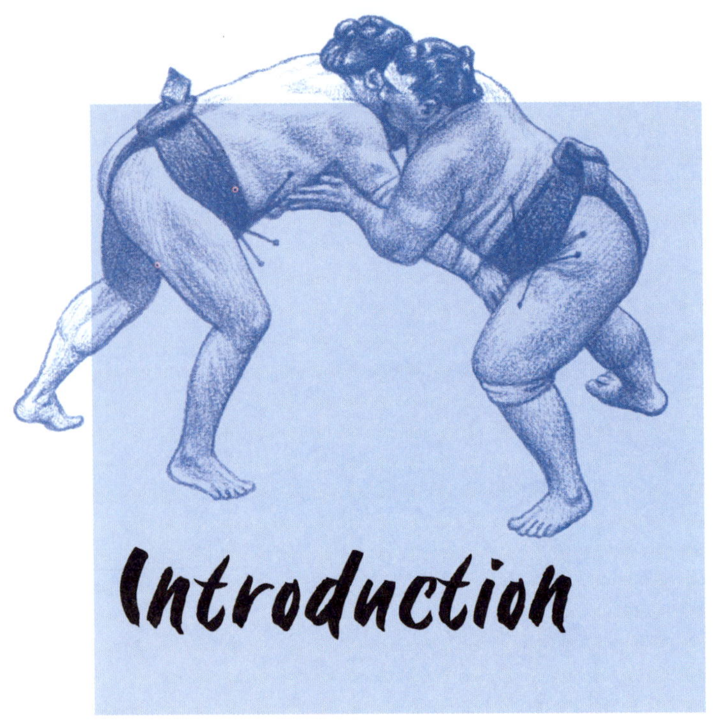

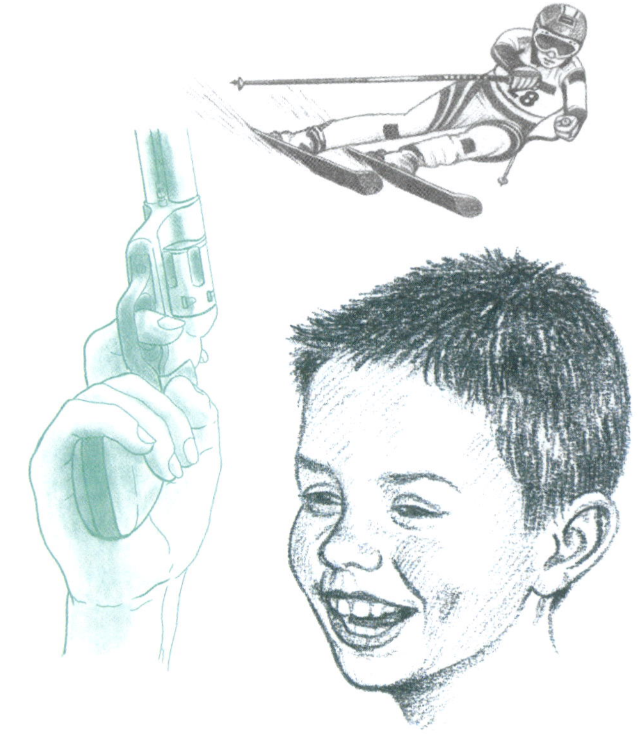

Introduction

This book is a collection of exceptional models for any artist who would like to be able to draw expressive, realistic characters. The book is divided into three chapters, progressing from the global to the more detailed.

The first chapter is devoted to movements of the body as a whole. We discuss "body language"—it's true that it can be read, and that people won't believe in your characters unless their movements are just right and make sense. To fully understand the workings of the human machine, we must start by looking "under the hood." Therefore, the first chapter starts with pages on anatomy, offers some rules on proportion, and then goes into detail about the limbs, which are the main actors in the body's movements—this includes the hand, which later has an entire chapter dedicated to it.

The pages on construction will teach you how to draw a skeleton, over which you can then place muscles, and then clothing. If bodies talk, then clothes are their makeup, and in their folds, they reveal the shape of the muscles that they cover, as well as the direction of movement, its speed, and its weight. After having considered all viewing angles using a superhero, you will approach a number of different aspects of movement in the form of a "databank" made up of suggestions and, on every page, sequences that break down the steps of an action. The process of creating these drawings will use a variety of techniques, using a 4B lead pencil, colored pencils, or a felt-tip pen.

The second chapter is dedicated to facial expressions. Knowing how to create a portrait means giving the right expression to the model, no matter what they are feeling. Painters and illustrators often find themselves in difficulty when they are trying to recreate the emotion that emanates from a face. This chapter explains how to give it the appropriately serious, sad, tired, or playful look without falling into caricature.

By studying this catalogue of portraits, you will see that people's faces can move very easily from the expression of one feeling to a very different one—from fatigue to sadness, for example—just through the simple emphasis of a mouth fold or by the crooking of an eyebrow into a frown. Studying the face muscles and a few rules about proportions will allow you to better understand how a face comes alive.

Looking at a comic strip or graphic novel, the reader sometimes must immediately

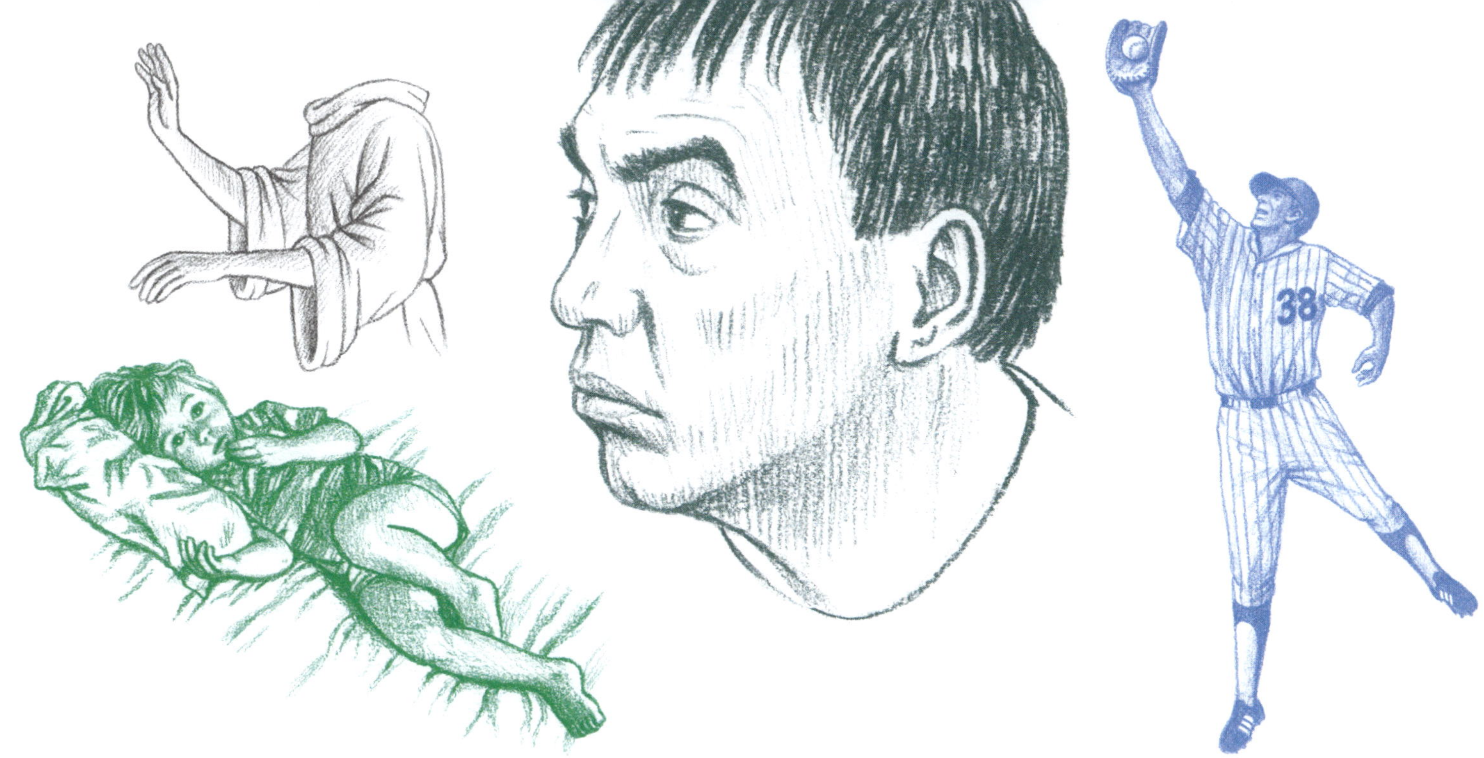

understand an image that has no words; so that the emotions can be clearly and unambiguously communicated, you, as the artist, will sometimes have to exaggerate the expression. We offer sequences that show the various steps in the evolution of a feeling. The other reason for these sequences is to spotlight the movements of a head in space and the way that the light creates its topography. In this chapter, you will find a large variety of human types so that you can find the character that you need.

The third chapter is devoted to the drawing of hands. The hand is a precise and powerful gripping body part, and without a doubt the most extraordinary tool available to the human being. it can detect the slightest roughness, the most diverse textures. The hand has many joints, which give it extreme mobility and make it very expressive. And it hardly ever stays in one position, adapting to every situation.

These characteristics make the hand the hardest part of the human body to draw. And yet, every artist must become familiar with it, because, like the face, it emerges from our clothing and is only occasionally hidden.

Thus, the hand is essential in any representation of the human body, and particularly in comic strips or graphic novels, where movements and positions must be varied and expressive.

Of course, the catalogue of models that makes up this book cannot be exhaustive. It is up to you to flesh it out. If you are imagining a movement and can't find any documentation for it, don't hesitate to act out the action yourself or to ask your friends and family to pose for you. And if you must choose one image to represent an action, choose the most expressive moment—in other words, the one that allows the viewer to guess what has just happened or what is about to take place. In the same way, to give a particular expression to a specific character, take up your pencil and sketch everyone around you!

But before you begin, remember this piece of advice, the only truly useful one when you are starting out: do not expect perfection from the first stroke of your pencil. It is better to make ten rough drawings in one hour than one single drawing, even if it is perfect, in ten hours. Expertise will come from constant repetition of the same theme, and the main thing is not to get discouraged: even if talent makes learning easier, it is, most importantly, hard work and discipline that will lead to success.

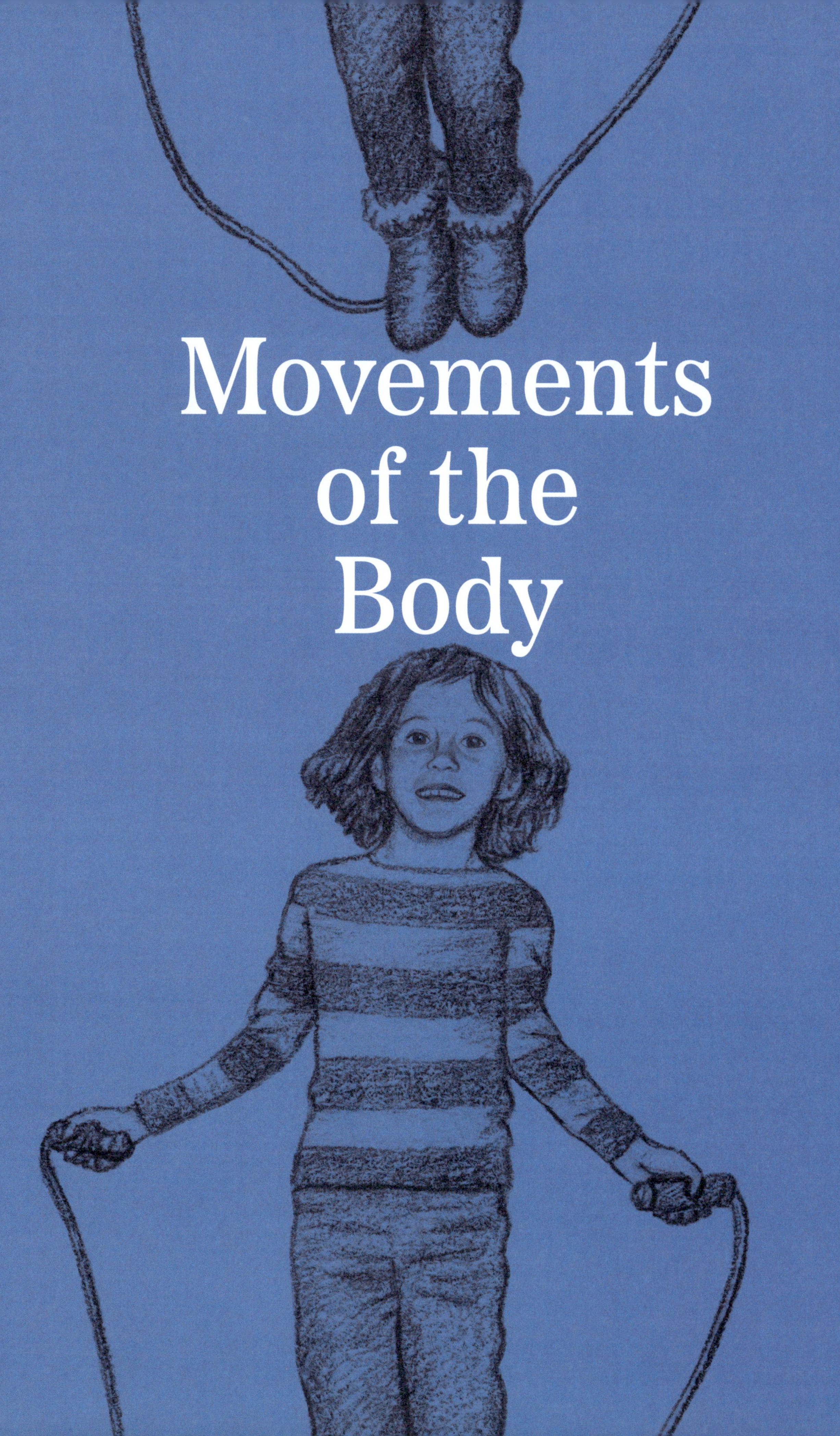

Movements of the Body

The Skeleton

To make your characters come alive, it is important to understand their bone structure. Here are some basic anatomical concepts to help you get started.

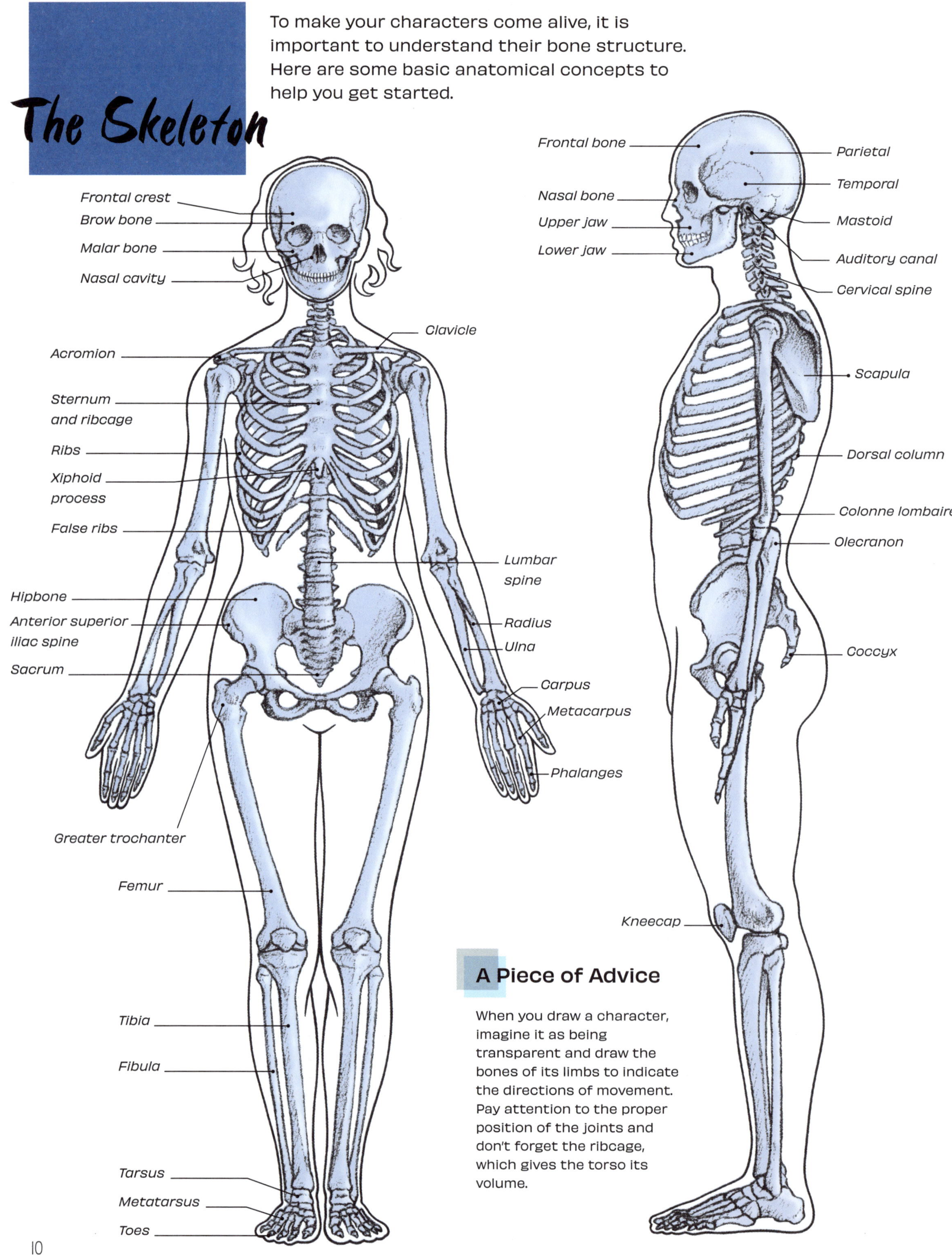

A Piece of Advice

When you draw a character, imagine it as being transparent and draw the bones of its limbs to indicate the directions of movement. Pay attention to the proper position of the joints and don't forget the ribcage, which gives the torso its volume.

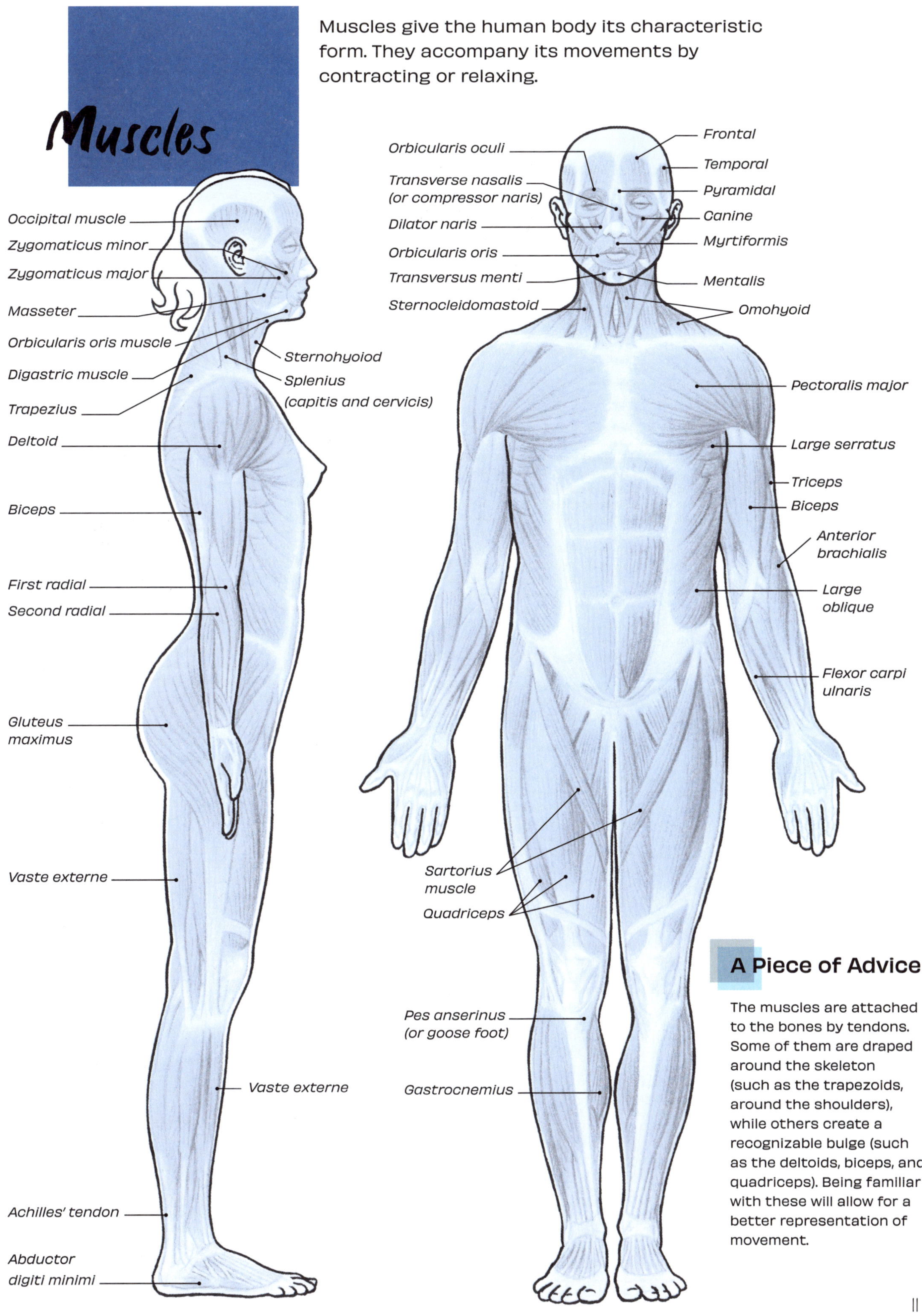

A Piece of Advice

The muscles are attached to the bones by tendons. Some of them are draped around the skeleton (such as the trapezoids, around the shoulders), while others create a recognizable bulge (such as the deltoids, biceps, and quadriceps). Being familiar with these will allow for a better representation of movement.

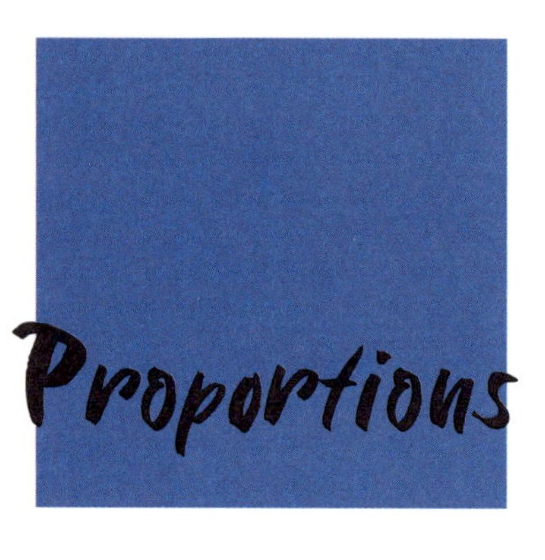

Proportions

The proportions of the human body vary from one individual to the next depending on body size and age. But there are some rules of thumb that will help you in your drawings.

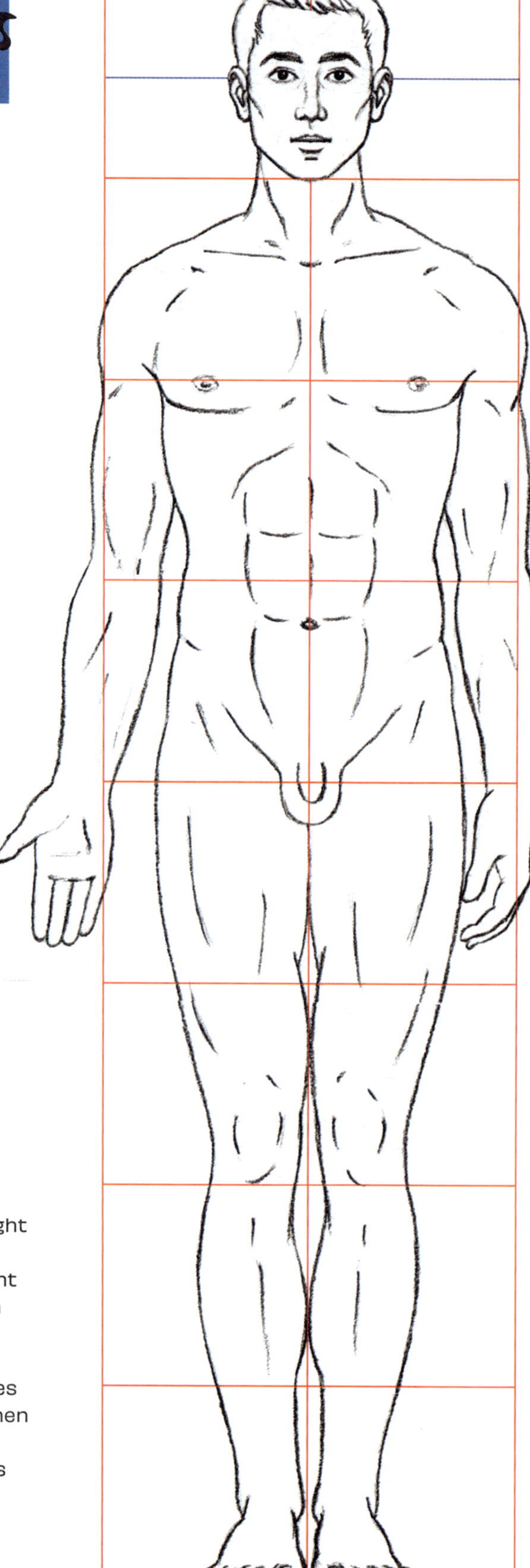

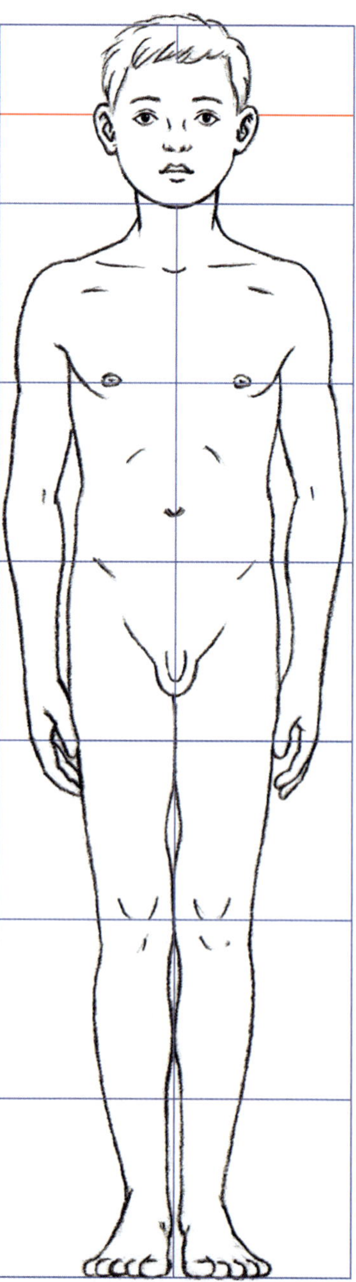

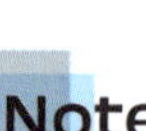

Note

You can figure that the height of a grown man is equal to about 7 or 8 times the height of his head (the man shown here is a tall man). A 10- or 12-year-old child's height is only about six or seven times the height of their head. When the arm is outstretched, the tip of the fingers comes almost to the mid-thigh.

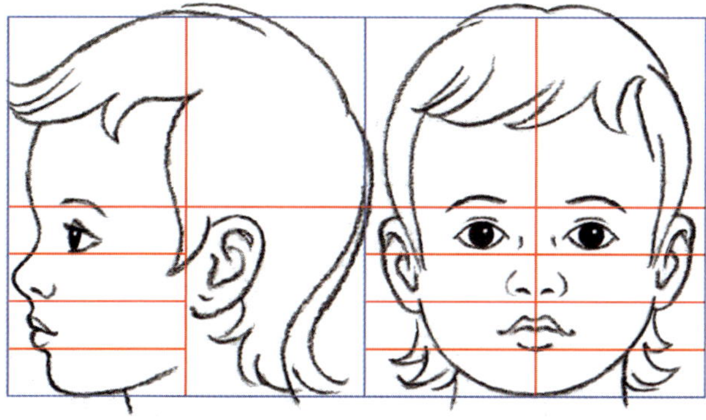

Note

The height of a grown woman is equal to about seven-and-a-half times the height of her head. You can count about four head heights from the top of the head to the crotch, and four head heights up from the bottoms of the feet to the hips. The height of a two-to-five-year-old child is only equal to about five times the height of its head.

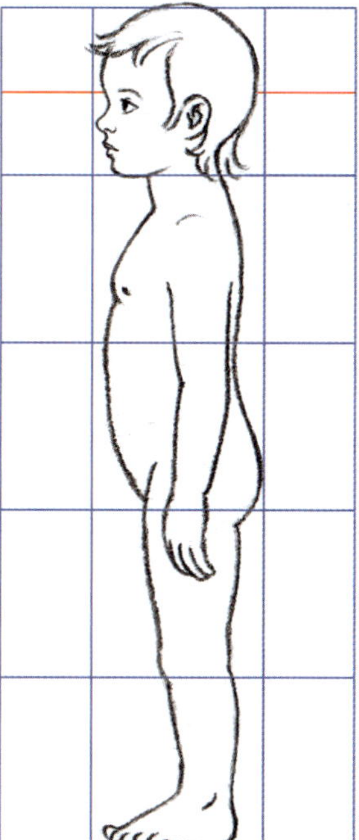

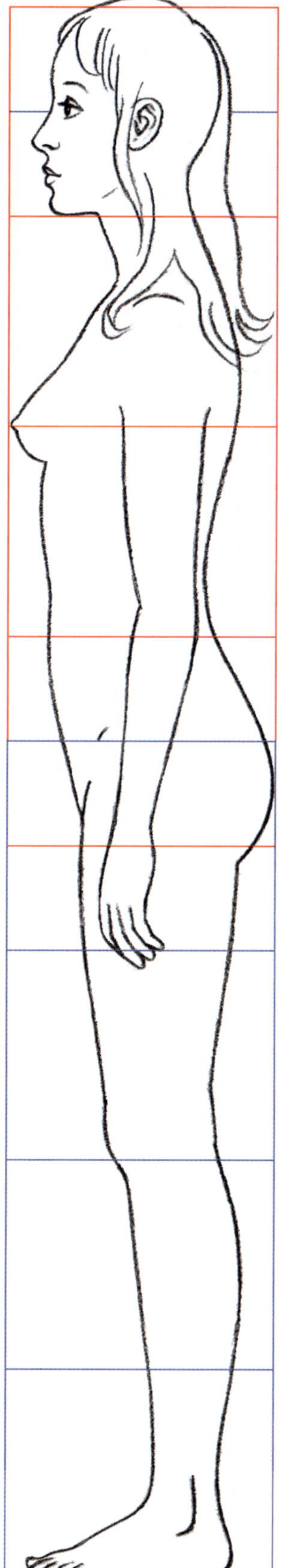

Constructing your character is a very important step: it helps lay the foundations for your drawing. It is a good idea to start with a very simplified drawing, a stick–figure person. This is a valuable aid that allows you to represent the human body in every position.

Construction

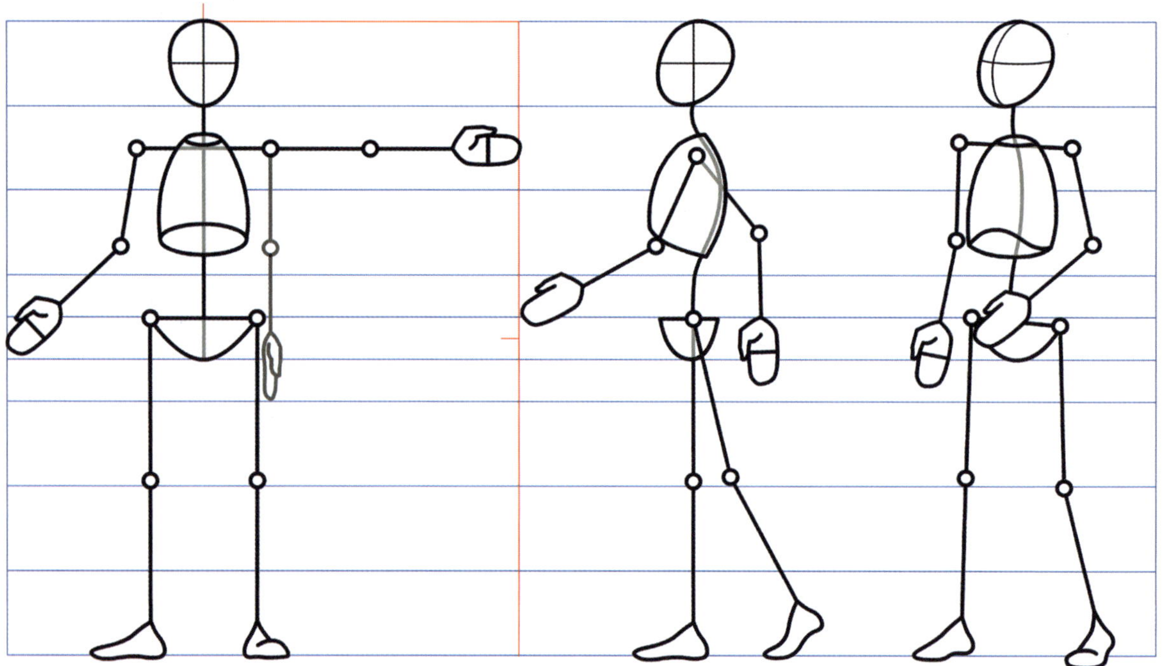

The total width of a human body with its arms outstretched is equal to the person's height.

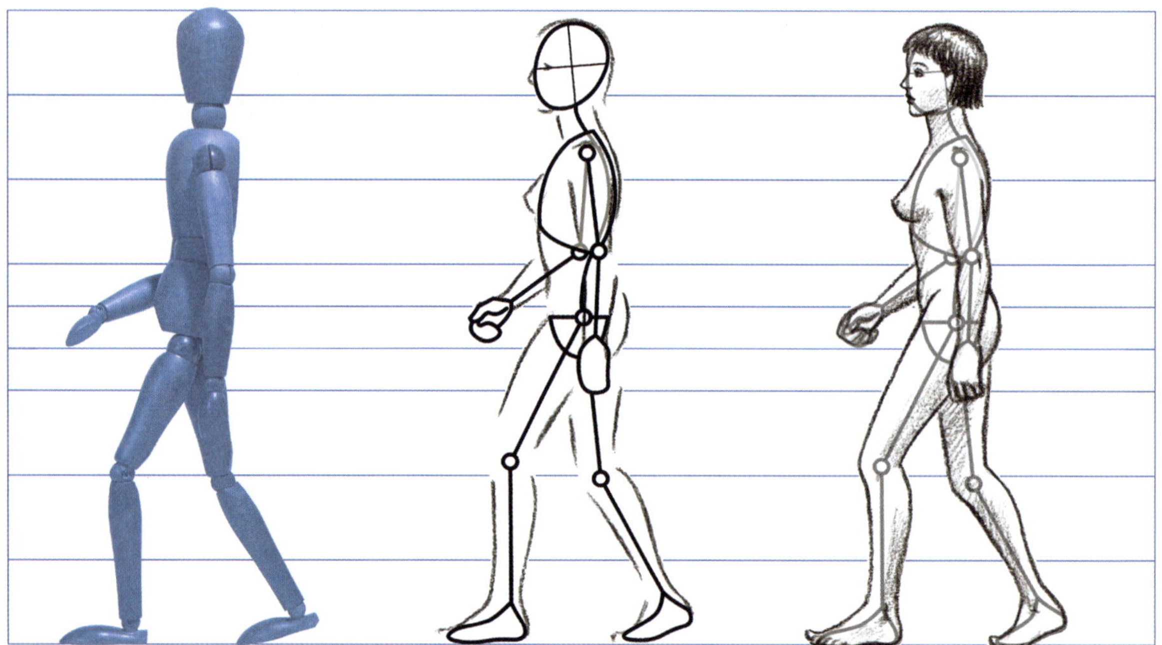

Sketch the most important muscles around the model. The muscles of the arms and legs are in the form of spindles: wide at the top and narrower at the bottom.

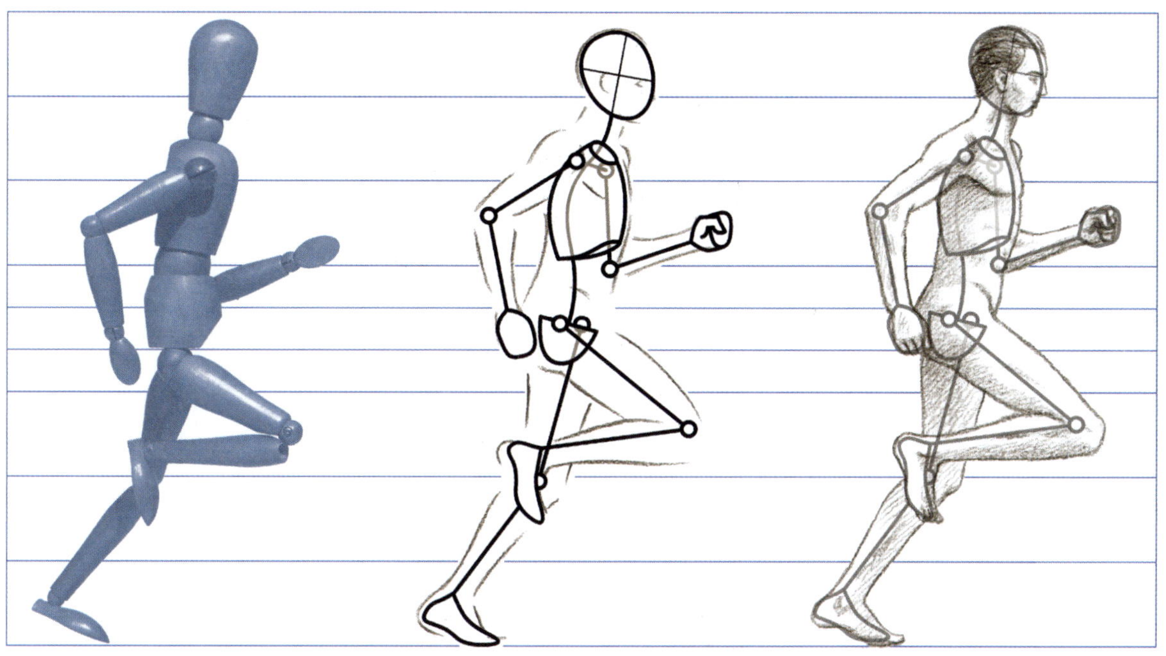

Draw a person running. In this position, the axis of the body is tilted forward.
Certain muscles stand out (shoulders, pectorals, thighs).

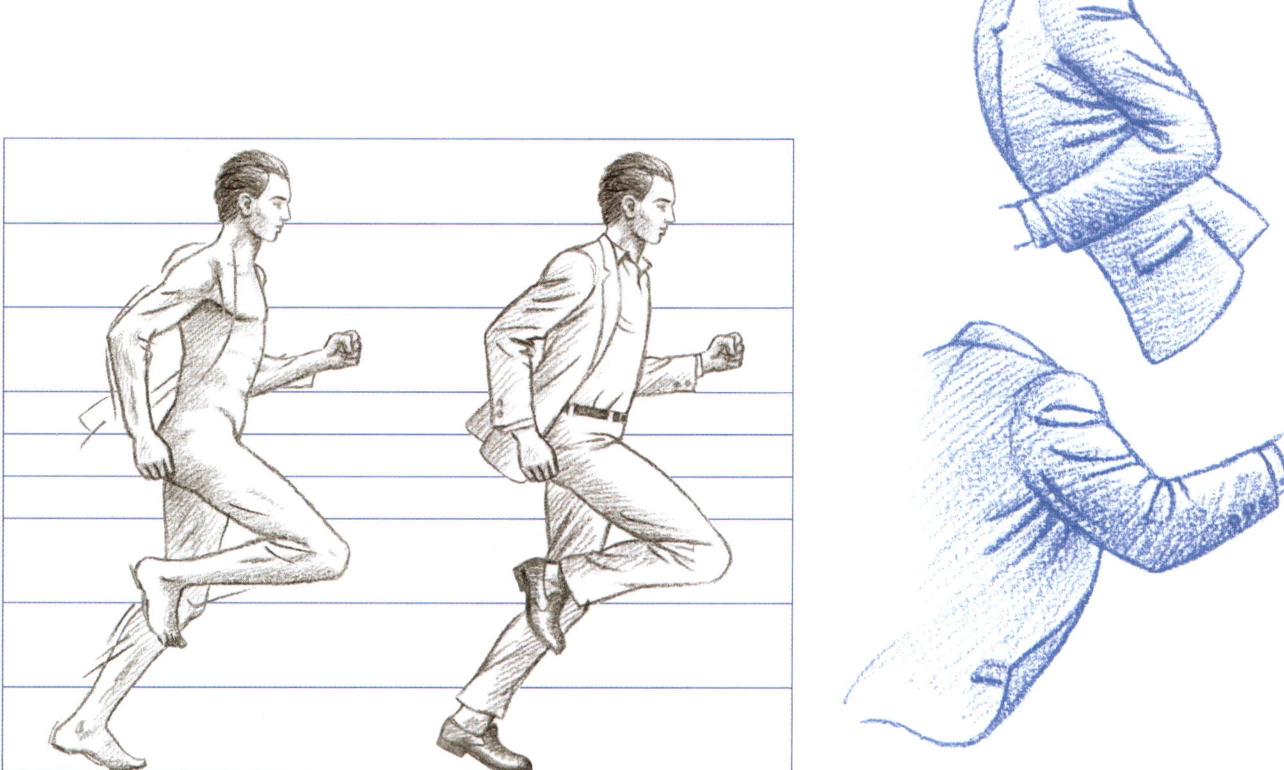

For a realistic effect, the clothes must follow the shape of the body.
Their folds show the tensions that are exerted in the direction of movement.
The jacket moves away from the body as a result of speed.

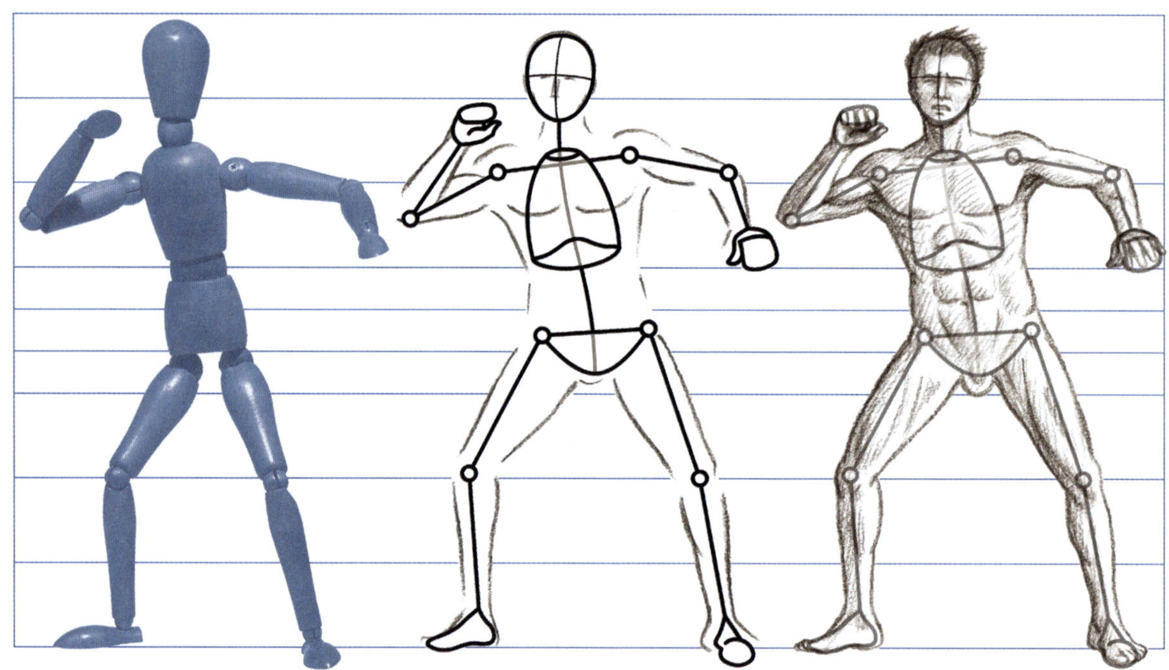

Now show a person gesticulating. The shoulder axis is not parallel to the axis of the pelvis. The head is tilted. The left forearm appears to be shorter. But trust your eyes: this foreshortening is a result of perspective.

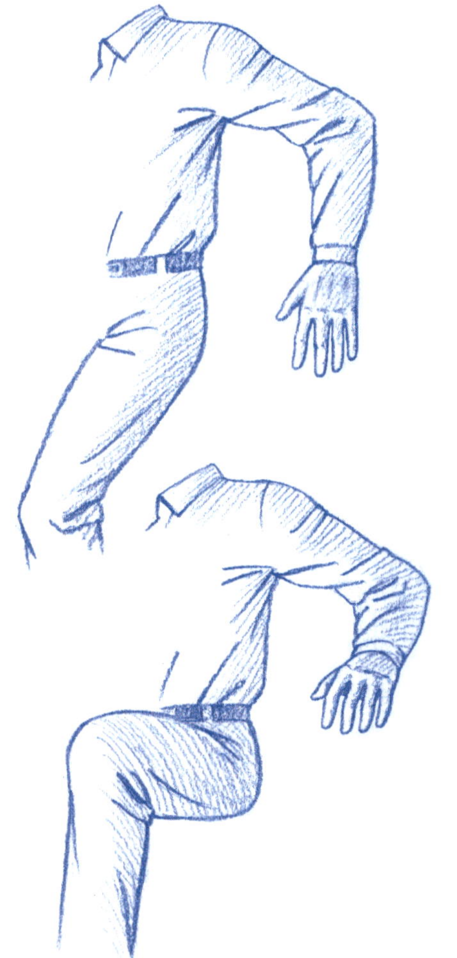

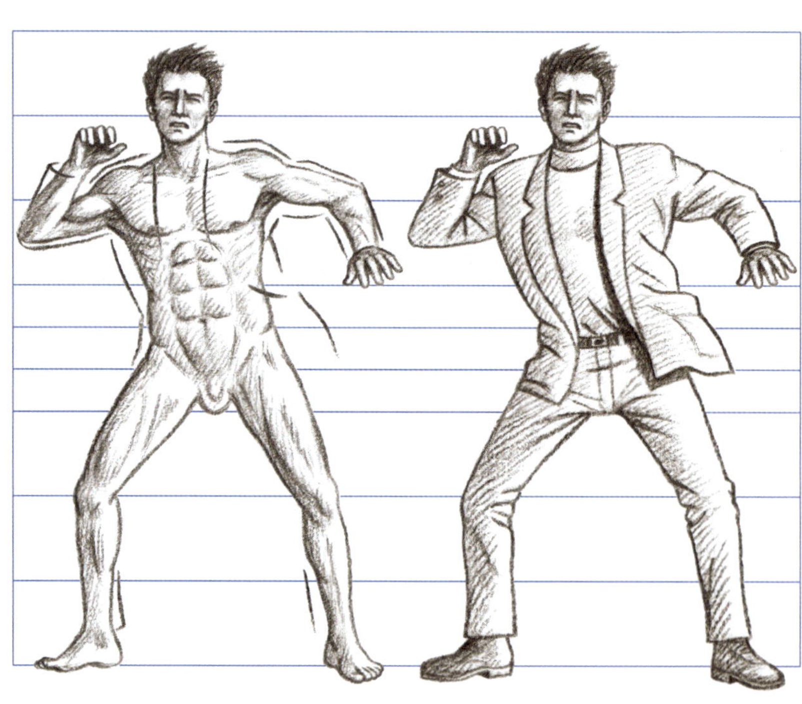

The wind flattens the jacket to the body on one side and makes it fly away on the other; the same is true for the hair. The folds of the clothing follow the movement of the body and of the wind.

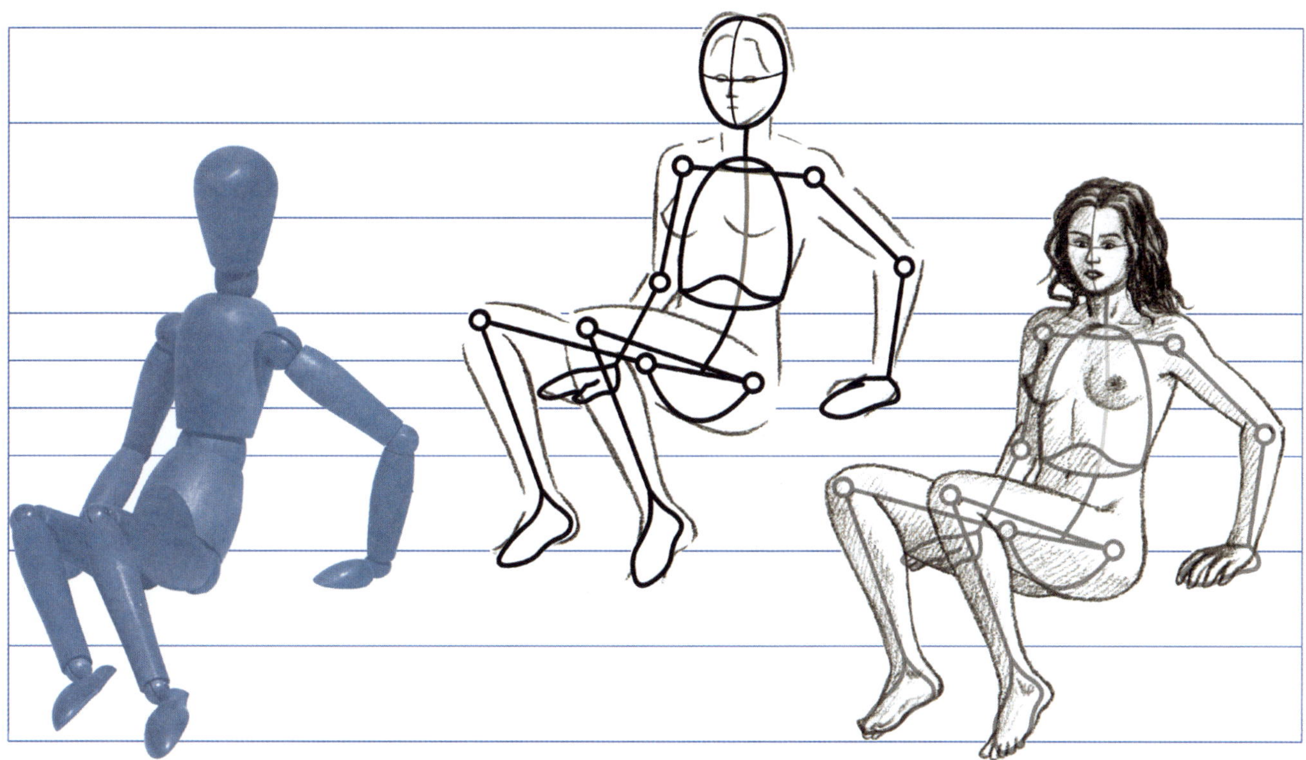

Draw a person sitting. The movement of leaning backward is shown by the
downward push of the hands and the foreshortening of the thighs.

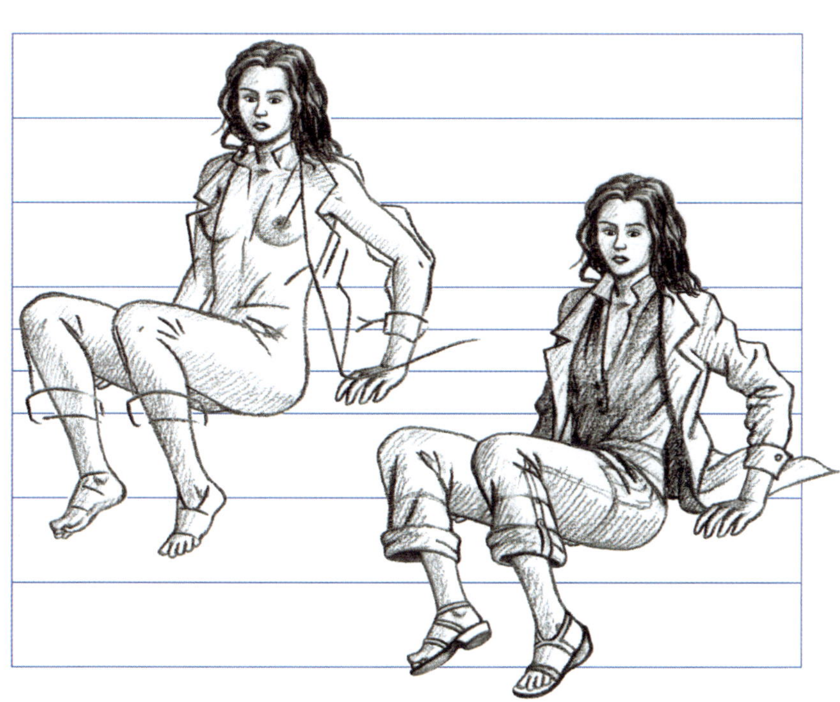

The folds of the coat highlight the angle that the body is making with
the ground. The clothes move away from the body due to gravity.

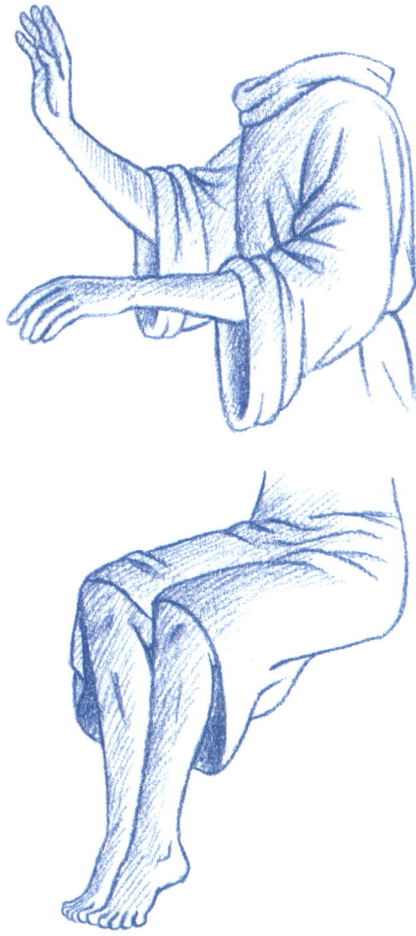

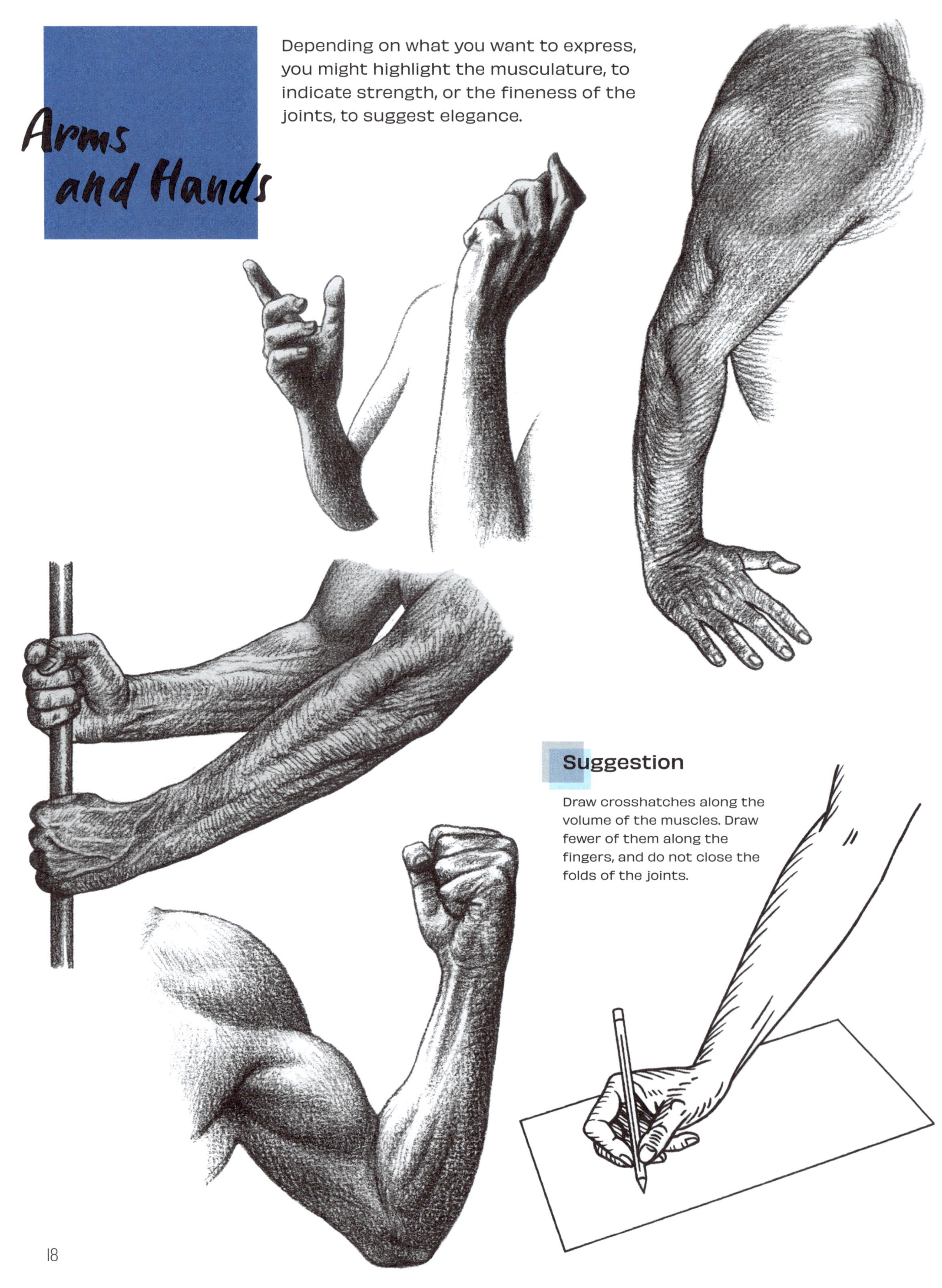

Arms and Hands

Depending on what you want to express, you might highlight the musculature, to indicate strength, or the fineness of the joints, to suggest elegance.

Suggestion

Draw crosshatches along the volume of the muscles. Draw fewer of them along the fingers, and do not close the folds of the joints.

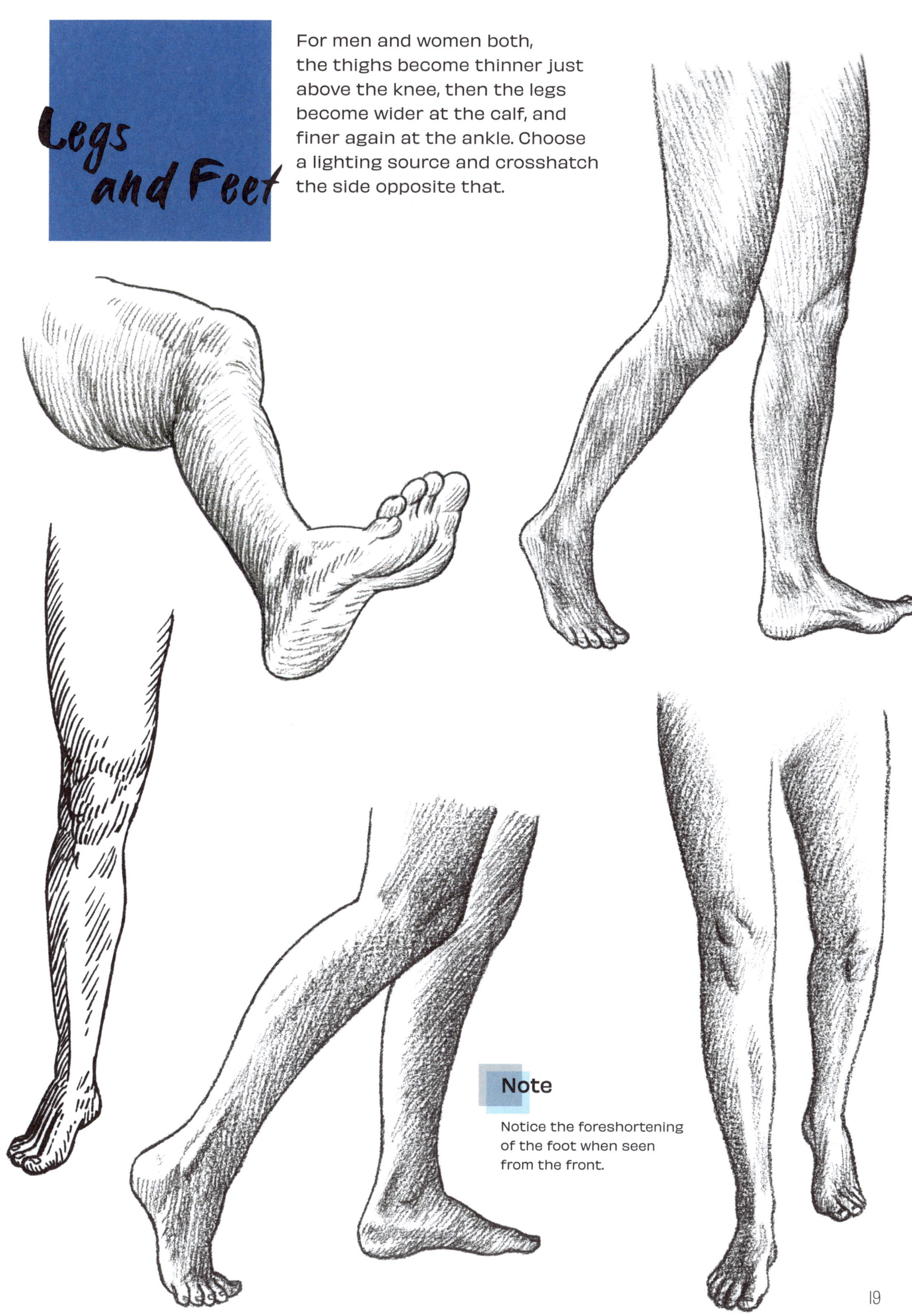

Legs and Feet

For men and women both, the thighs become thinner just above the knee, then the legs become wider at the calf, and finer again at the ankle. Choose a lighting source and crosshatch the side opposite that.

Note

Notice the foreshortening of the foot when seen from the front.

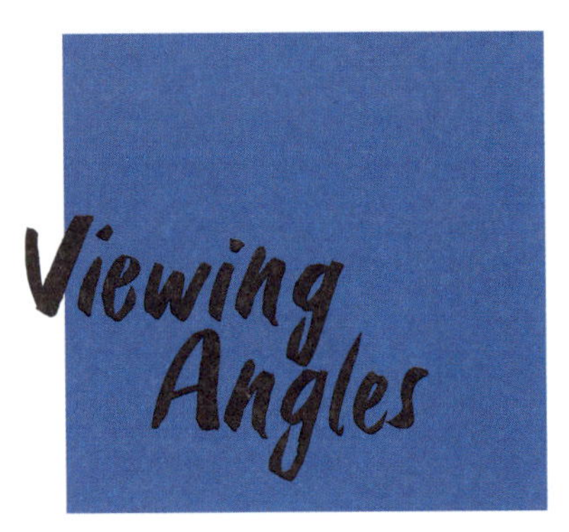

Viewing Angles

American comic book artists are the champions of the foreshortened view. To help you understand this technique, here are a few different views, from different angles, of the same pose. Working on perspective will allow you to achieve the most exaggerated views.

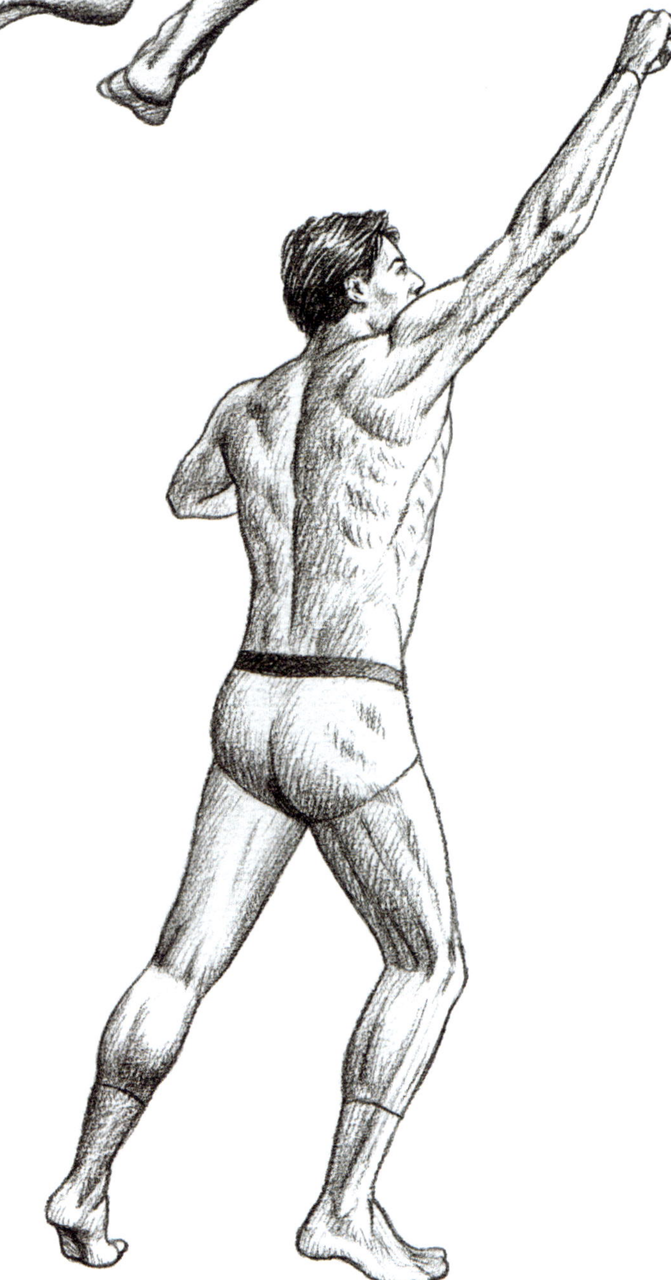

The character is seen here from below, from a low-angle perspective. His foot appears to be disproportionately large compared to the rest of his body.

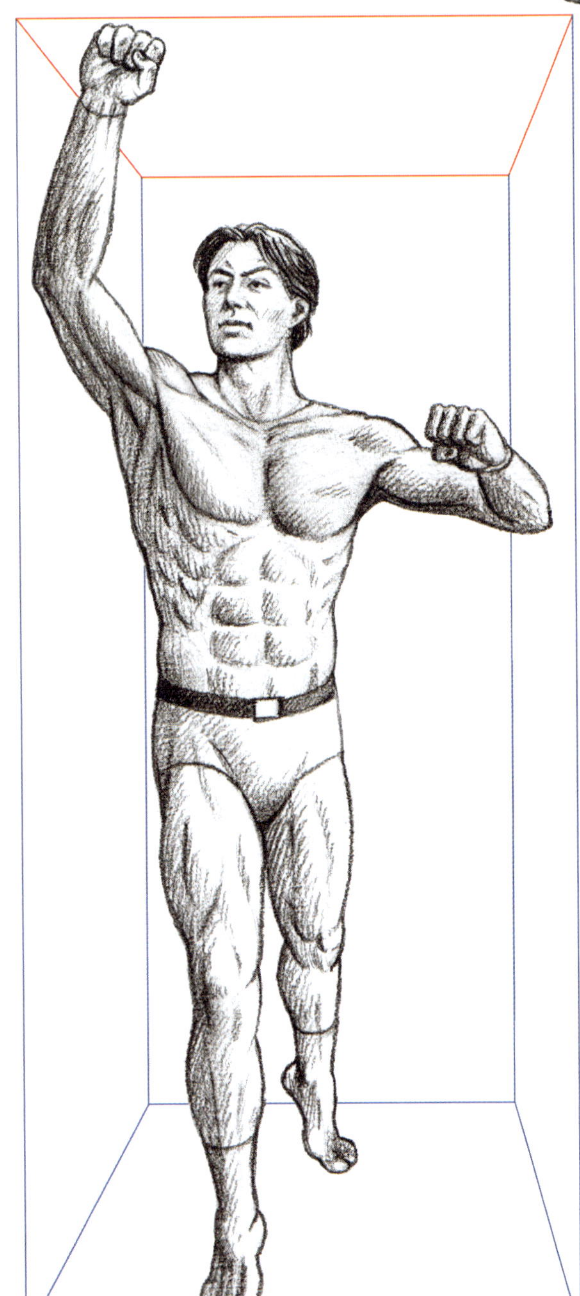

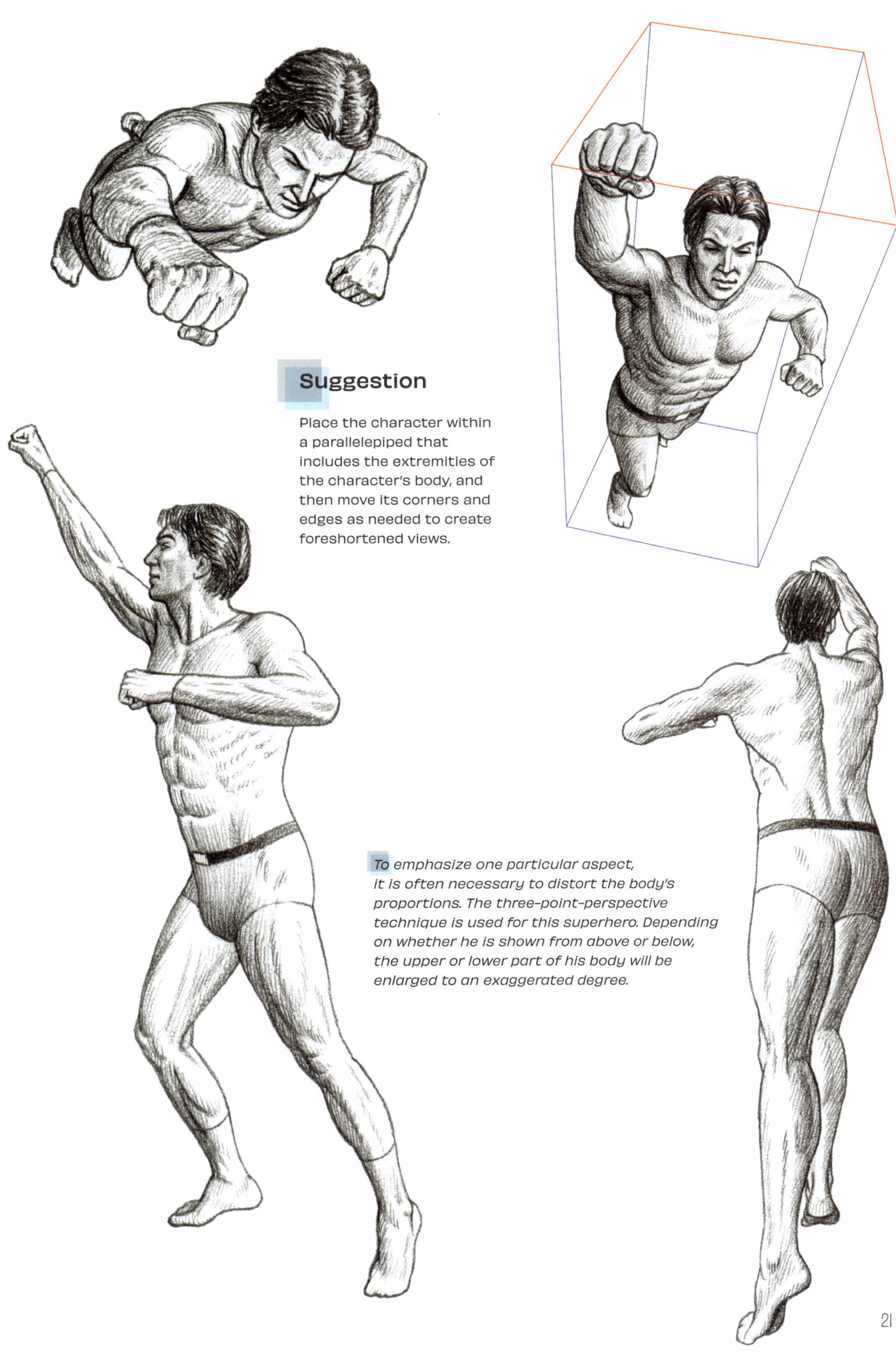

Suggestion

Place the character within a parallelepiped that includes the extremities of the character's body, and then move its corners and edges as needed to create foreshortened views.

To emphasize one particular aspect, it is often necessary to distort the body's proportions. The three-point-perspective technique is used for this superhero. Depending on whether he is shown from above or below, the upper or lower part of his body will be enlarged to an exaggerated degree.

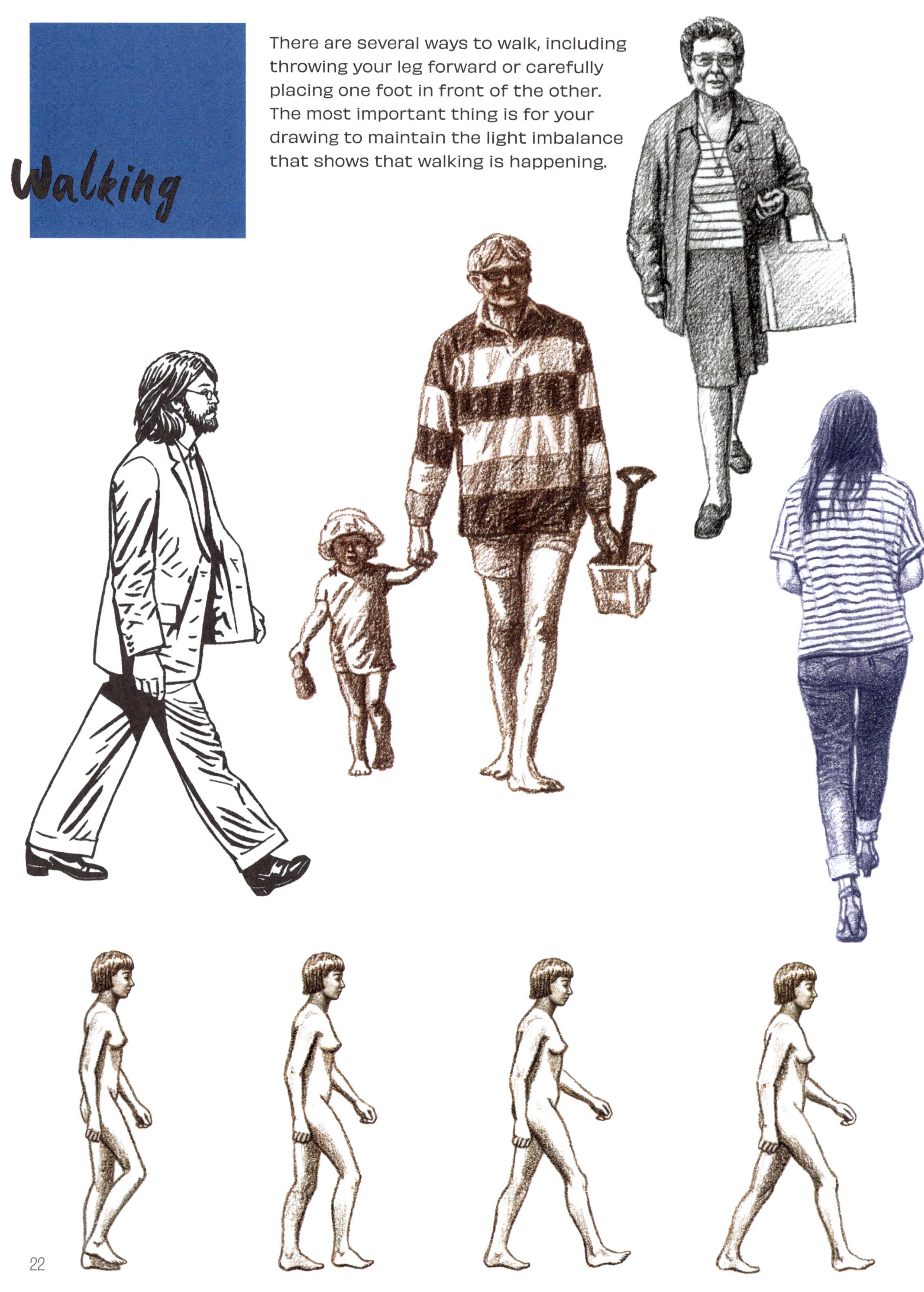

There are several ways to walk, including throwing your leg forward or carefully placing one foot in front of the other. The most important thing is for your drawing to maintain the light imbalance that shows that walking is happening.

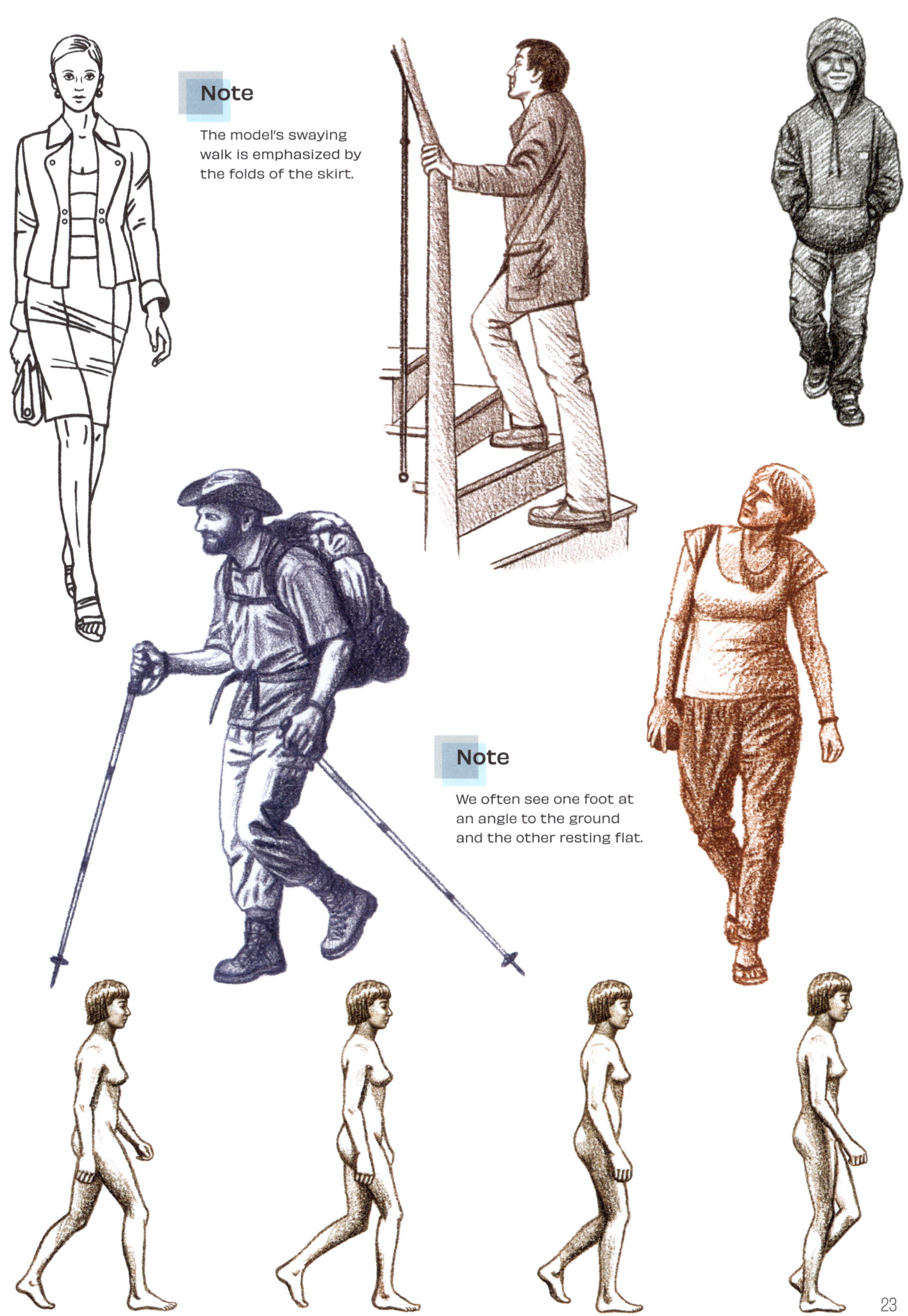
Note
The model's swaying walk is emphasized by the folds of the skirt.
Note
We often see one foot at an angle to the ground and the other resting flat.

Running

A frozen image depicting someone running is always off-balance. The axis of the body is often leaning in one direction, and one foot is touching the ground while the other is in the air.

Note

The way that the side of the jacket is floating emphasizes the movement.

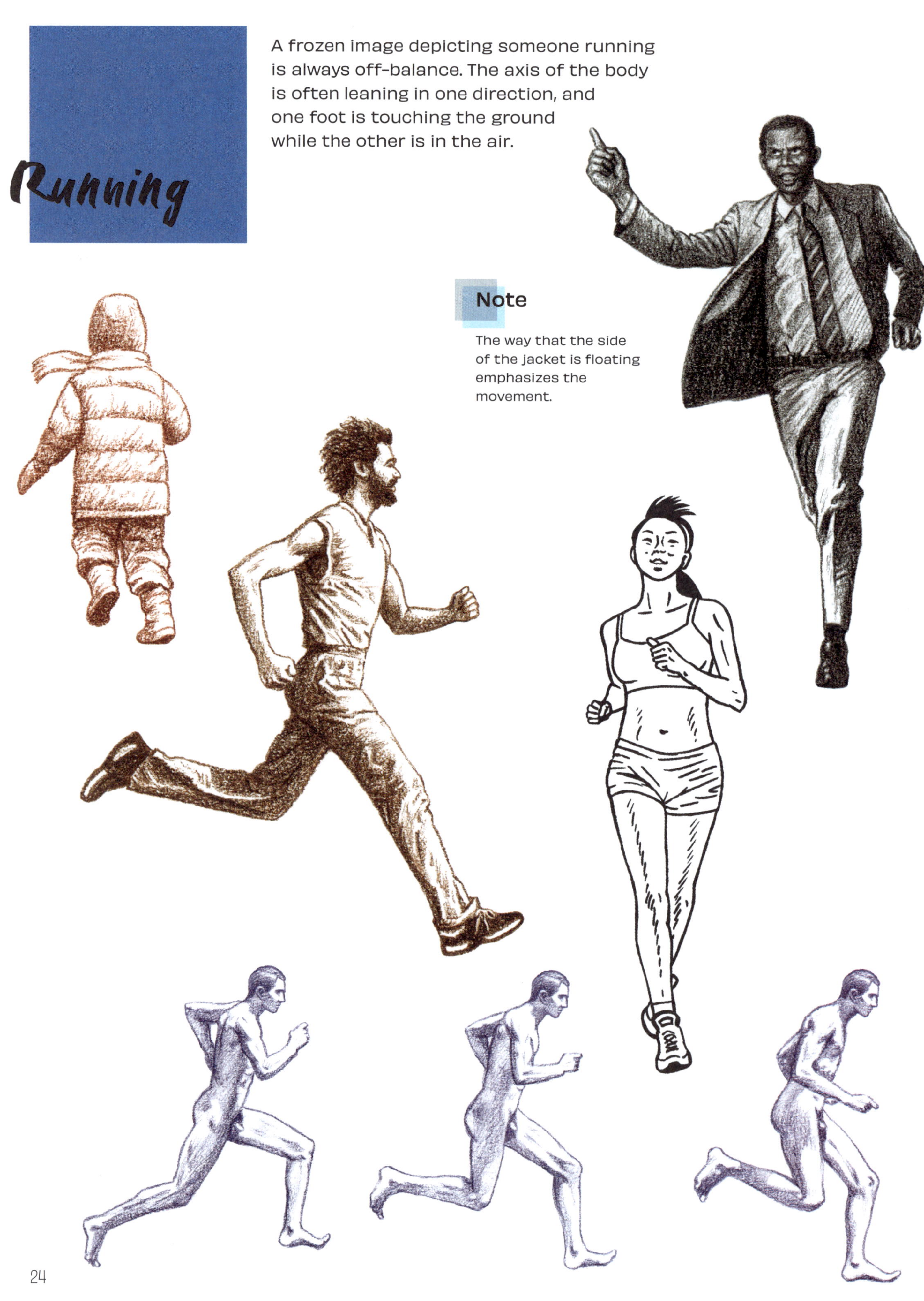

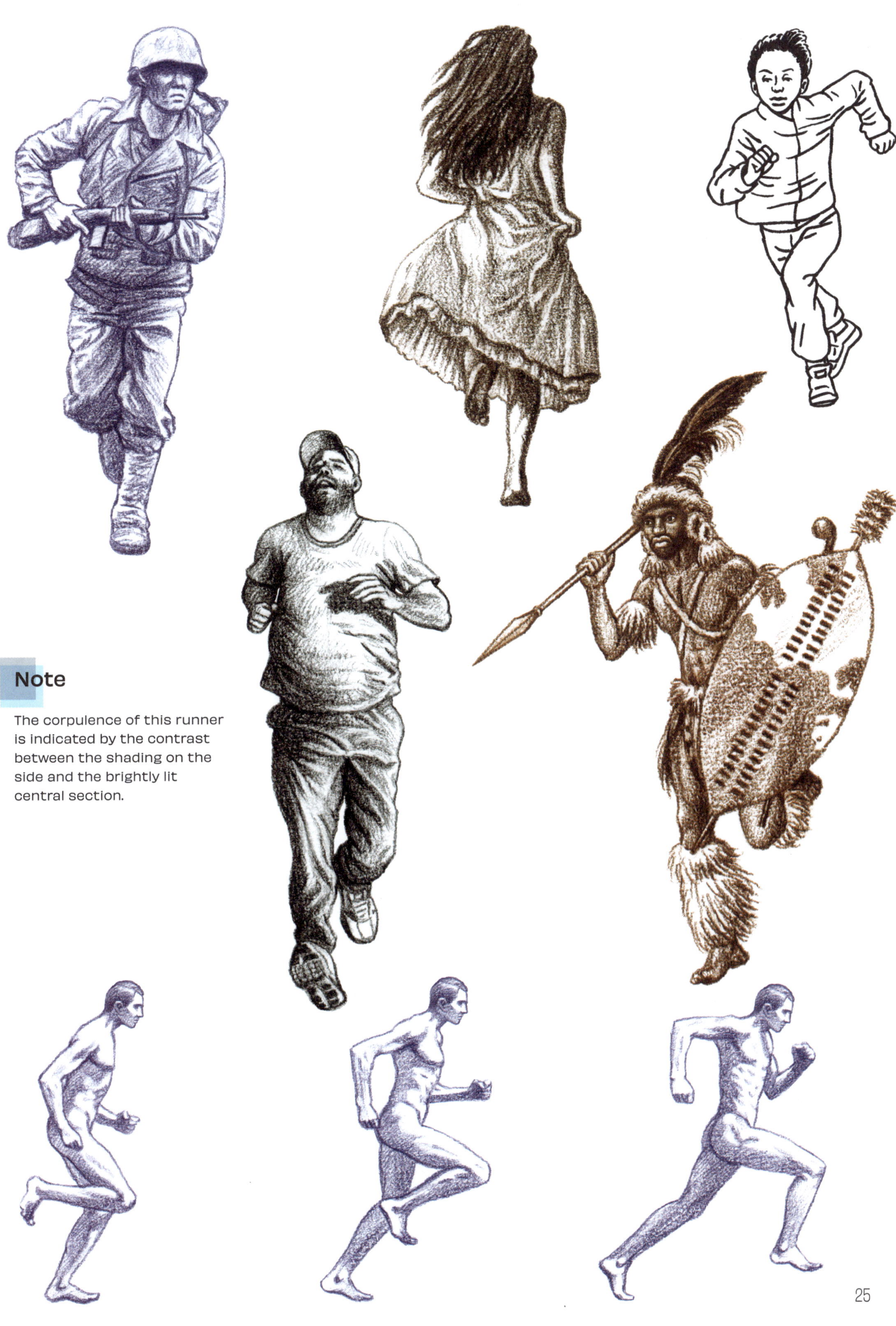

Note

The corpulence of this runner is indicated by the contrast between the shading on the side and the brightly lit central section.

To efficiently illustrate a jump in one single image, you need to choose the moment when the body is suspended in the air. The sense of levitation is accentuated by the way the clothes float.

Note

In this felt-pen treatment, the crosshatches indicating the shadows stop before the contour line, creating a backlighting effect.

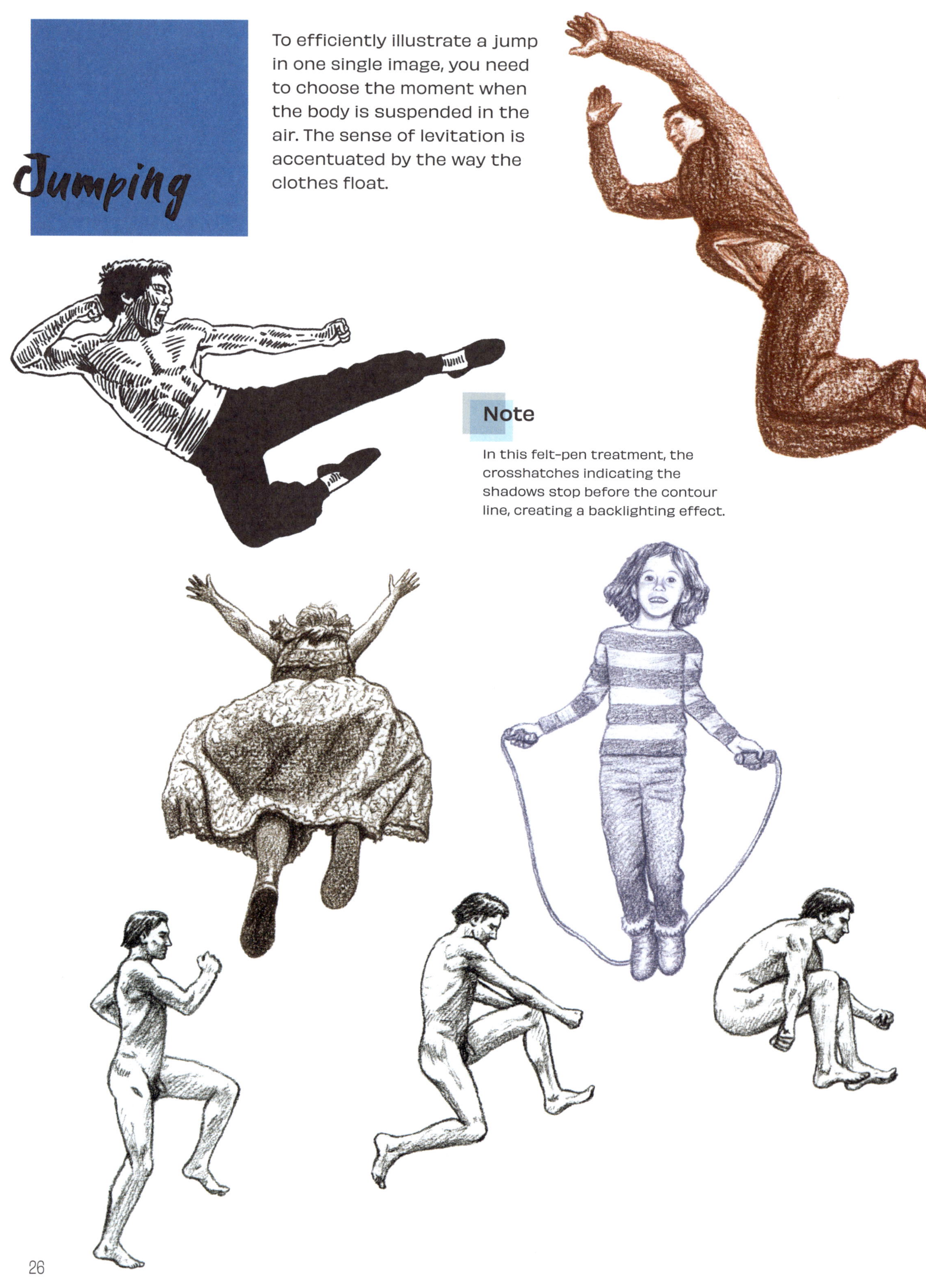

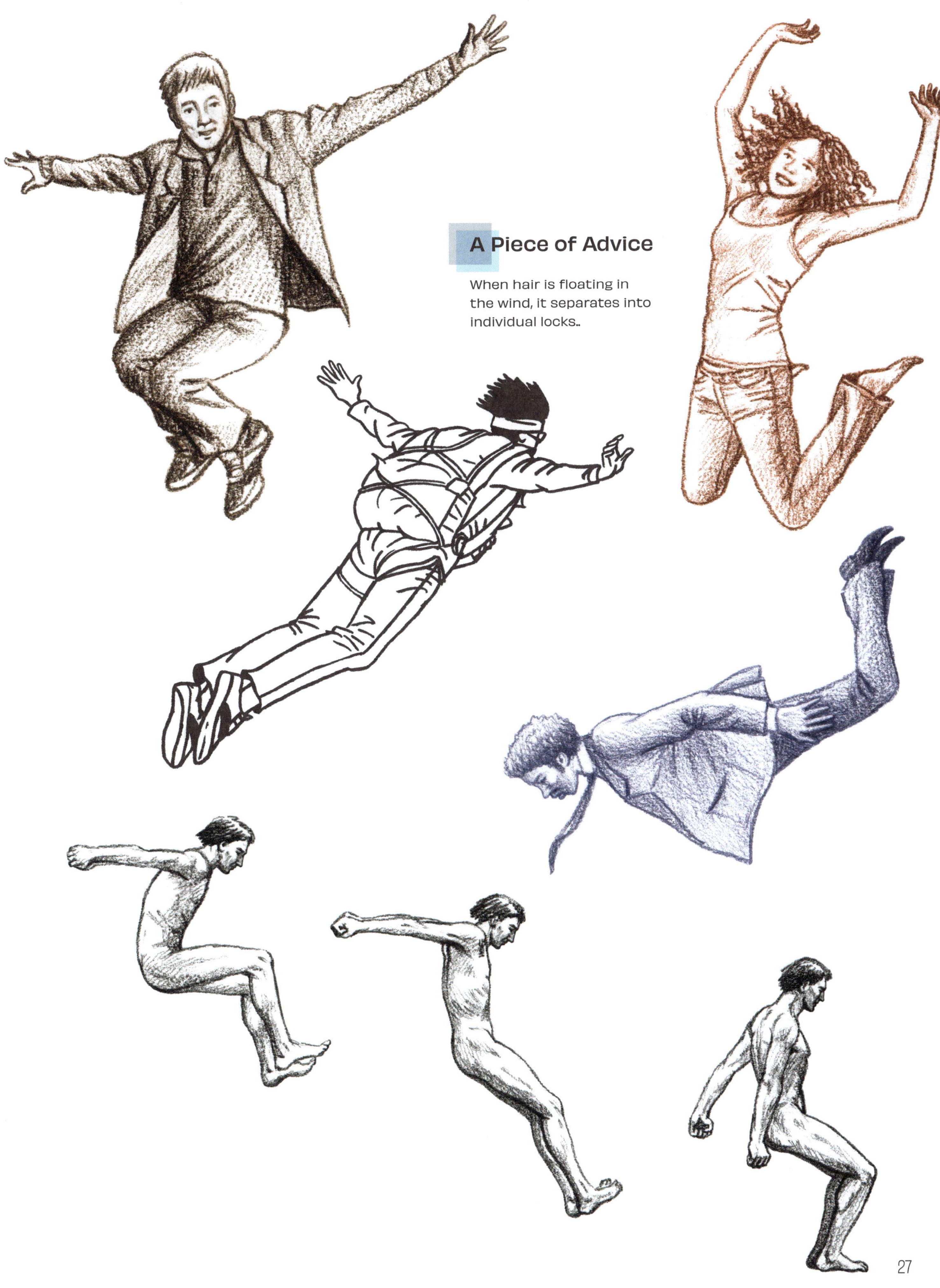
A Piece of Advice

When hair is floating in
the wind, it separates into
individual locks..

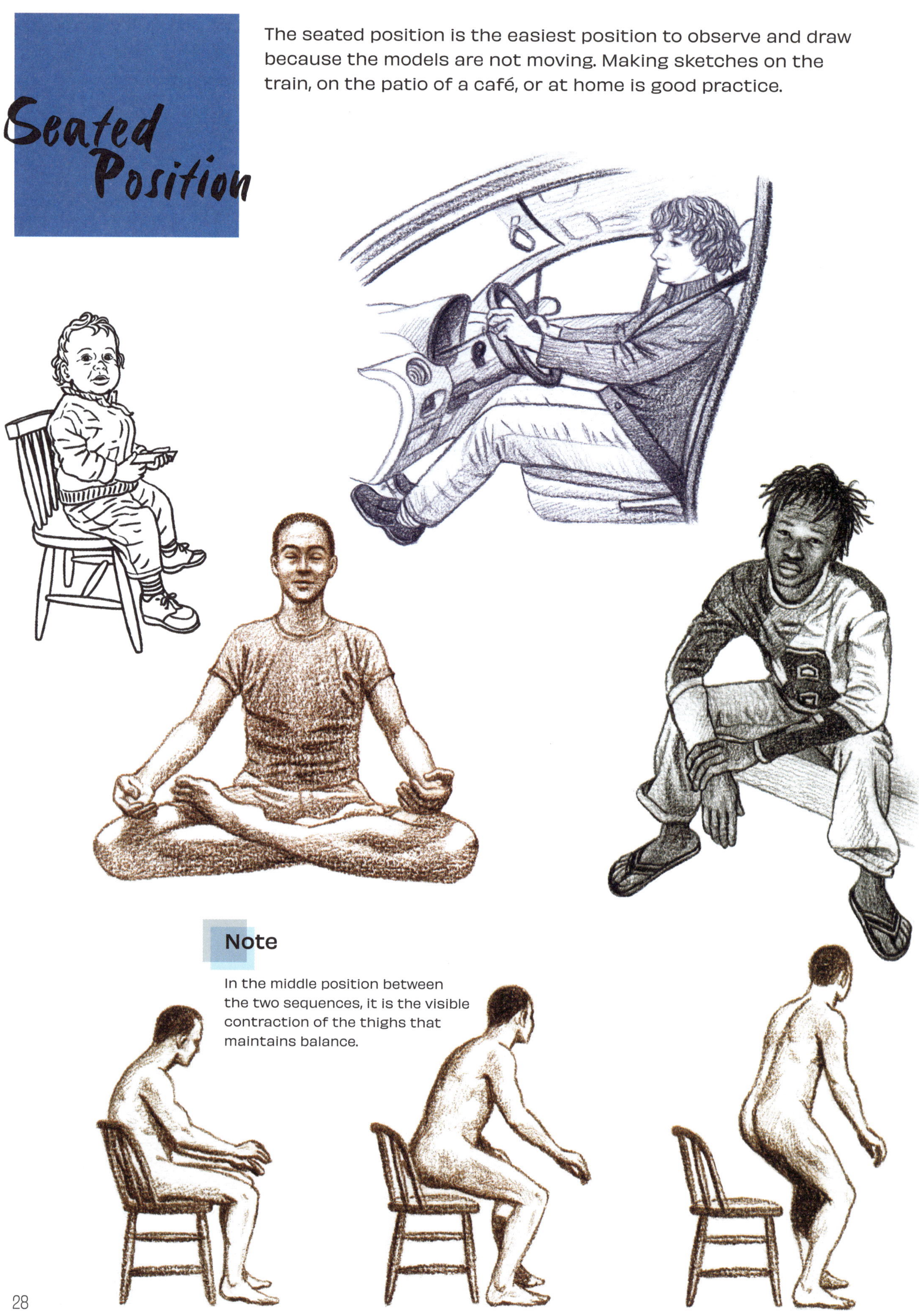

The seated position is the easiest position to observe and draw because the models are not moving. Making sketches on the train, on the patio of a café, or at home is good practice.

Seated Position

Note

In the middle position between the two sequences, it is the visible contraction of the thighs that maintains balance.

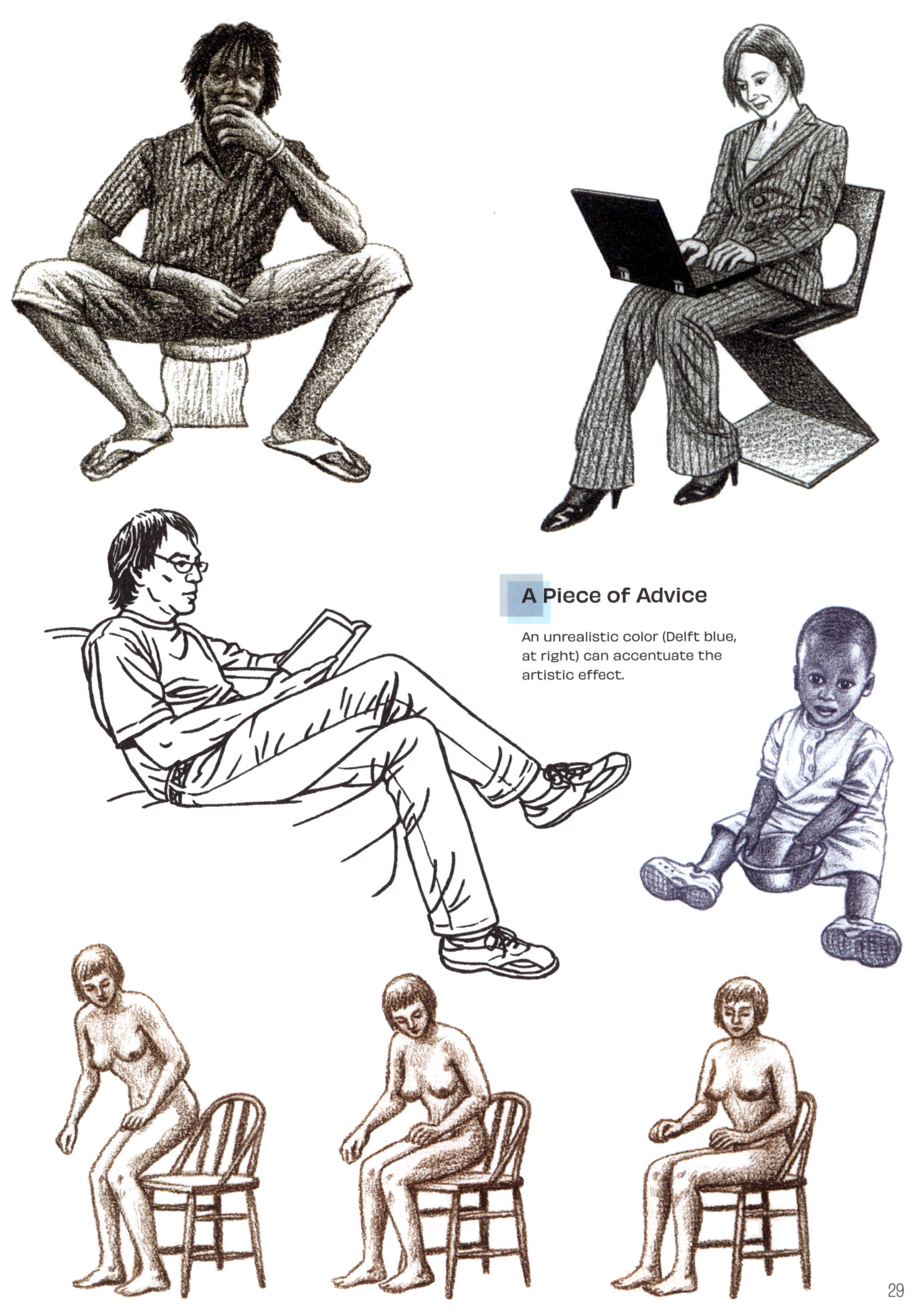

A Piece of Advice

An unrealistic color (Delft blue, at right) can accentuate the artistic effect.

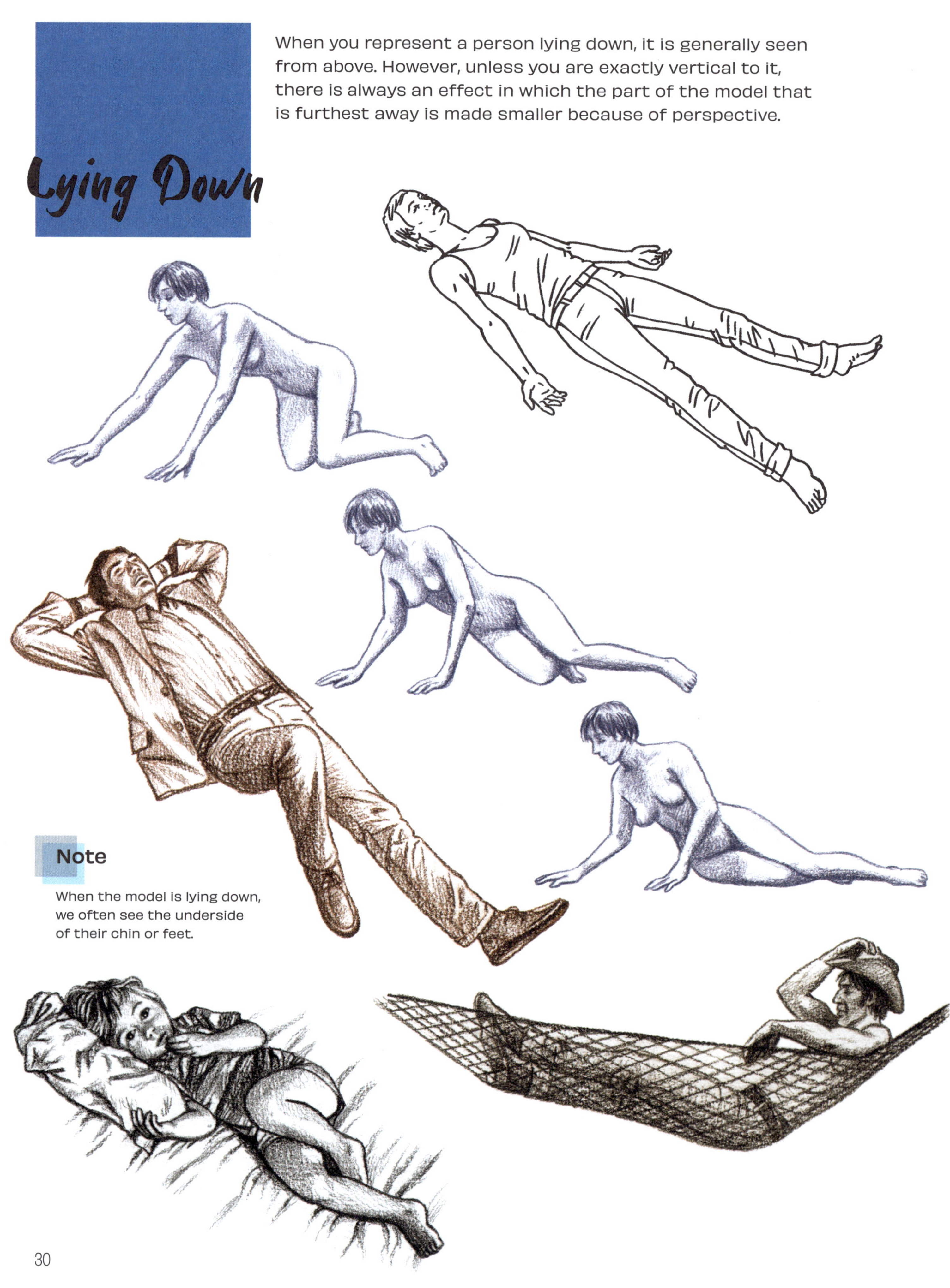

When you represent a person lying down, it is generally seen from above. However, unless you are exactly vertical to it, there is always an effect in which the part of the model that is furthest away is made smaller because of perspective.

Lying Down

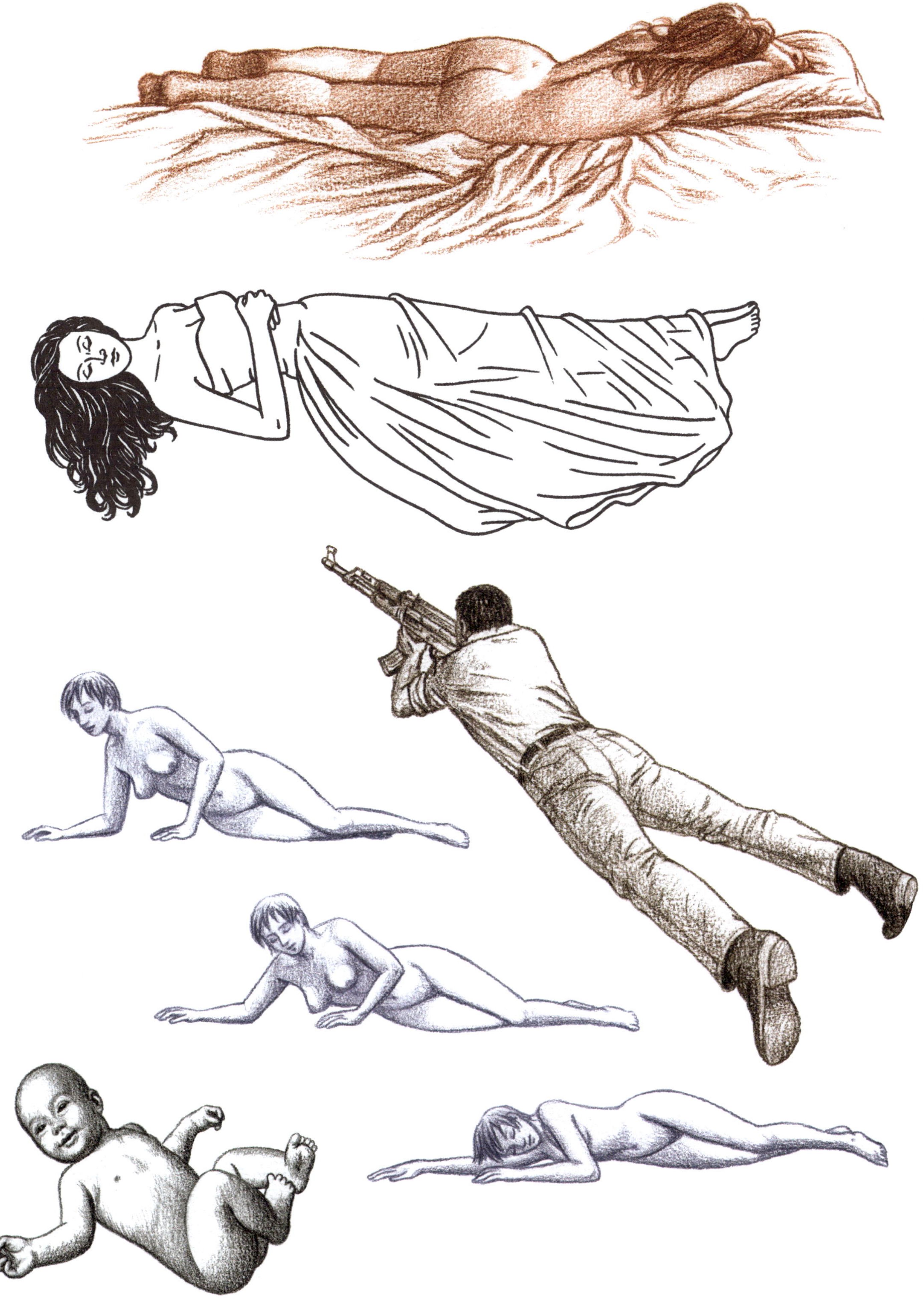

To capture the intensity of an attack, choose a moment when the action has a visible consequence, for example when a head is spinning away after a blow.

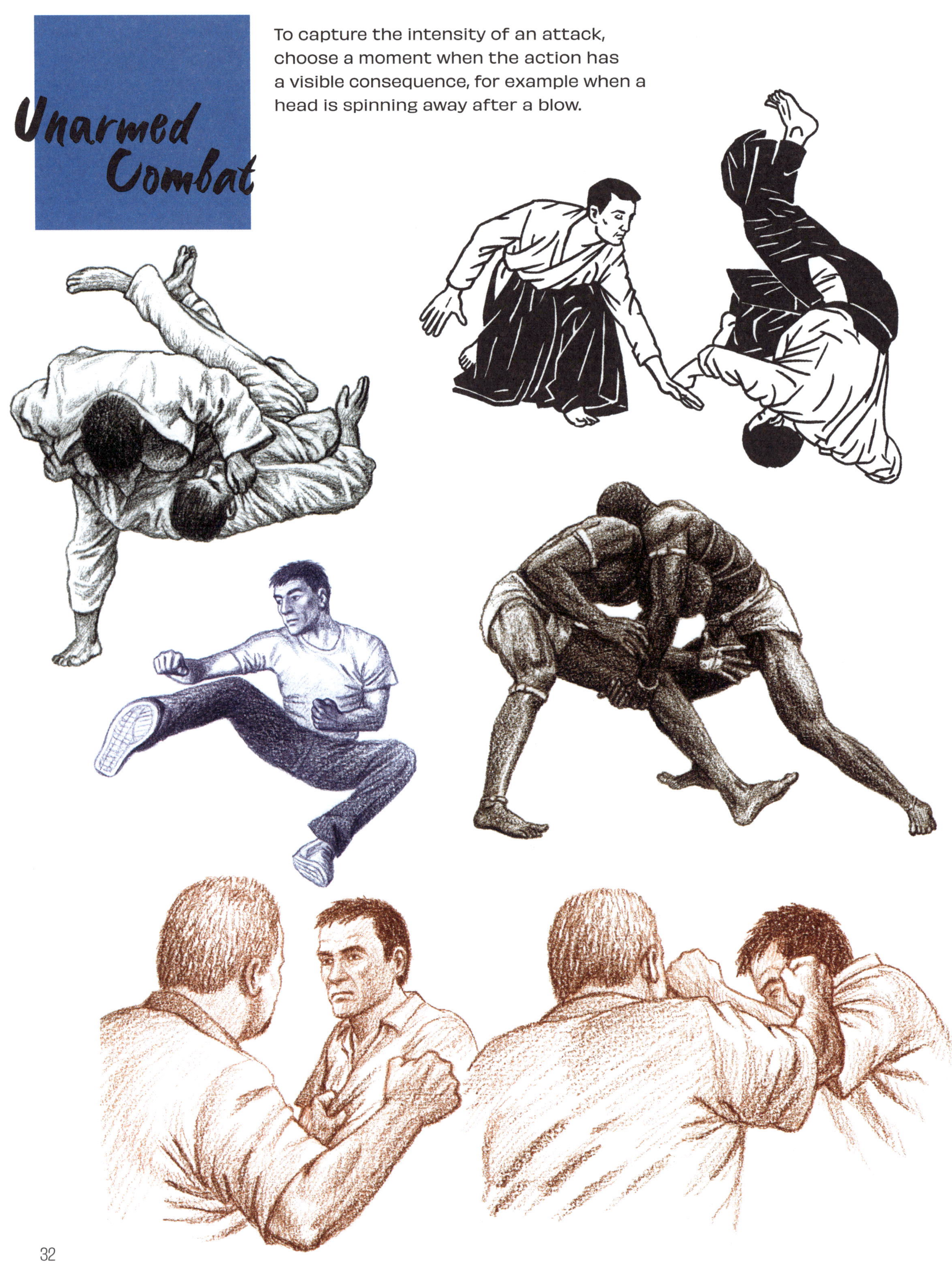

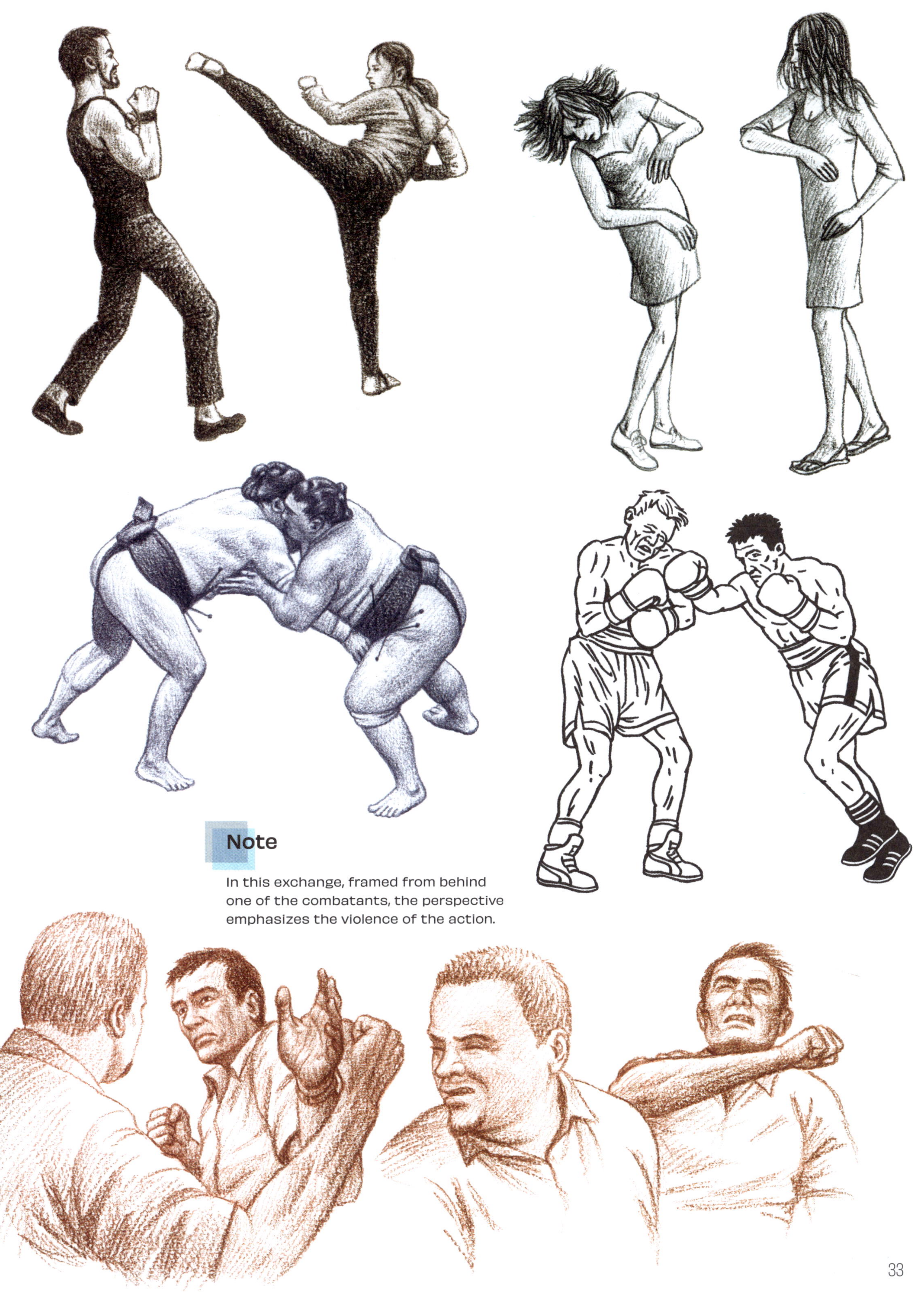

Note

In this exchange, framed from behind
one of the combatants, the perspective
emphasizes the violence of the action.

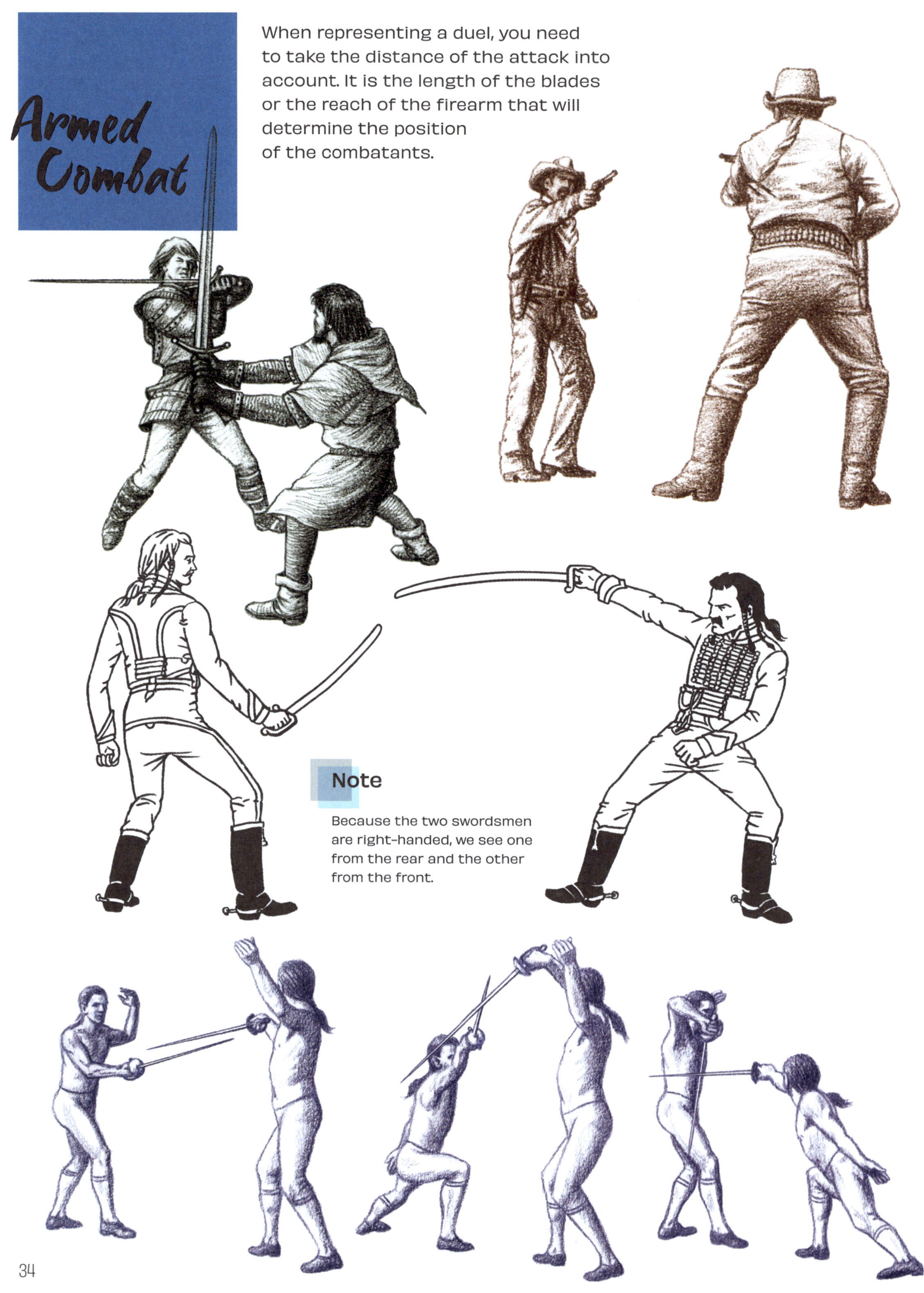

Armed Combat

When representing a duel, you need to take the distance of the attack into account. It is the length of the blades or the reach of the firearm that will determine the position of the combatants.

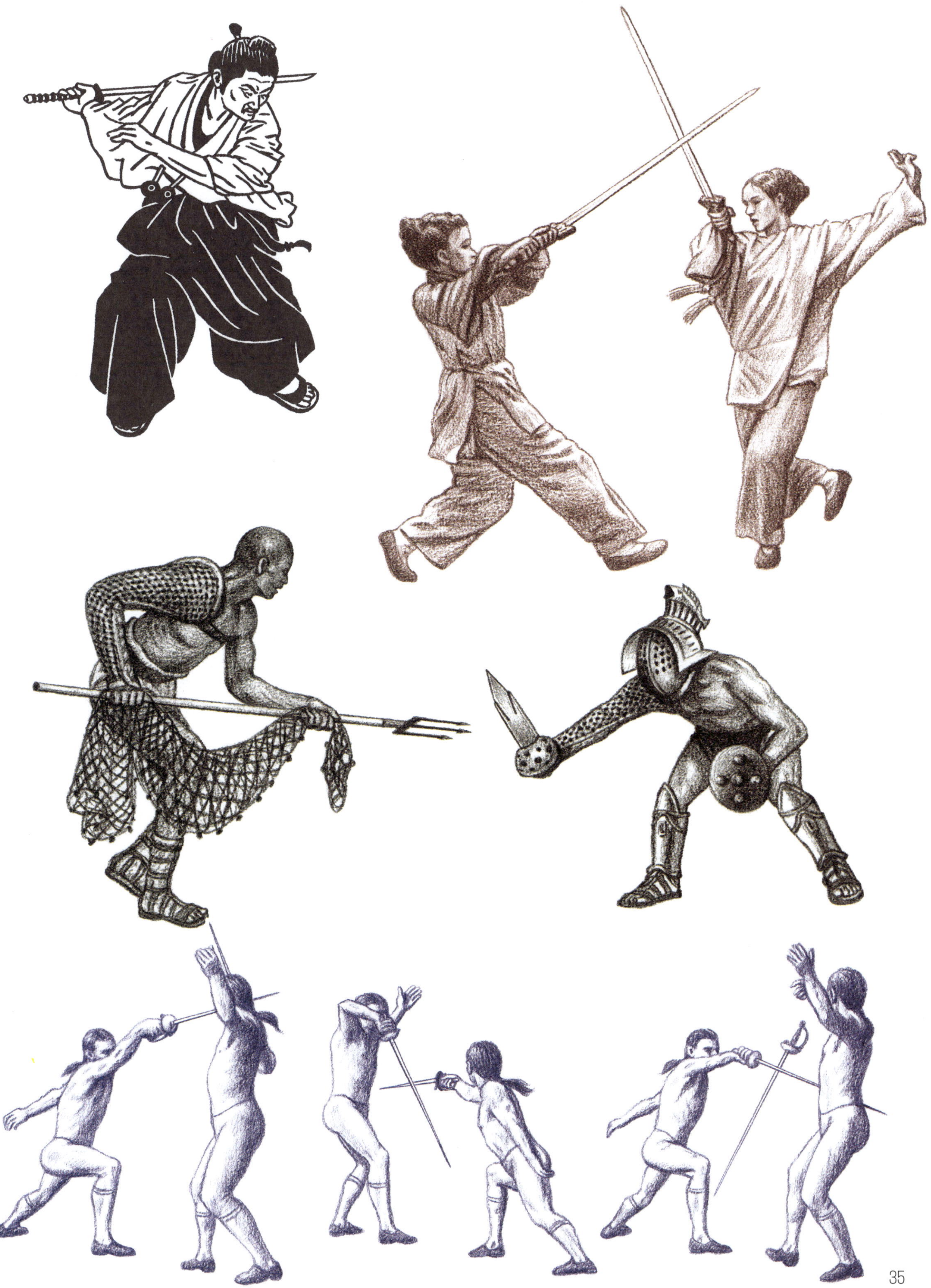

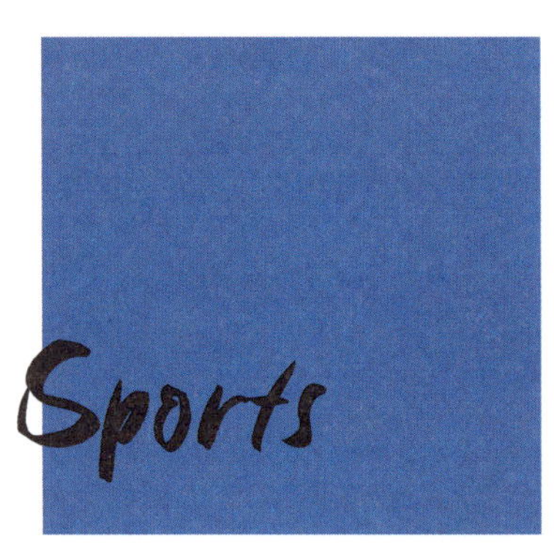

Sports

Athletic activity pushes the movement of the body to its limits. This is where you can best observe bodies in movement. We can see the functions of the muscles in the exertion or performance of strength, flexibility, or precision.

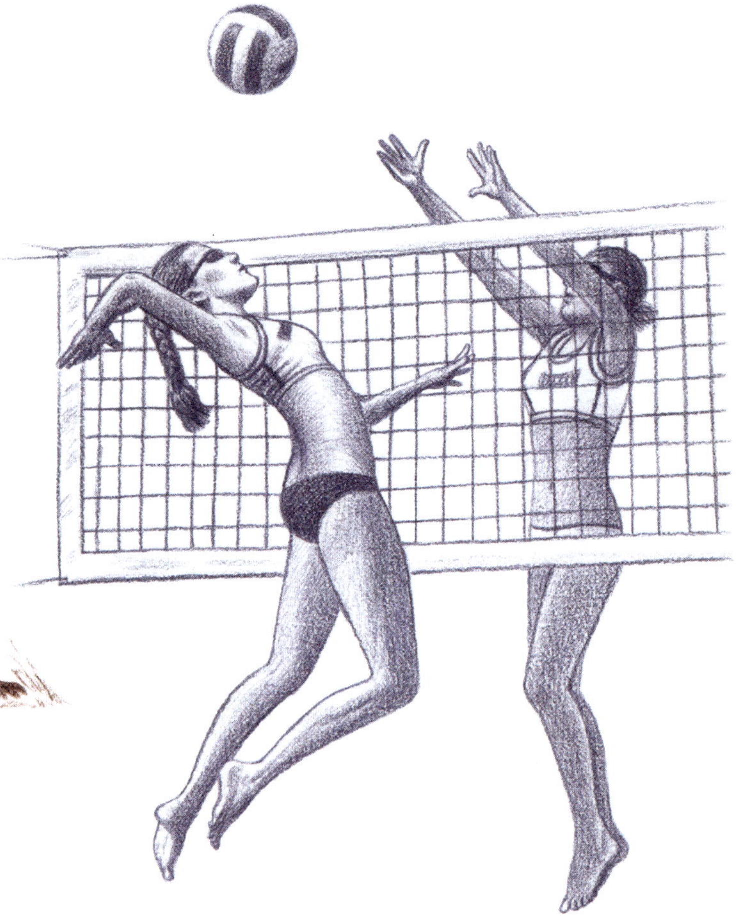

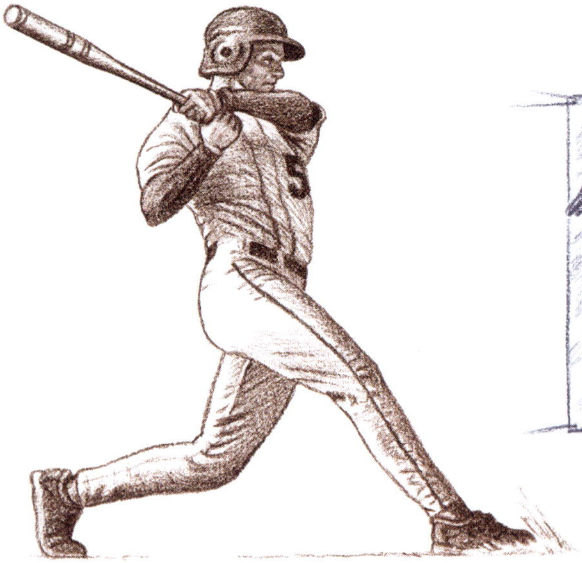

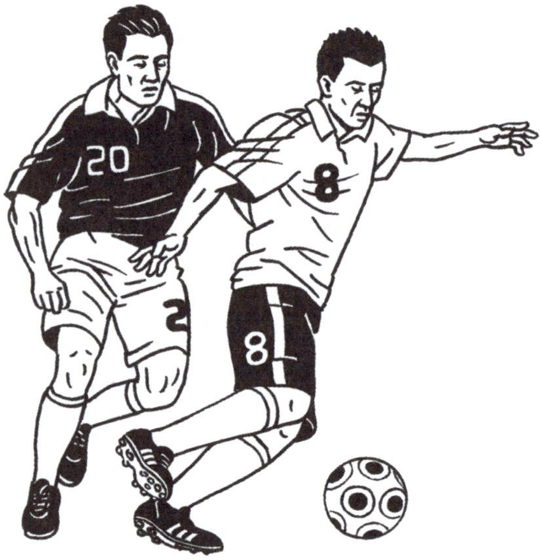

Note

When you need to use foreshortening, it is important to take anatomy into account to fully understand what you are trying to represent.

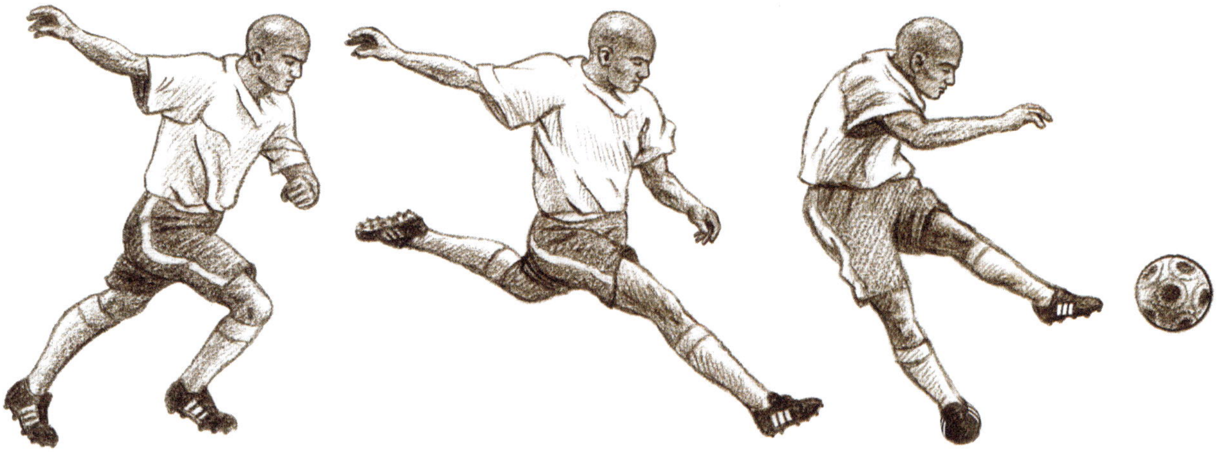

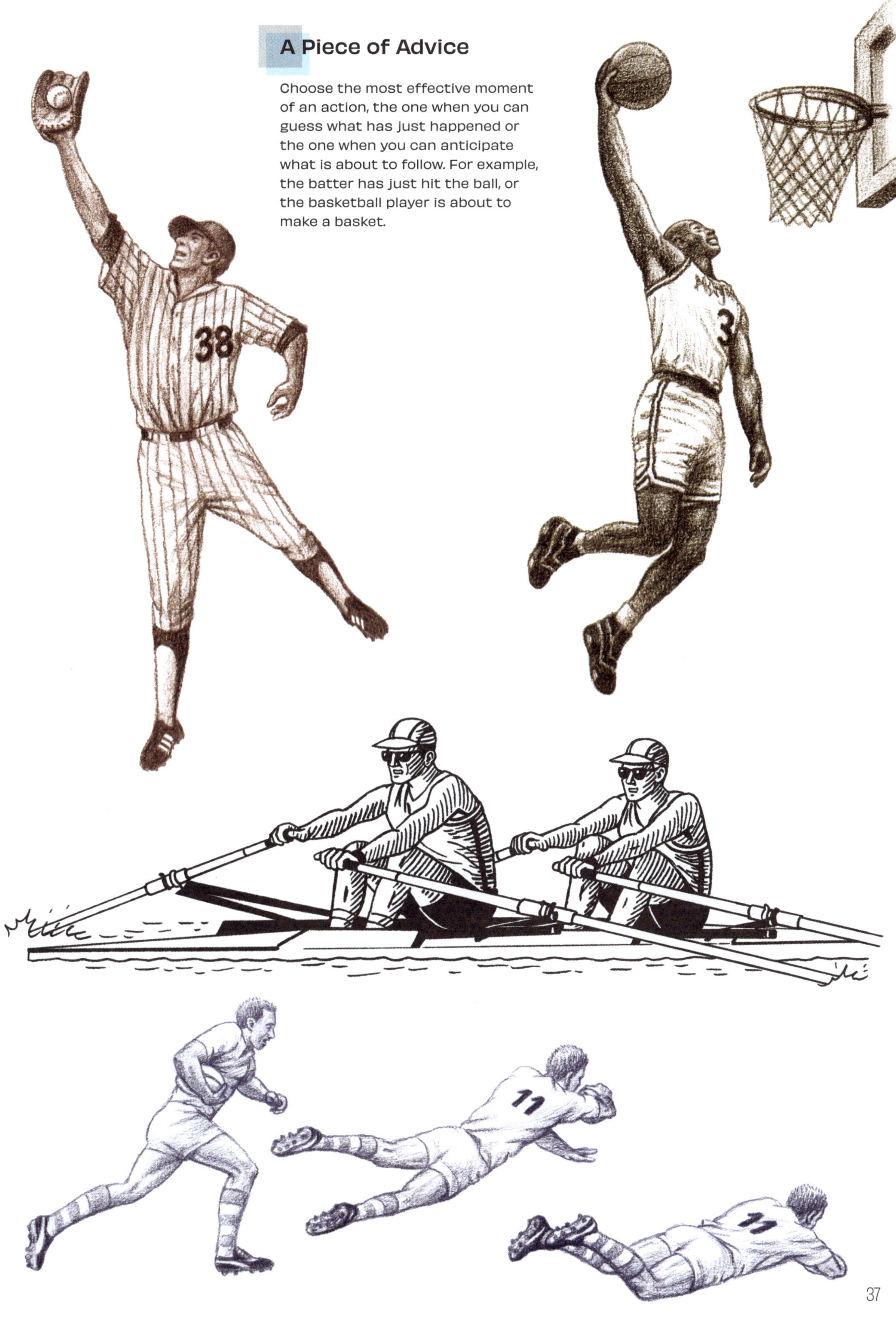

A Piece of Advice

Choose the most effective moment of an action, the one when you can guess what has just happened or the one when you can anticipate what is about to follow. For example, the batter has just hit the ball, or the basketball player is about to make a basket.

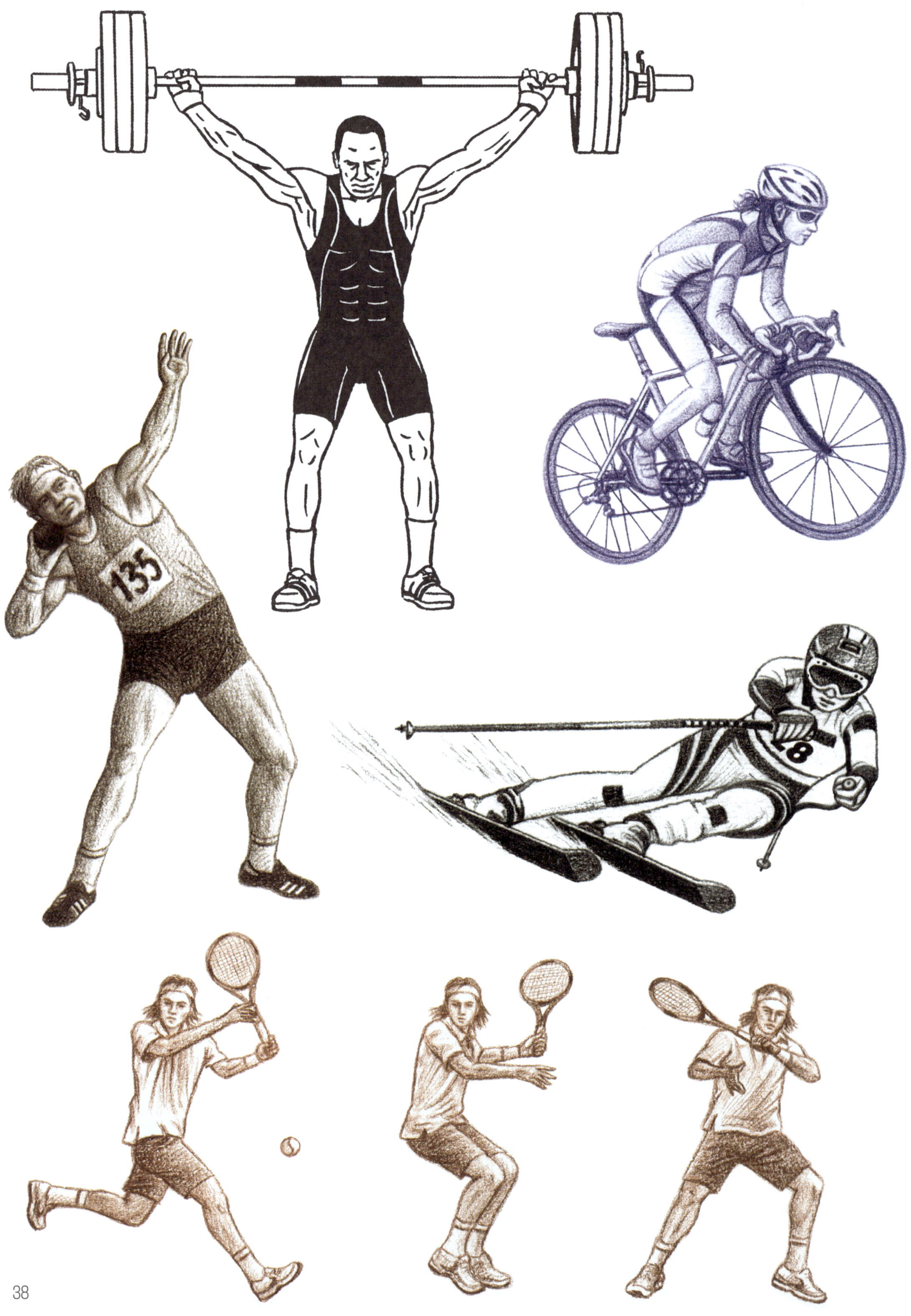

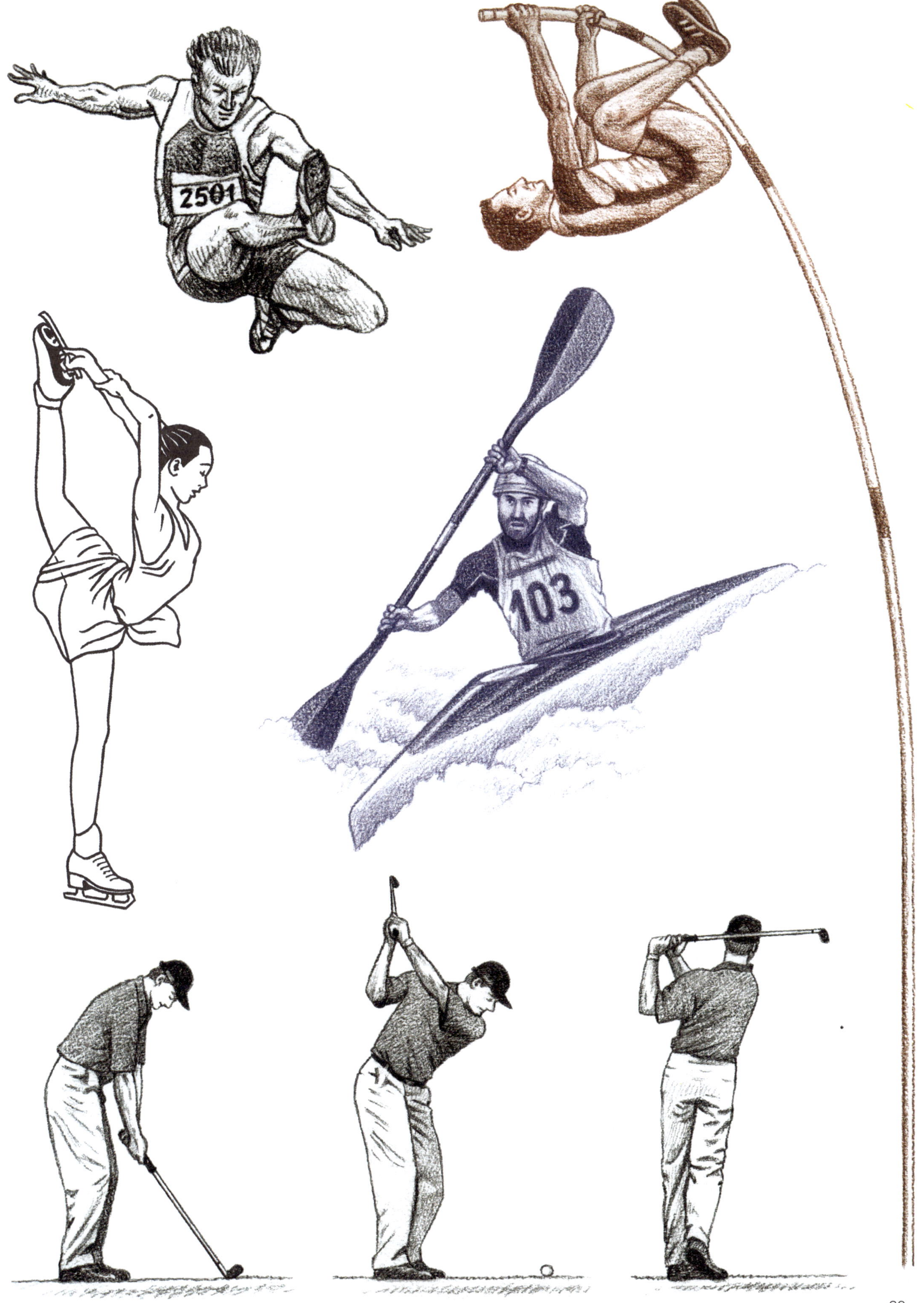
2501
103

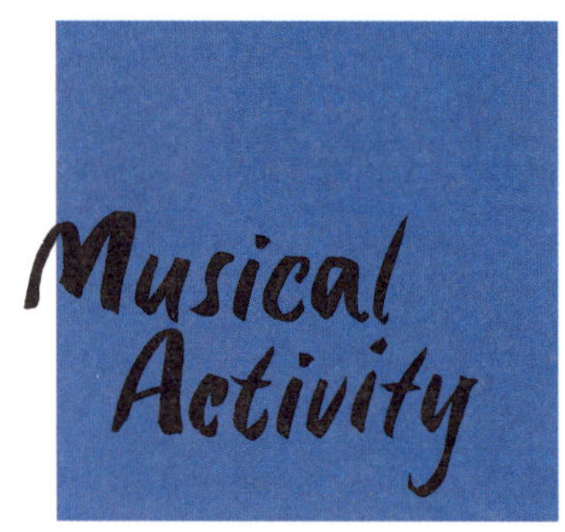

Musical Activity

Musicians' movements are specific and extremely precise because the accuracy of the notes depends on making the right gesture. Here we can only just touch on this subject, which would need much more space to treat fully, since the diversity of musical instruments means that there are many very specific poses and positions that musicians take.

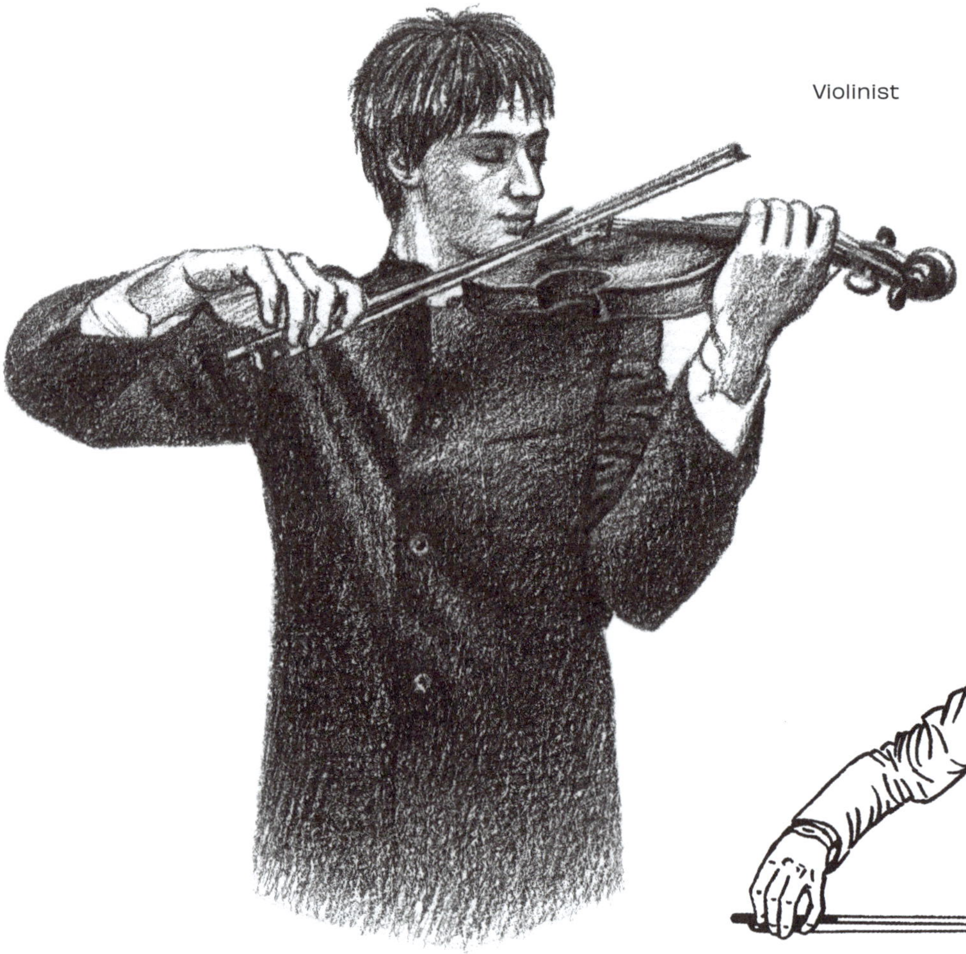

Violinist

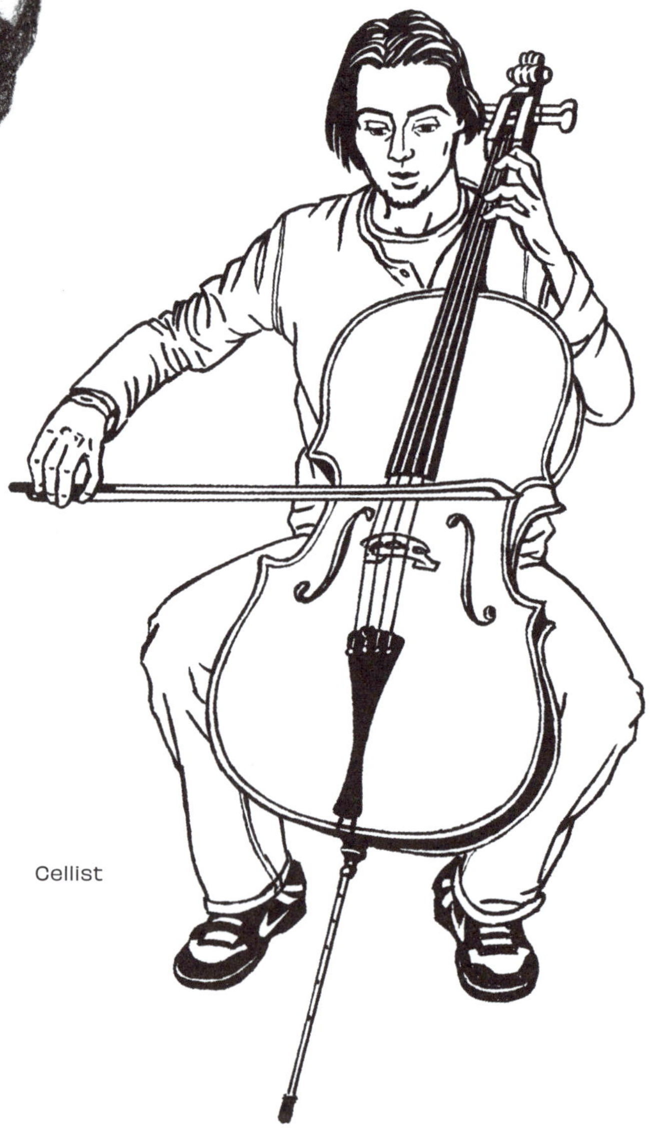

Cellist

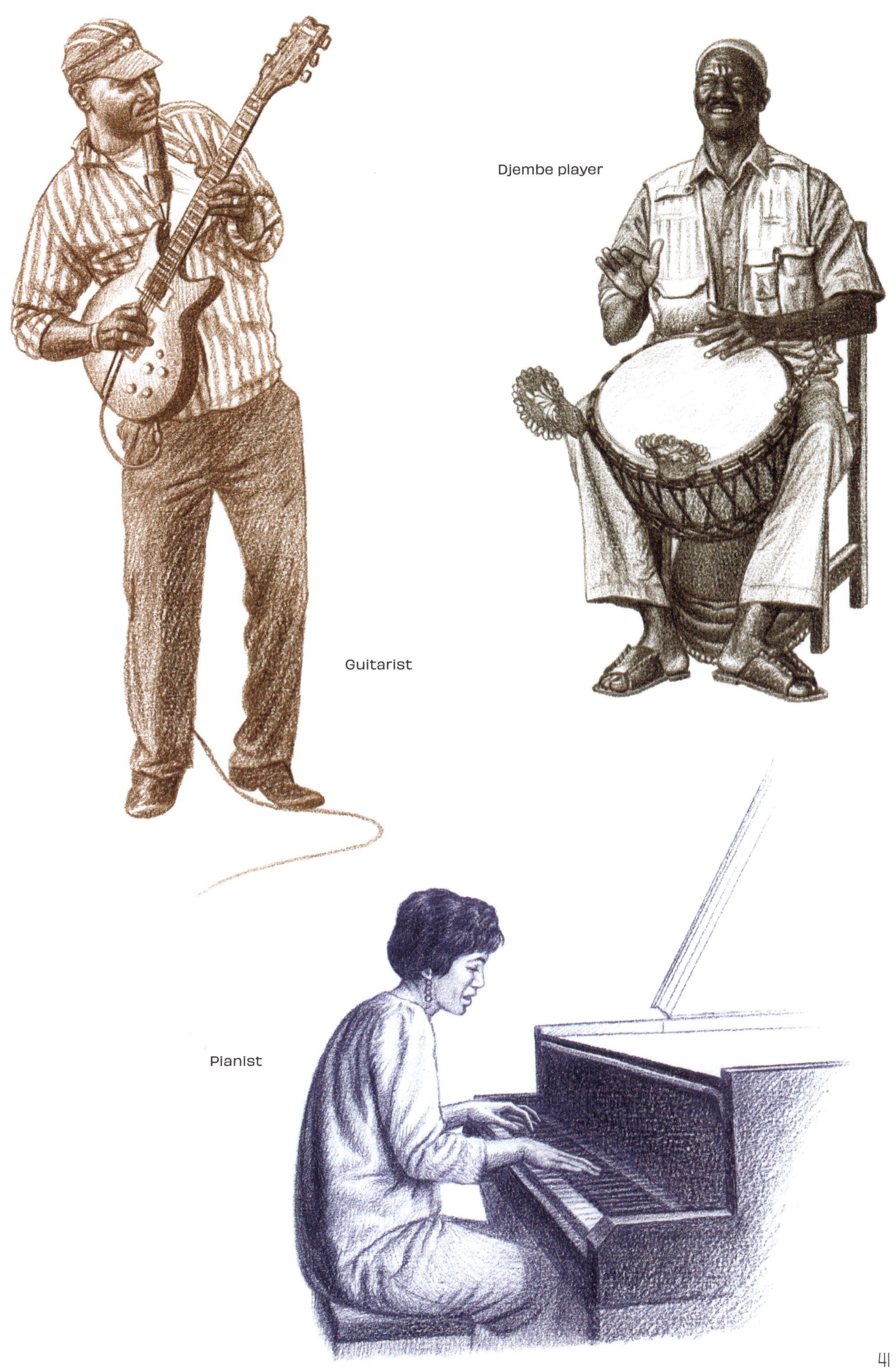
Djembe player
Guitarist
Pianist

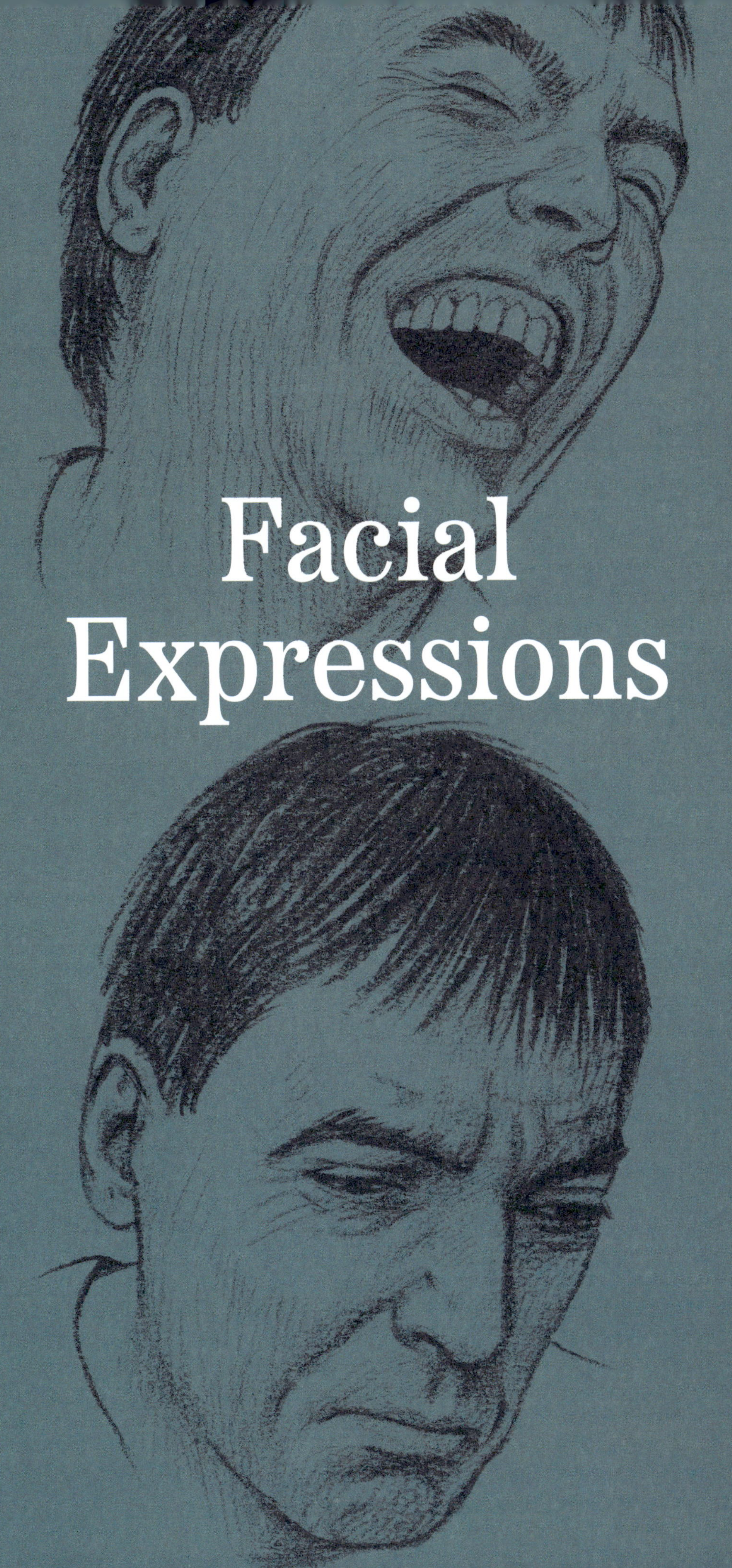

Facial Expressions

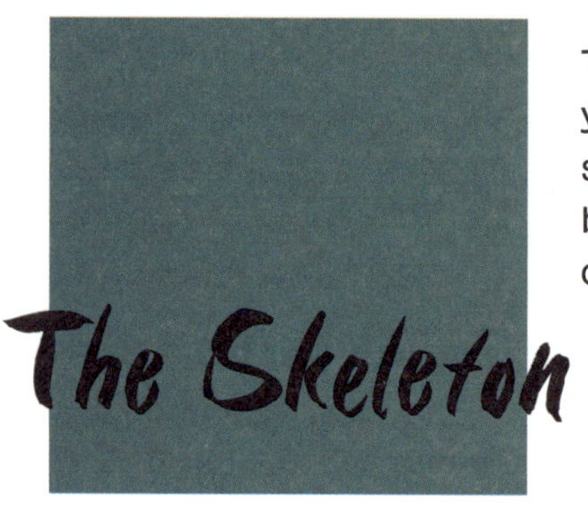

To capture the various different facial expressions, you need to know the general structure and shape of the skull. Here are some basic anatomical facts that can get you started.

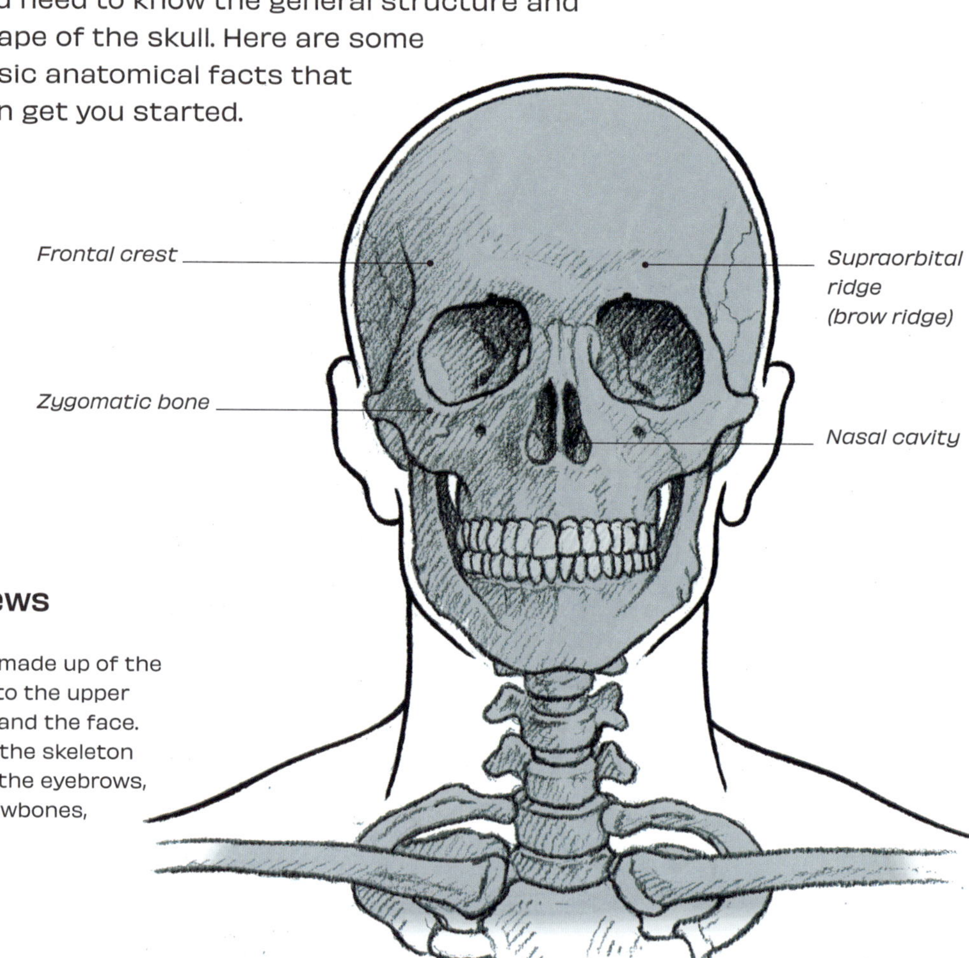

Front and Side Views

The skeleton of the head is made up of the cranial cavity, which refers to the upper and rear parts of the head, and the face. The shapes and volumes of the skeleton give the face its character: the eyebrows, cheekbones, nasal bones, jawbones, proportions, etc.

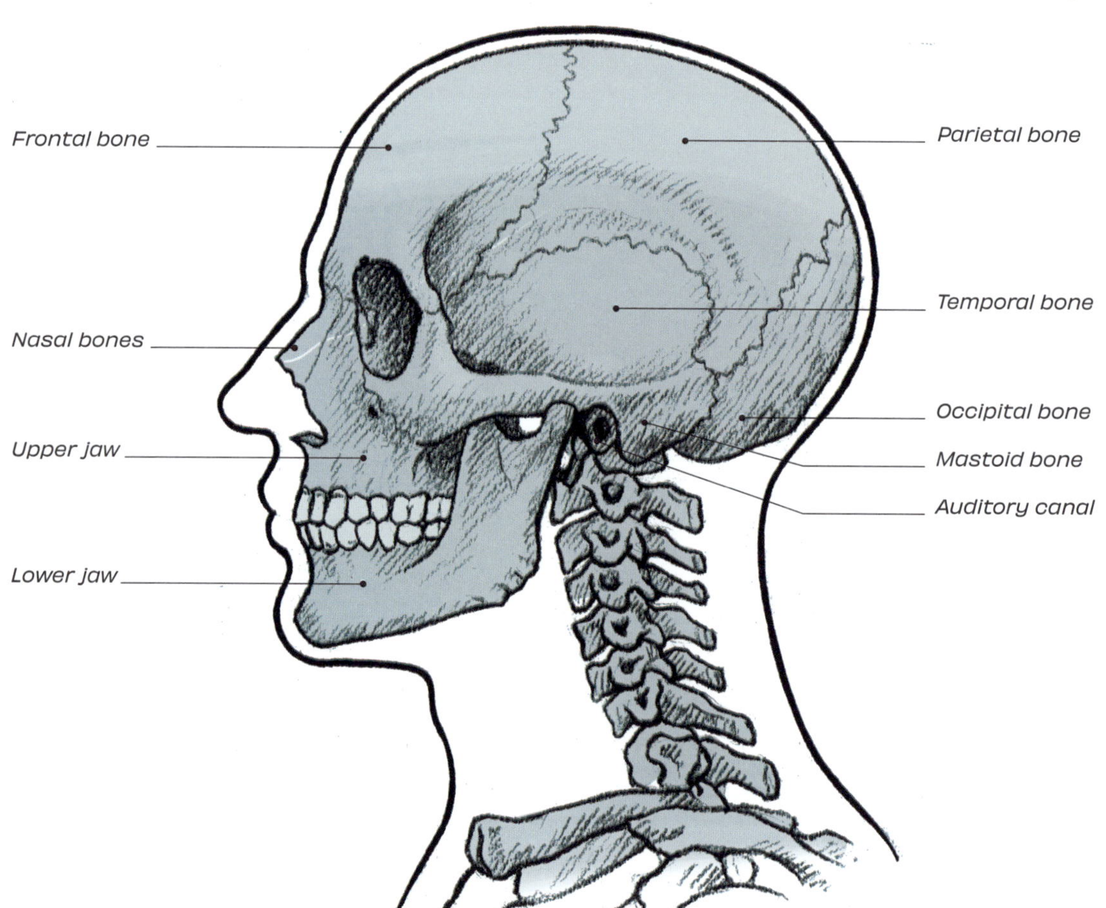

In the face, it is the skin muscles that make the tissues of the skin move and determine the different facial expressions.

Muscles

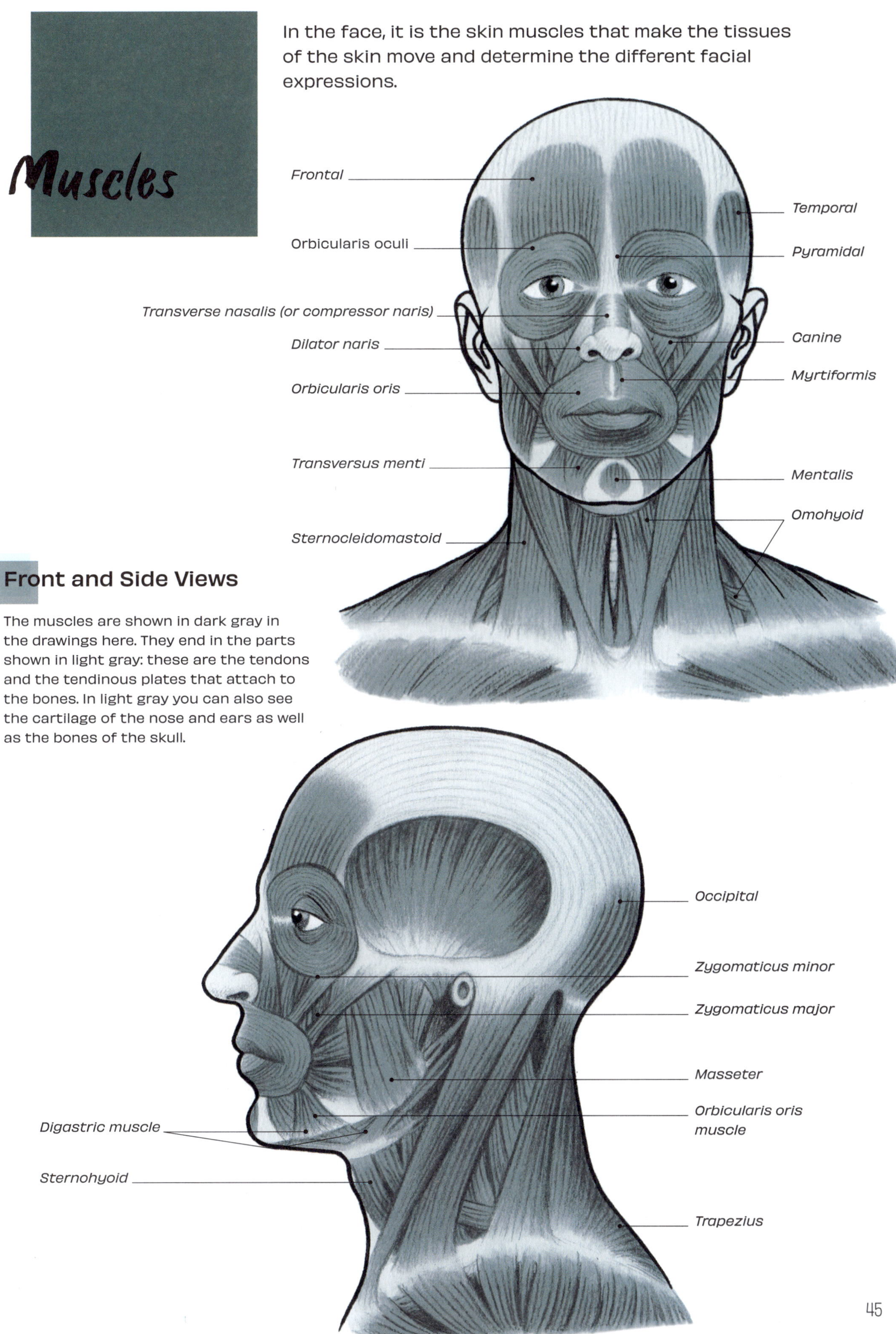

Front and Side Views

The muscles are shown in dark gray in the drawings here. They end in the parts shown in light gray: these are the tendons and the tendinous plates that attach to the bones. In light gray you can also see the cartilage of the nose and ears as well as the bones of the skull.

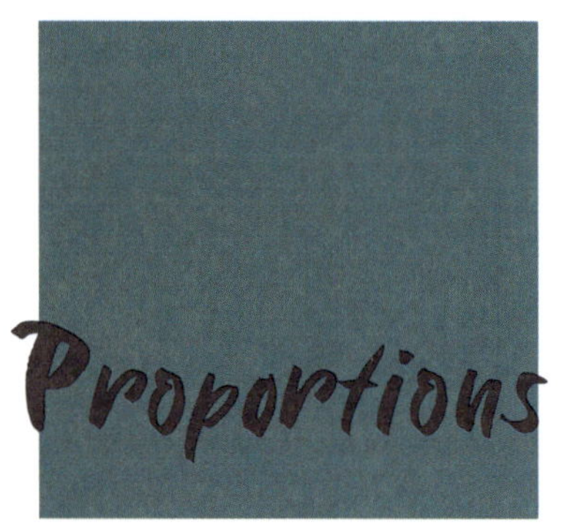

Even though there are rules of proportion that need to be respected, there is no perfect face; the two profiles of our face (from the two different sides) are never perfectly symmetrical. However, here are a few hints to help you correctly position the features of a face.

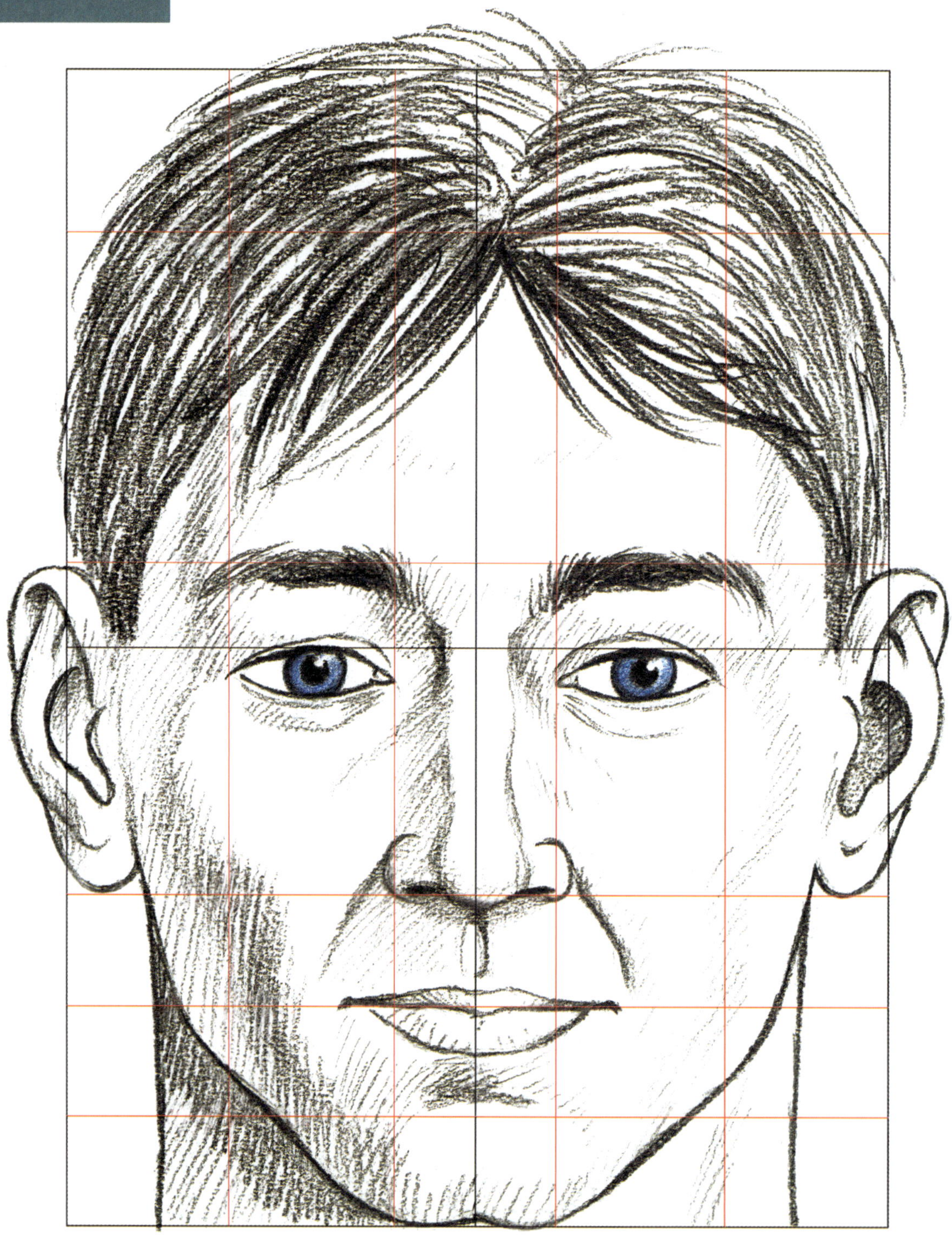

The hollow between the forehead and the nose is at the vertical halfway point of the head.
The width of one eye can fit in the space between the two eyes.
Starting from the hairline, the face can be divided into three equal parts:
hairline to eyebrows, eyebrows to base of nose, and base of nose to chin.

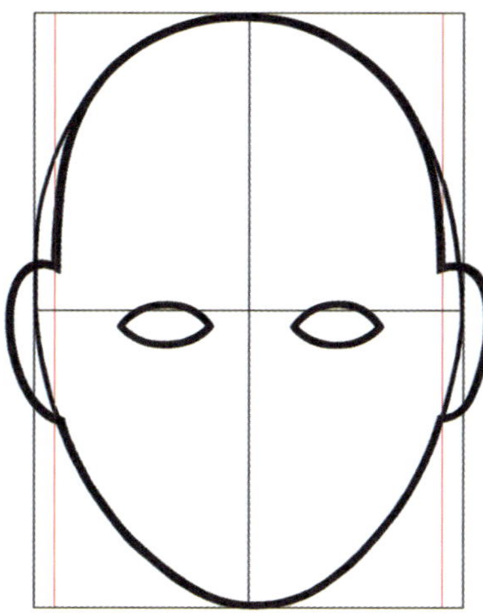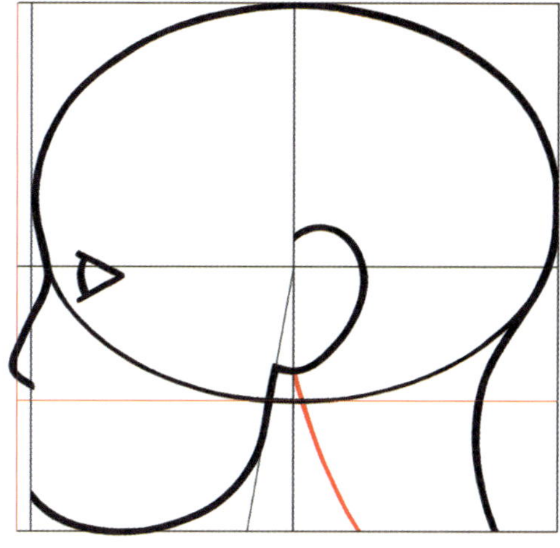

*The entirety of the face fits into just a little more than a quarter of the skull.
The ears attach to the vertical midline of the head. The line of the mouth is in the
first third of the space from the base of the nose to the chin.*

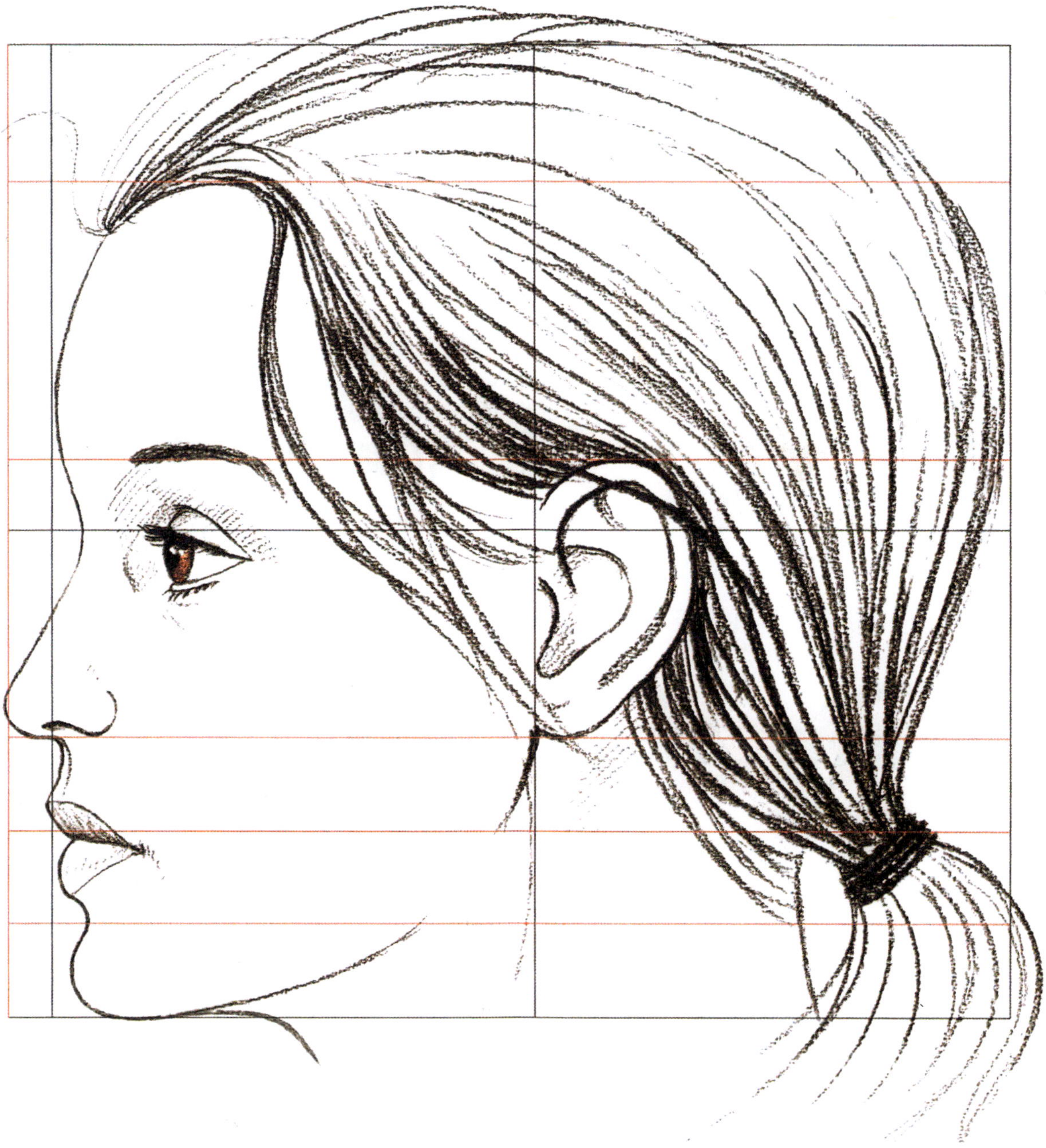

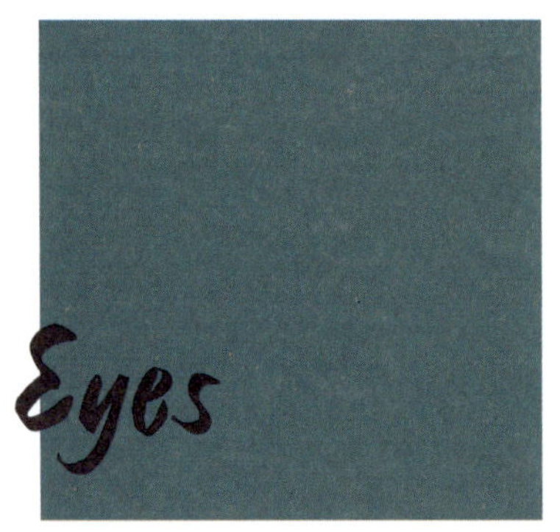

Eyes

Knowing how to draw eyes means being able to capture a look and, through that look, most of the emotion that emanates from the face. The motion of the eyebrows indicates a variety of very different emotions: they rise to indicate surprise and fear and they lower and pull together to express rage.

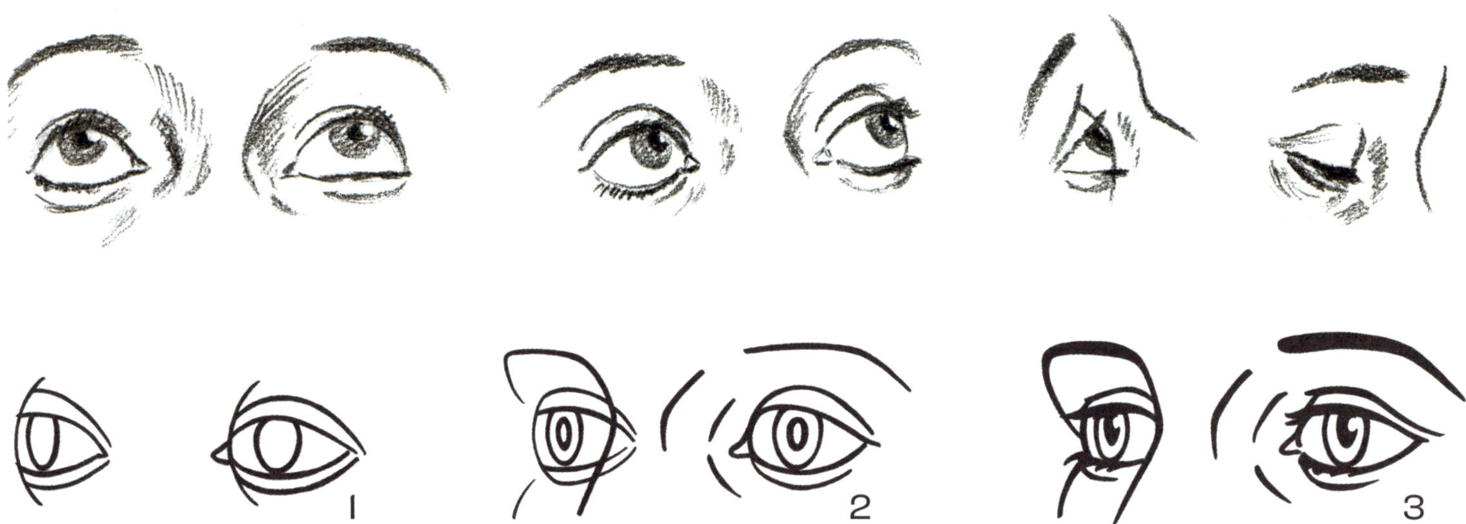

When the face turns toward its profile, the bridge of the nose partially hides the outside eye.

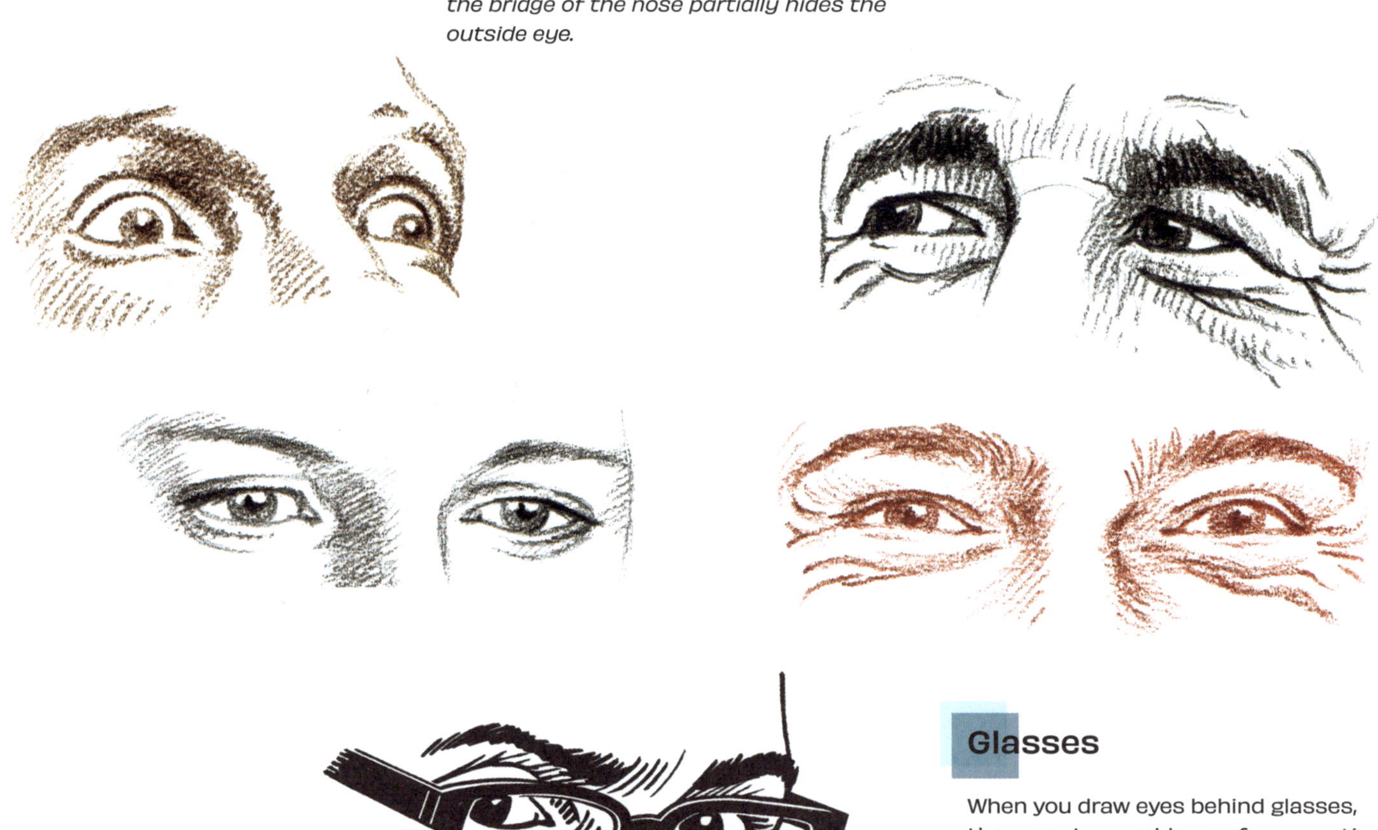

Glasses

When you draw eyes behind glasses, there are two problems of perspective: the issue of the eyes and that of the glasses, on a parallel plane.

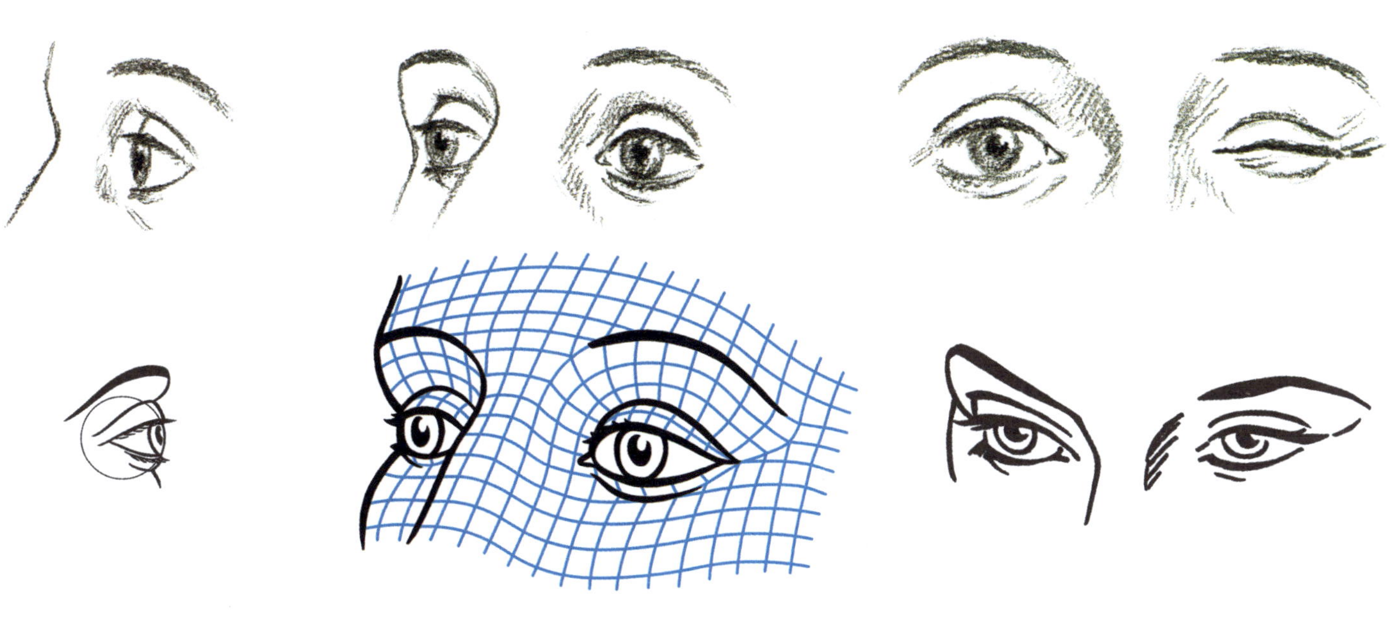

The Position of the Eyes

The eyes are orbs positioned at the back of the
eye sockets: they are rounded, and partially hidden
by the eyelids, which follow their rounded shape
and are surrounded by a hollow.

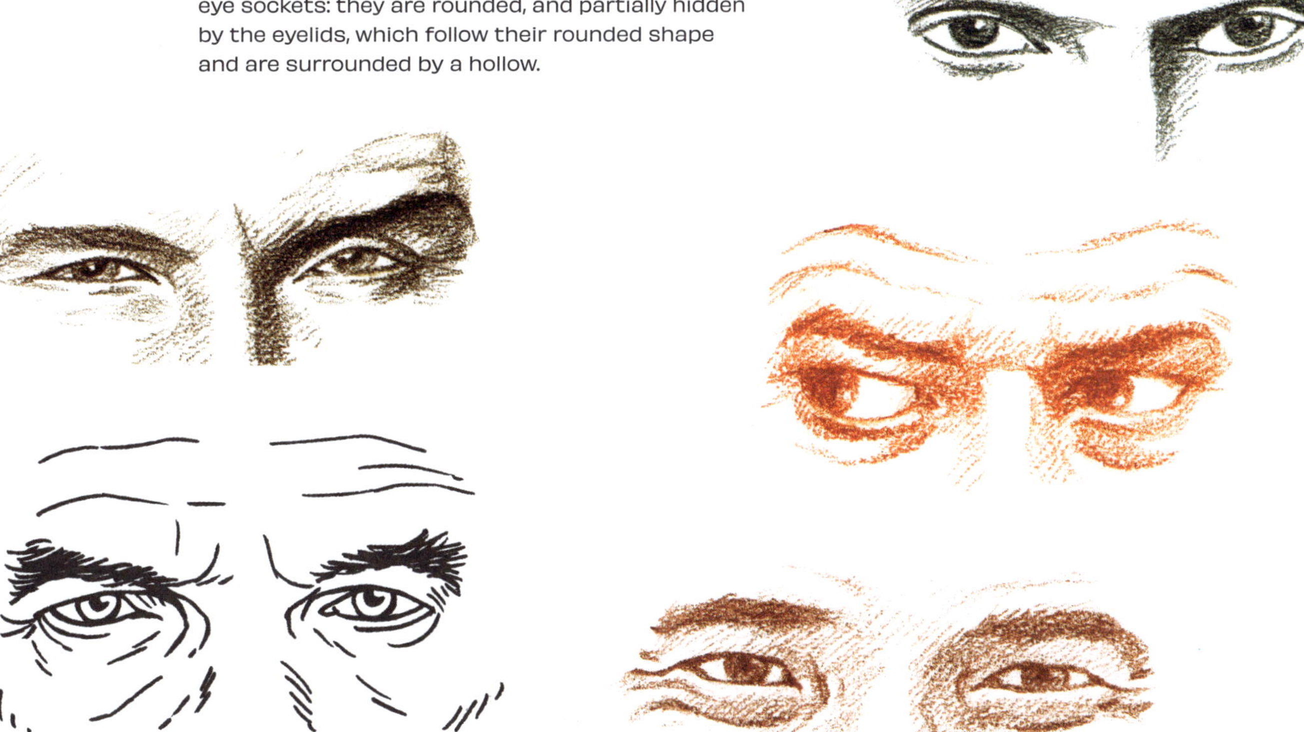

Noses

Rounded, aquiline, trumpet-shaped, or flattened, the nose can come in any shape. Do you have enough flair to draw it?

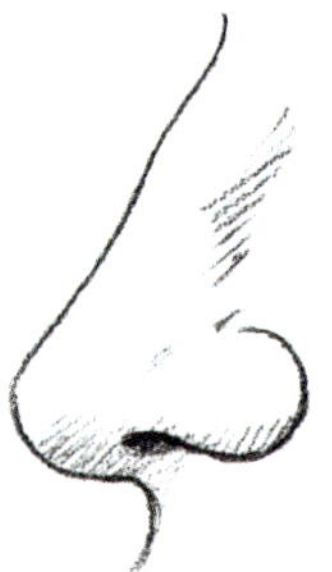 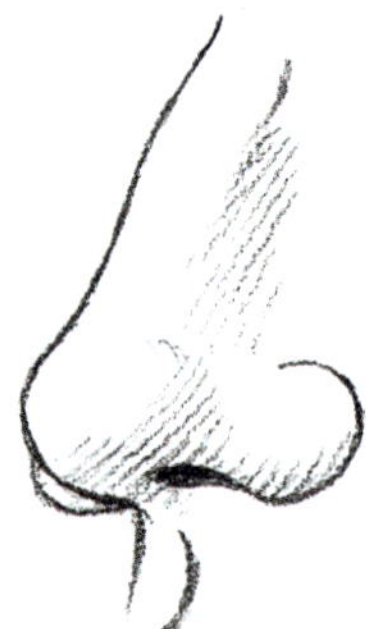 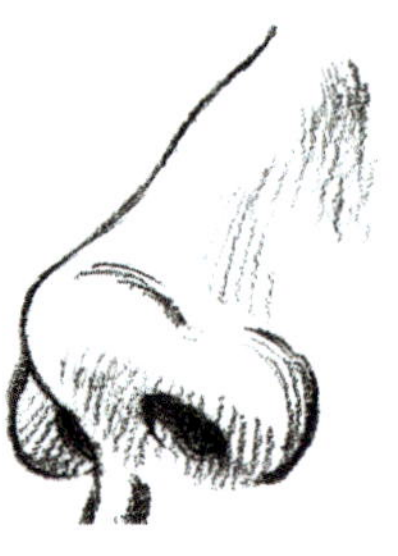 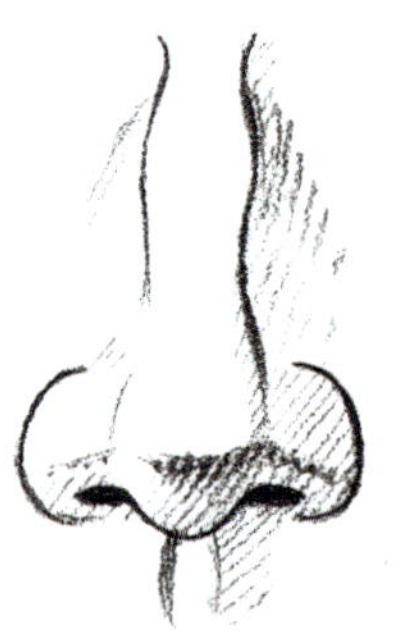 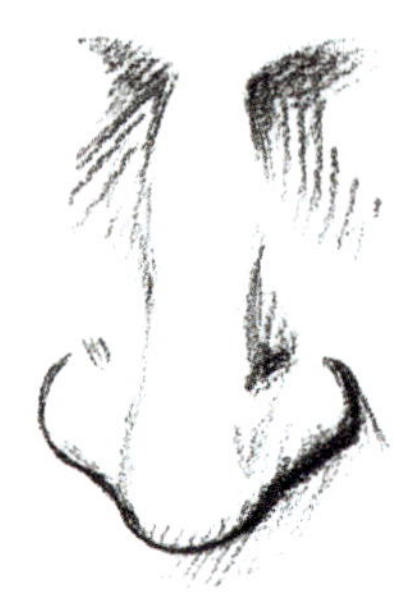

From the side, the bridge is very visible. It's important to pay attention to the way in which the nostril connects to the tip of the nose.

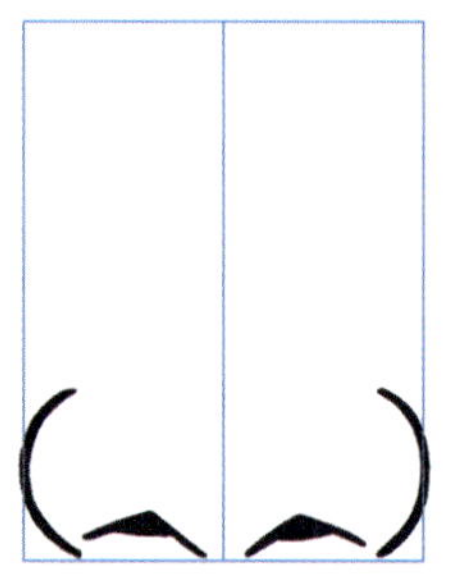 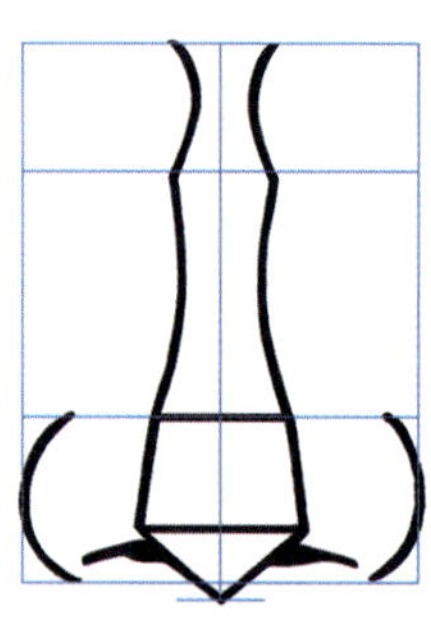 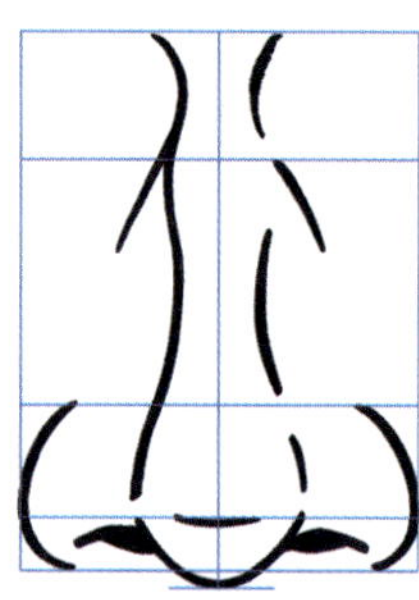 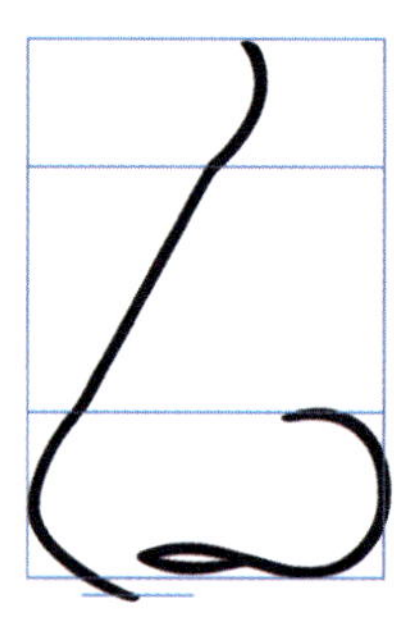 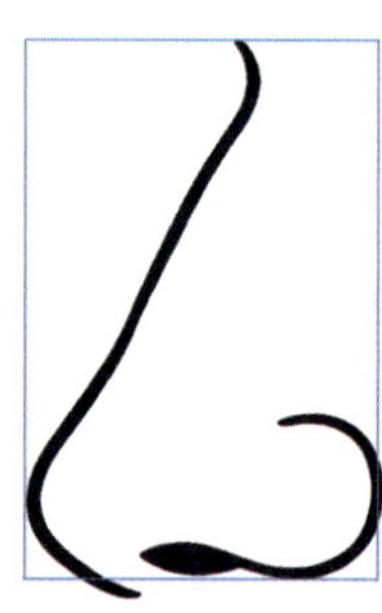

The nose is made up of a bridge and of two bulges, which are the nostrils.

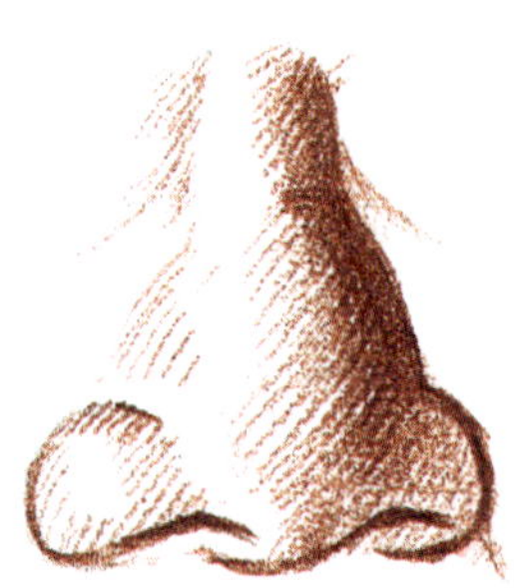 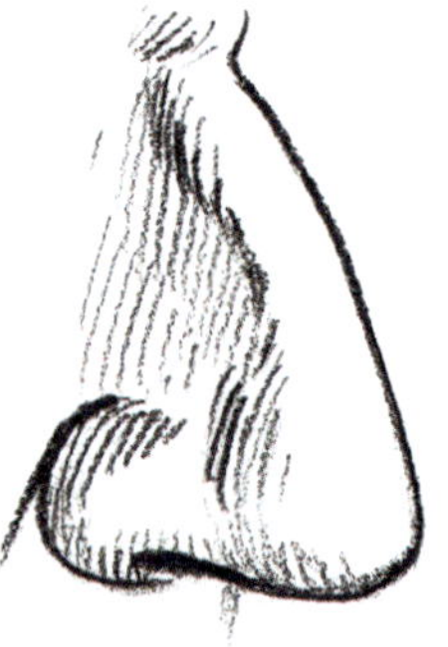 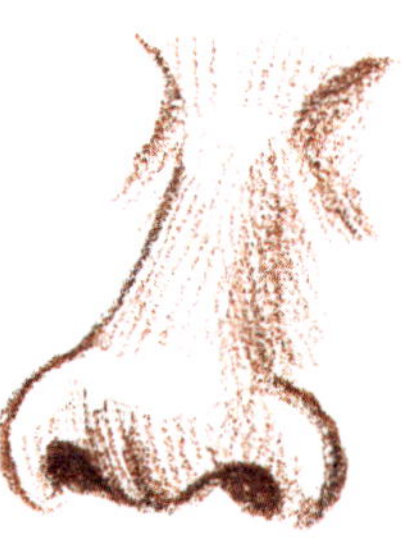

From the front, the bridge is only visible through the play of shadows. The tip of the nose is positioned either above, at the same level as, or below the line of the nostrils, depending on whether the nose is turned up, straight, or hooked.

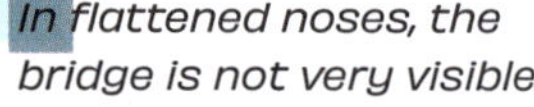 *In flattened noses, the bridge is not very visible.*

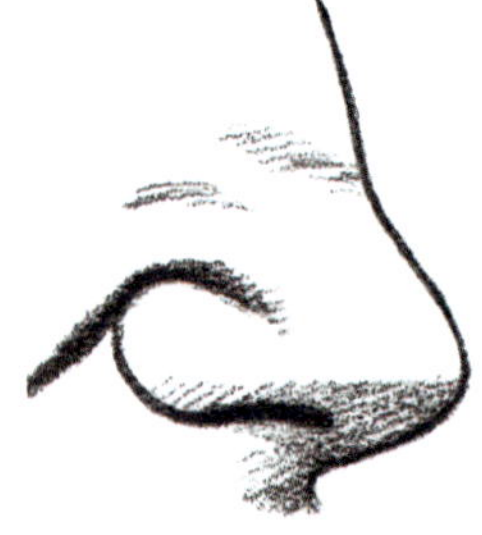 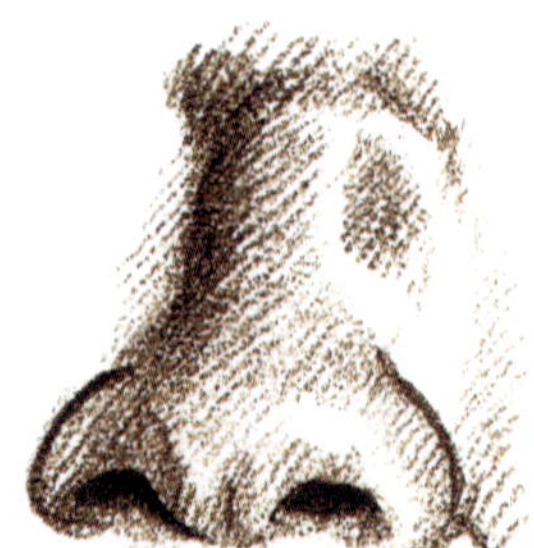

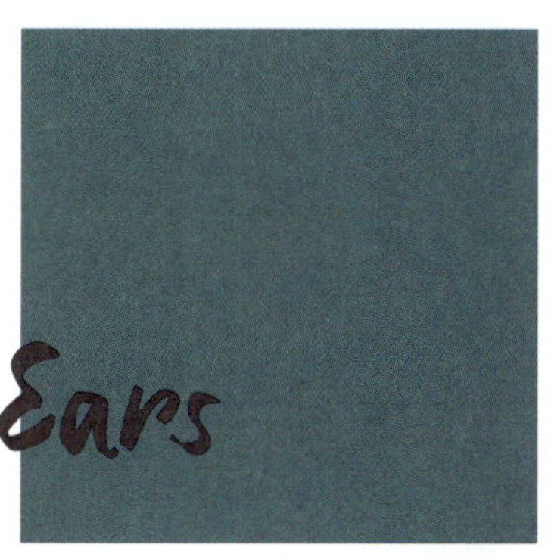

Ears

The constitution of the ear is the same for all ears. It is only its shape that varies from one individual to the next: ears can be flat or pointed, have large lobes, etc.

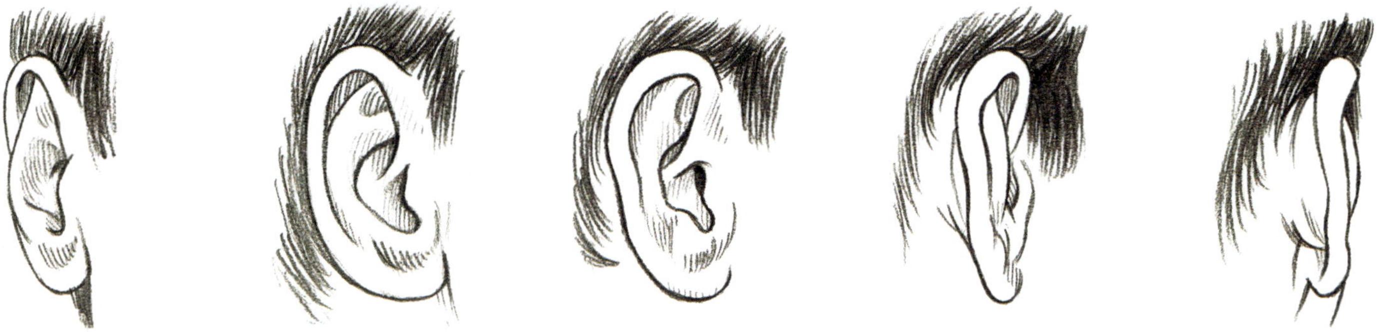

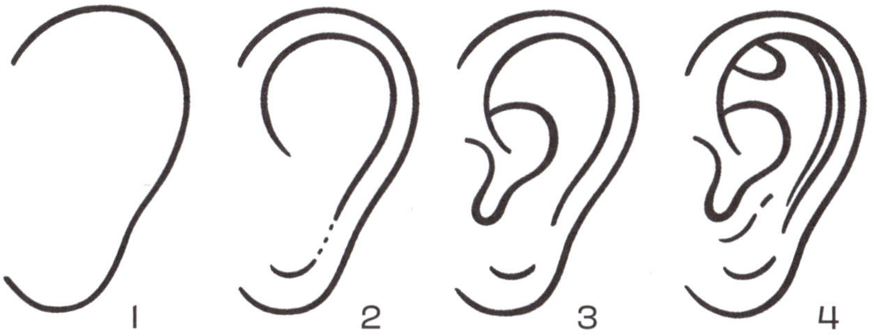

1   2   3   4

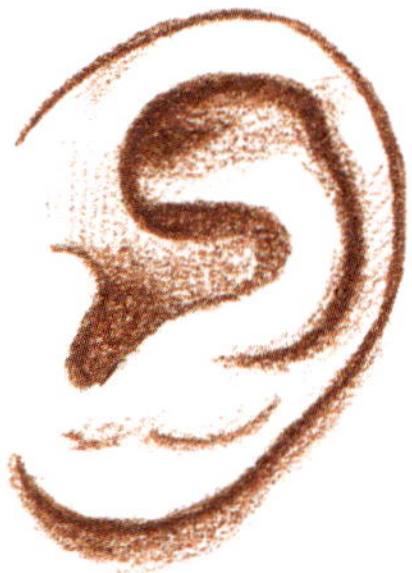

Child's ear

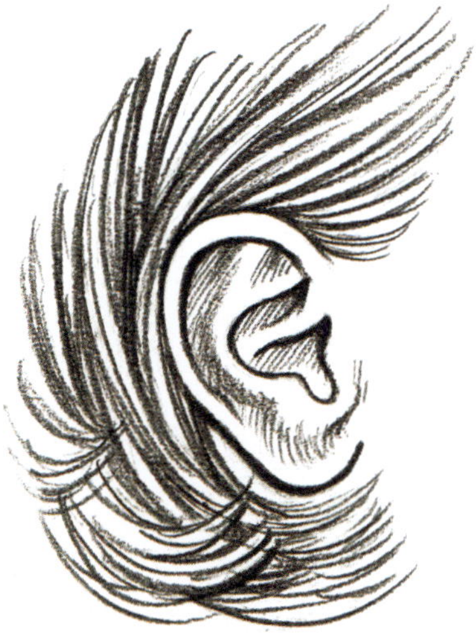

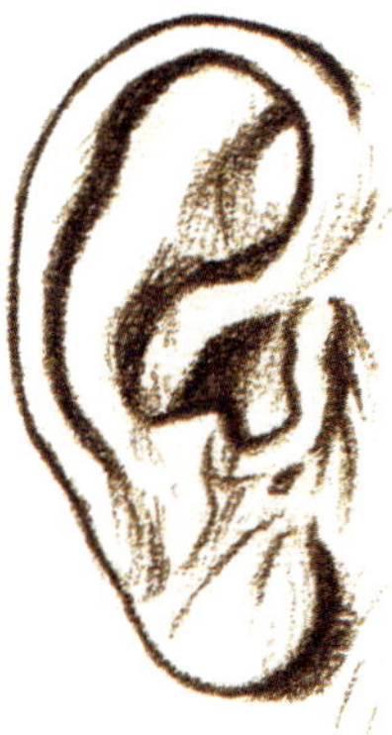

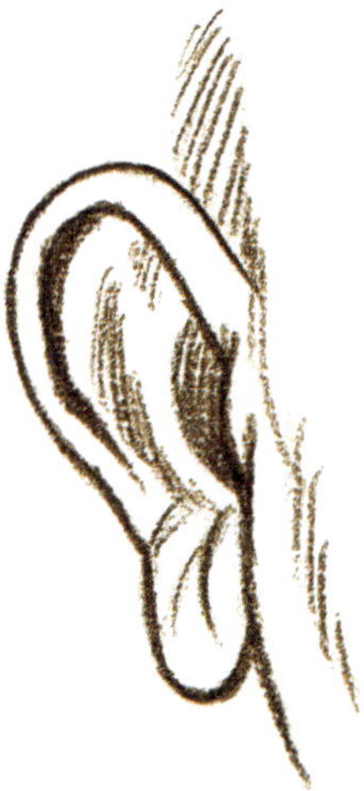

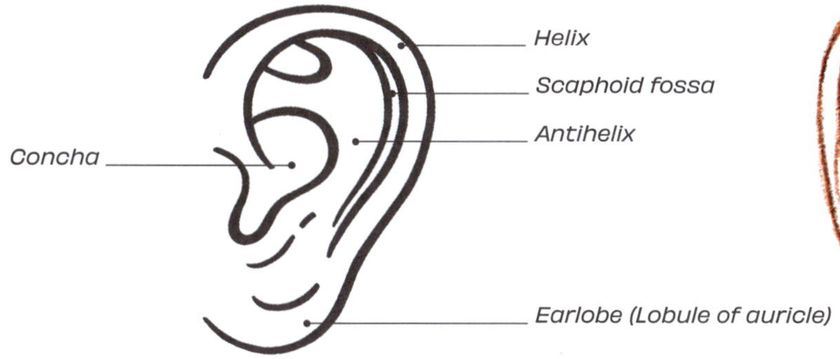

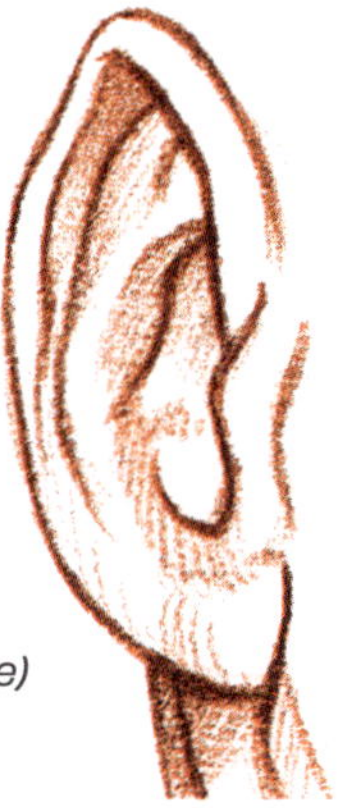

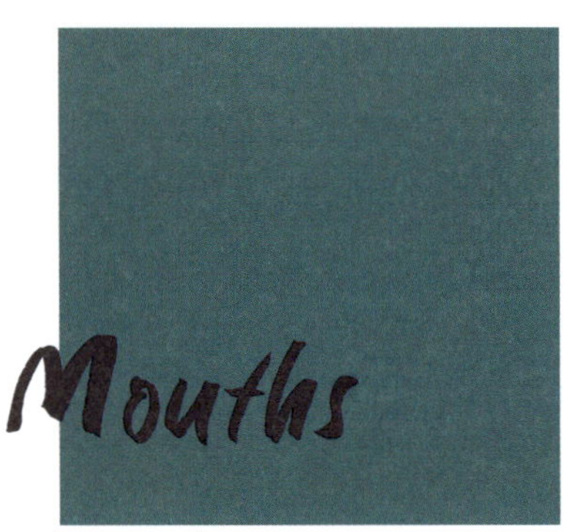

Open or closed, full or fine, smiling or sad, the mouth determines the whole lower part of the face.

Mouths

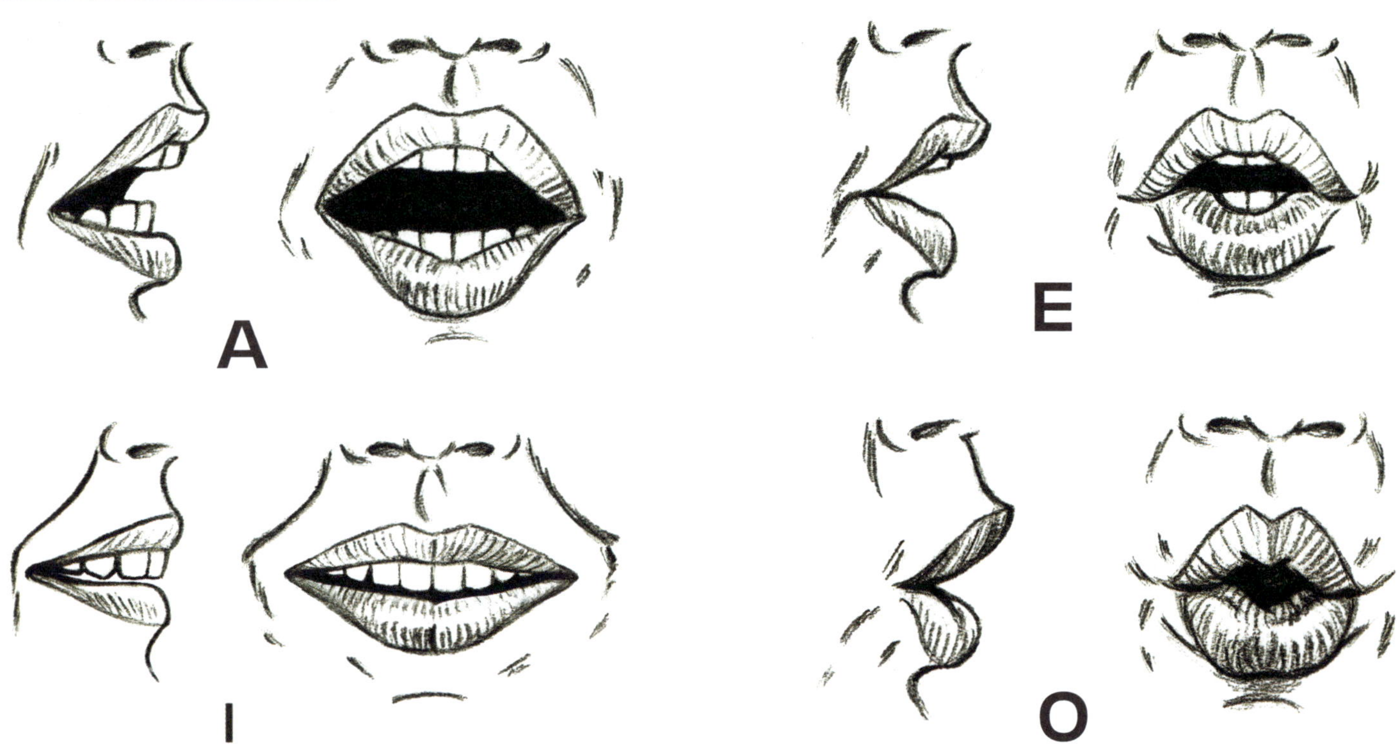

The movement of the mouth varies depending on what sound is being pronounced. The vowels are called "palatal" because they are articulated at the level of the palate.

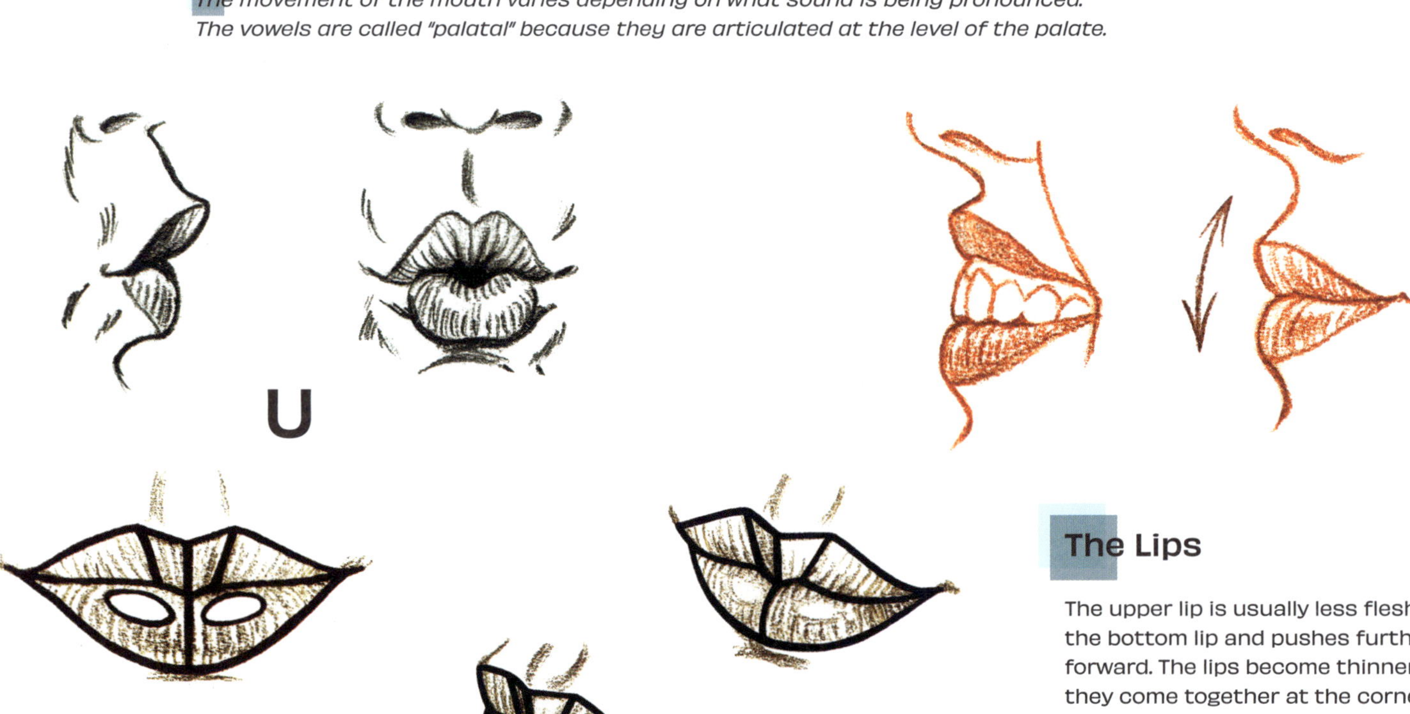

The Lips

The upper lip is usually less fleshy than the bottom lip and pushes further forward. The lips become thinner where they come together at the corners of the mouth, or "commissures."

Breakdown of the mouth

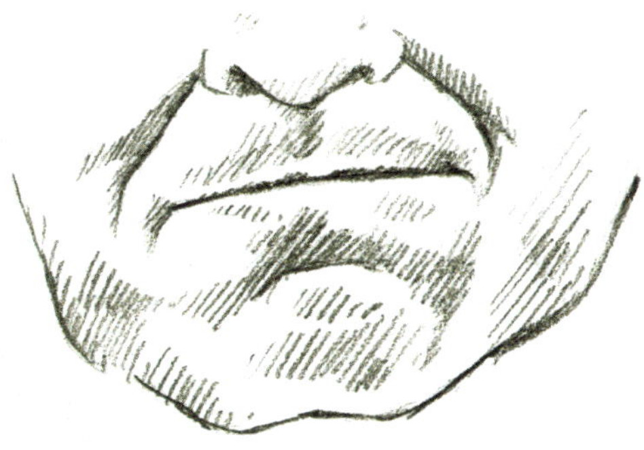

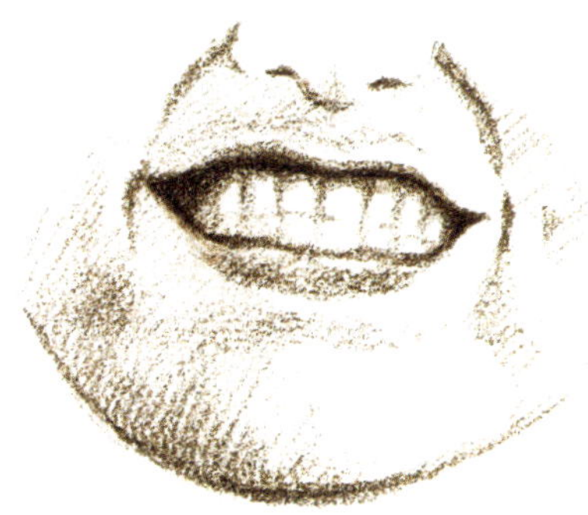

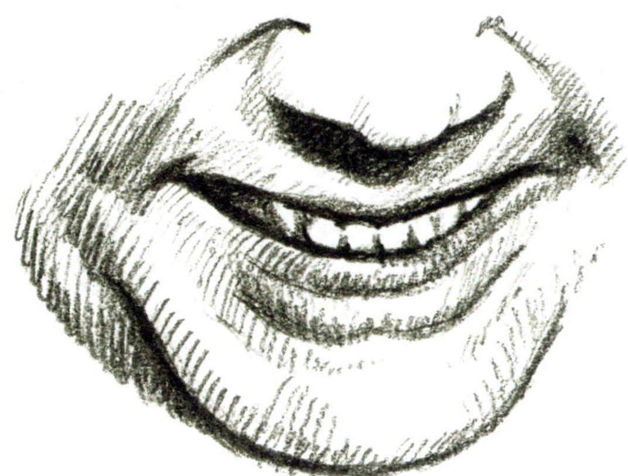

Even when the mouth is closed, even just a slight movement in the tension of the muscles is enough to give the face its expression.

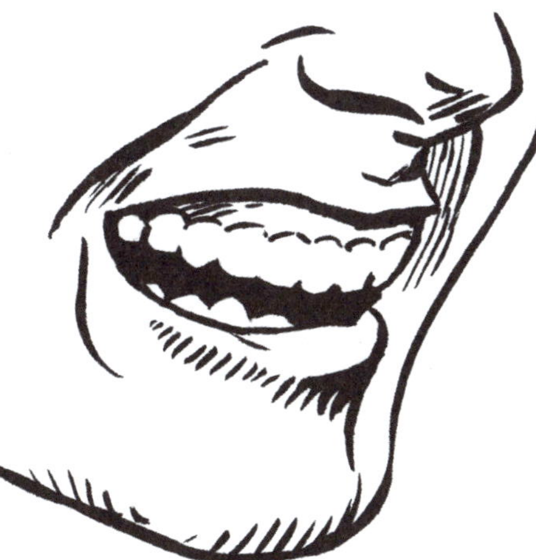

Just going by the shape that the mouth takes, it's easy to guess the expression on the face!

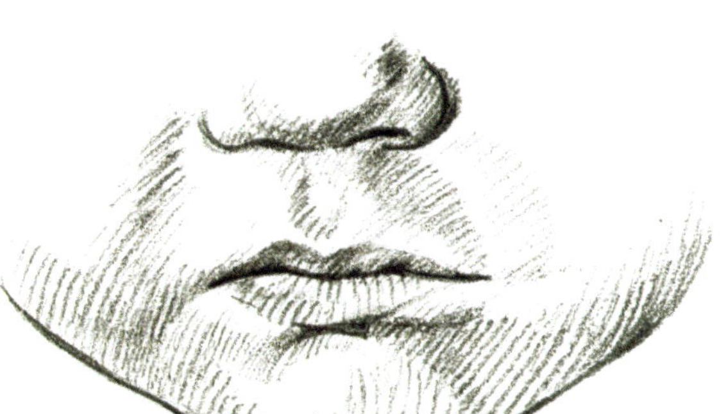

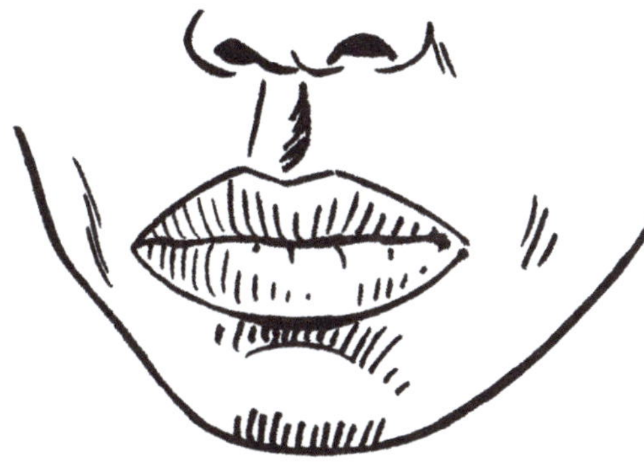

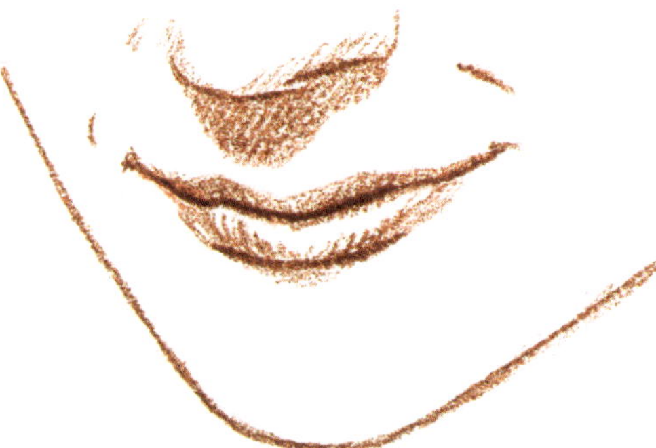

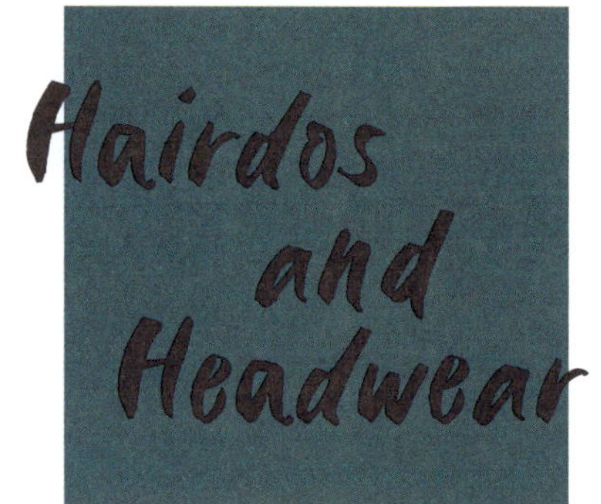

Hairdos and Headwear

The expression on the very same face can look very different depending on whether the hair is long or short, curly or straight, cut short or braided. Add to these variations the many possibilities offered by the different hats that you can use to give character to your faces.

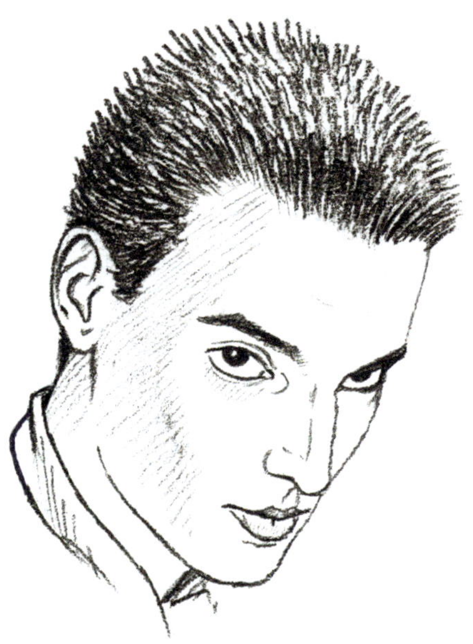

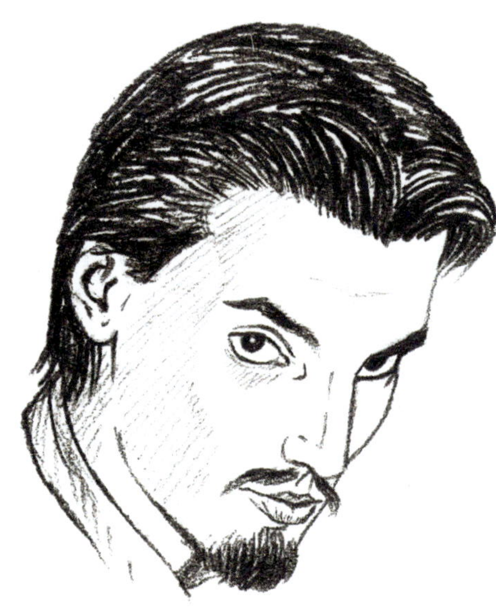

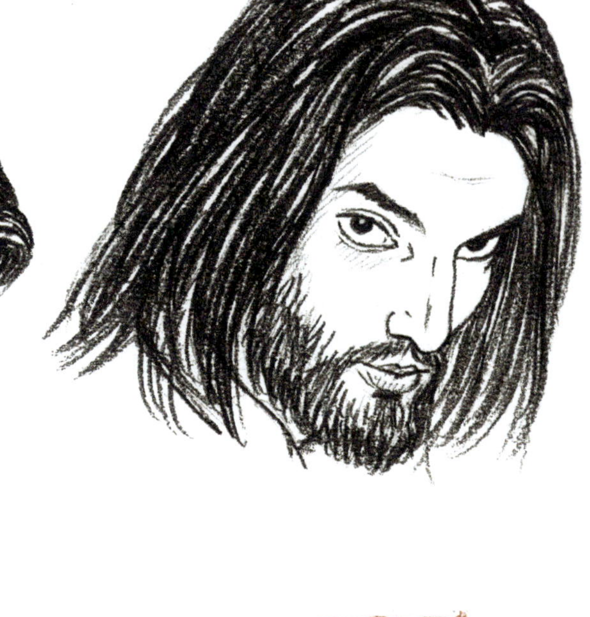

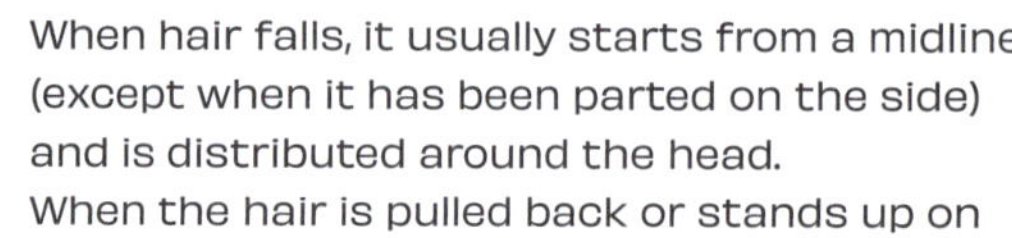

Base of the Hair

When hair falls, it usually starts from a midline (except when it has been parted on the side) and is distributed around the head.
When the hair is pulled back or stands up on the head, we can see the base of the hair (or hairline) in a crown around the face.

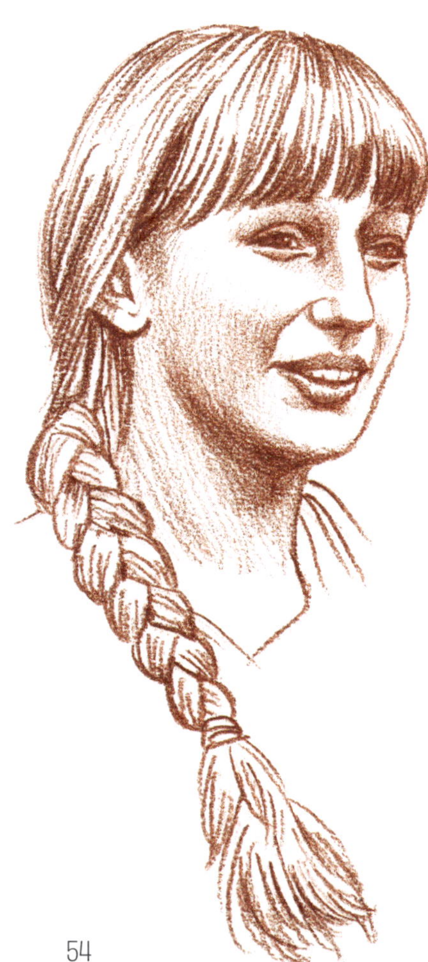

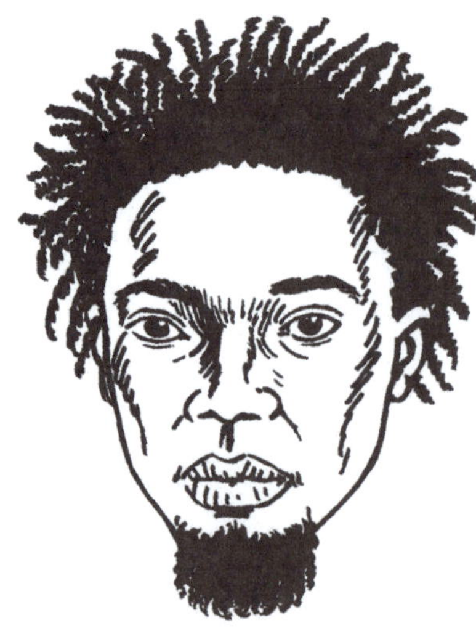

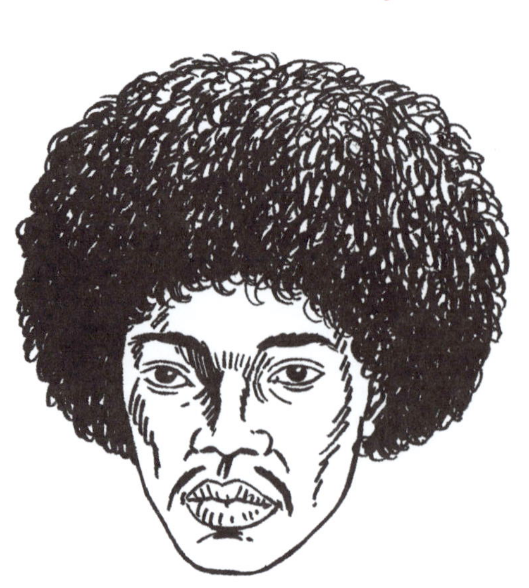

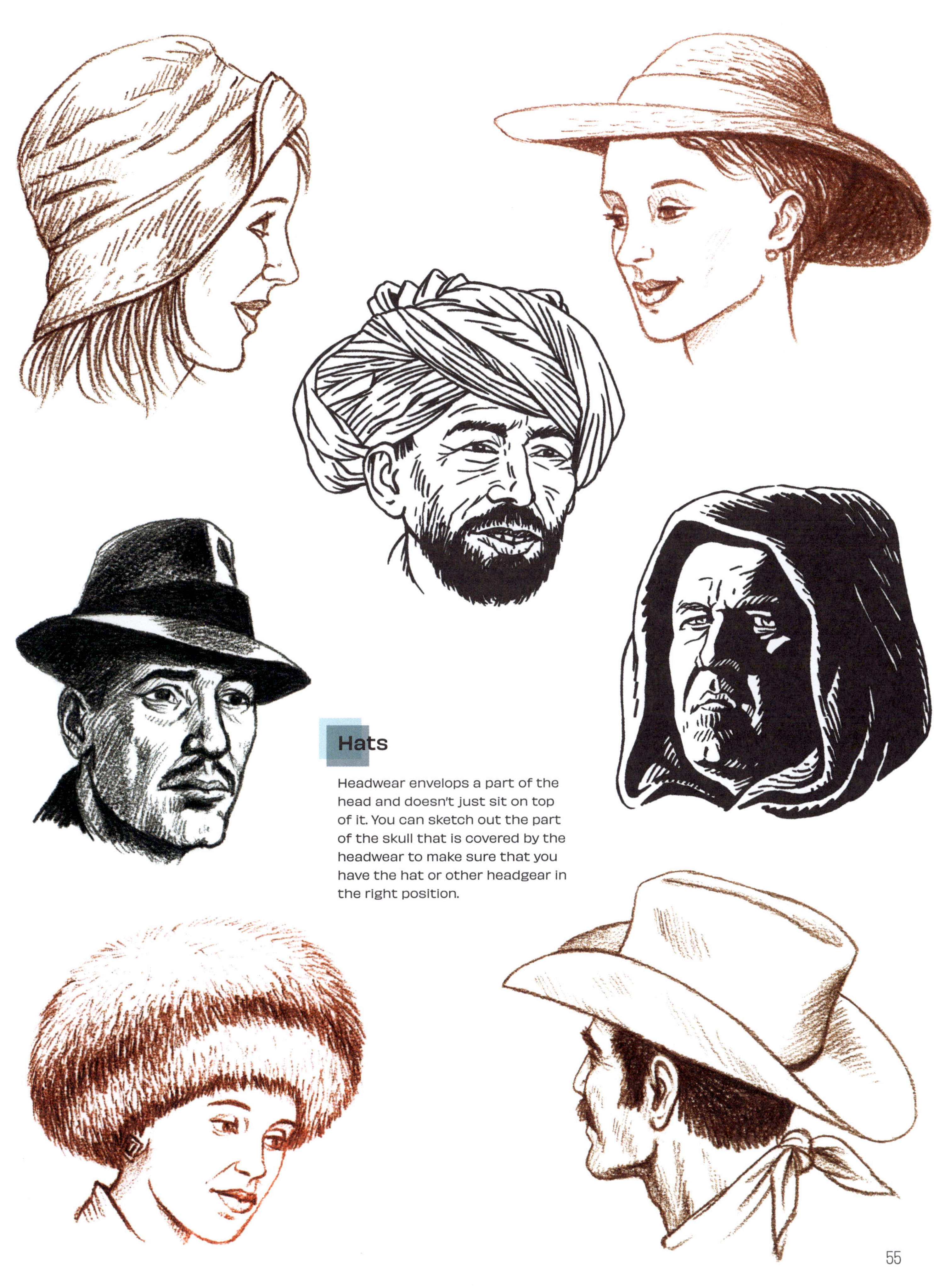

Hats

Headwear envelops a part of the head and doesn't just sit on top of it. You can sketch out the part of the skull that is covered by the headwear to make sure that you have the hat or other headgear in the right position.

As people grow older, their head grows and its proportions change: the facial features move further apart, and the face grows longer. Then some wrinkles appear, the skin becomes lax in some places, and some hair begins to disappear.

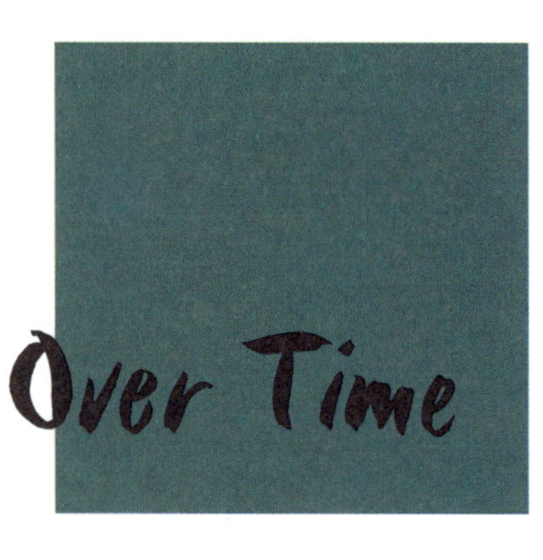

Over Time

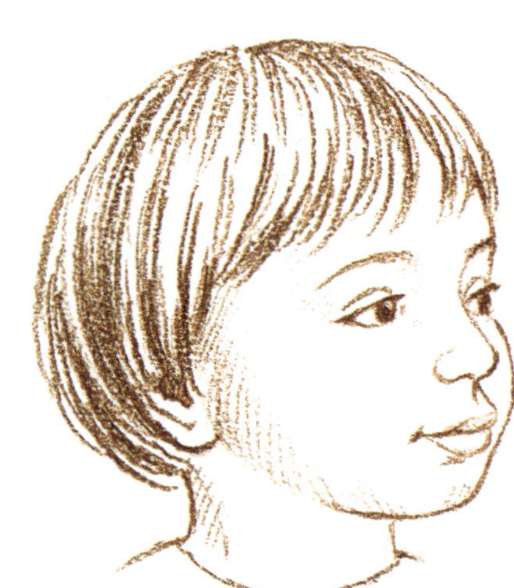

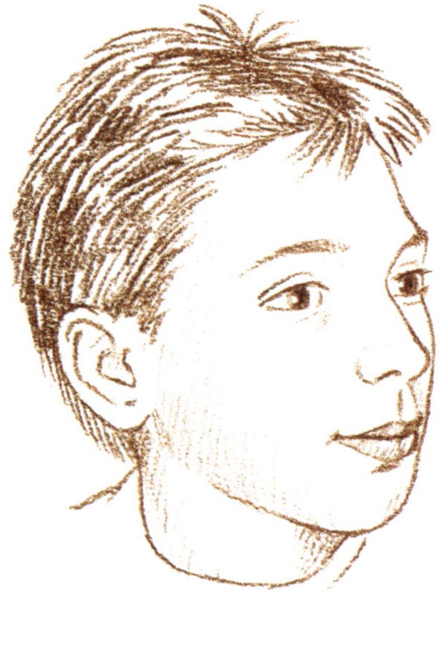

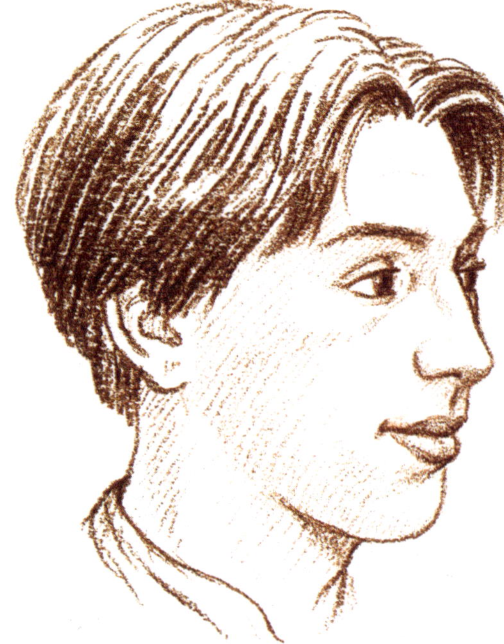

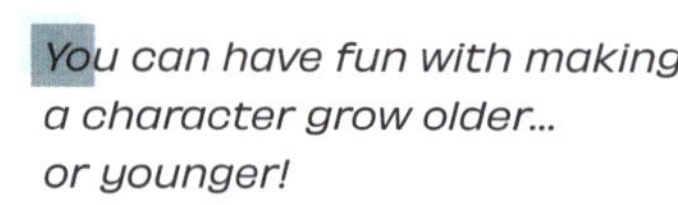

You can have fun with making a character grow older... or younger!

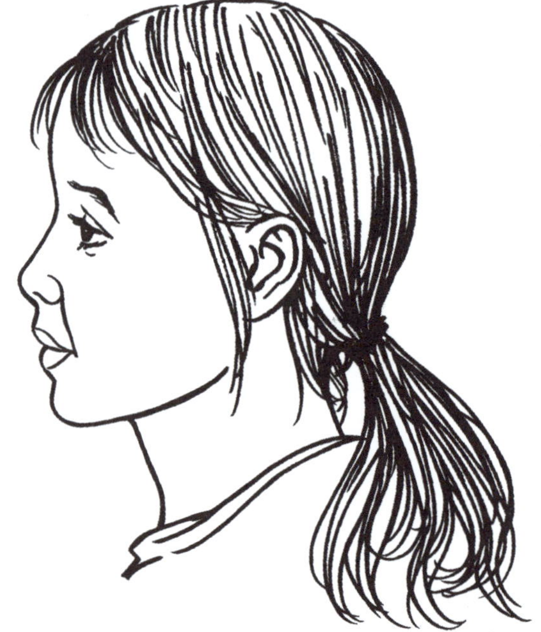

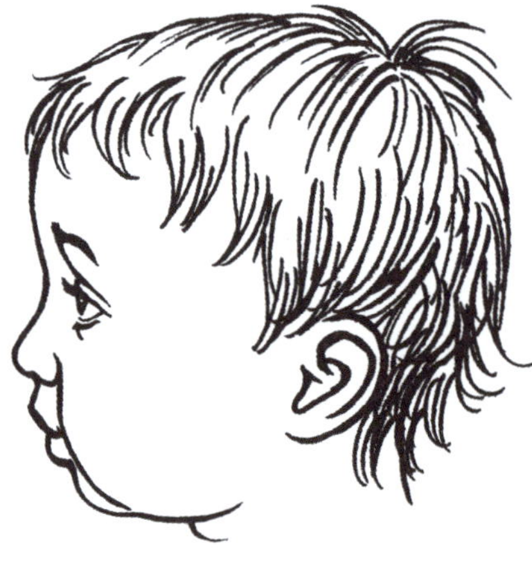

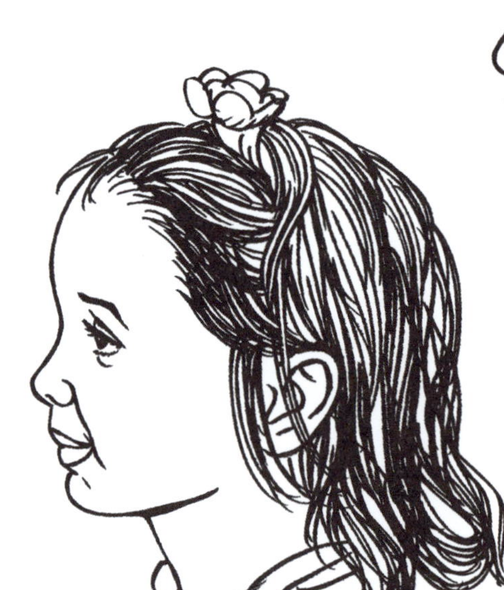

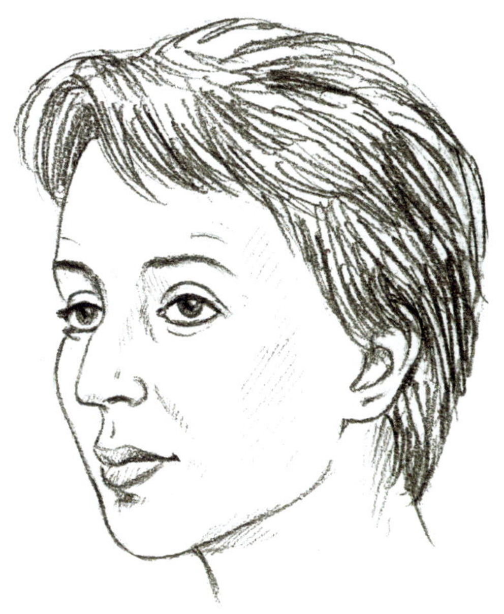

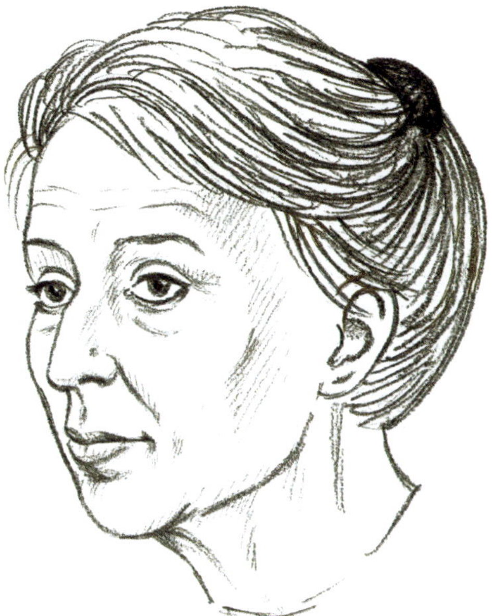

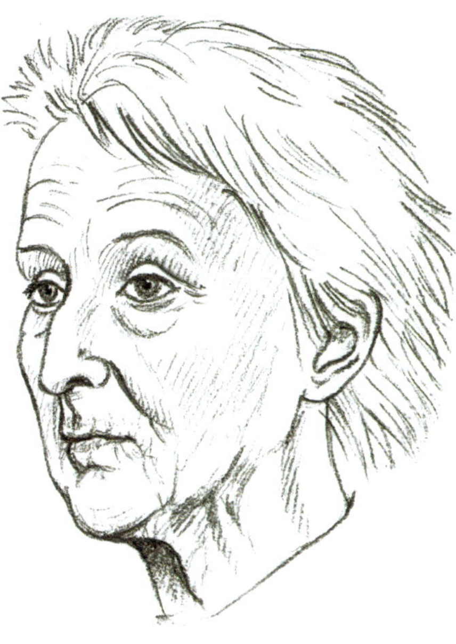

The facial features are more strongly marked, and the hair has become white.

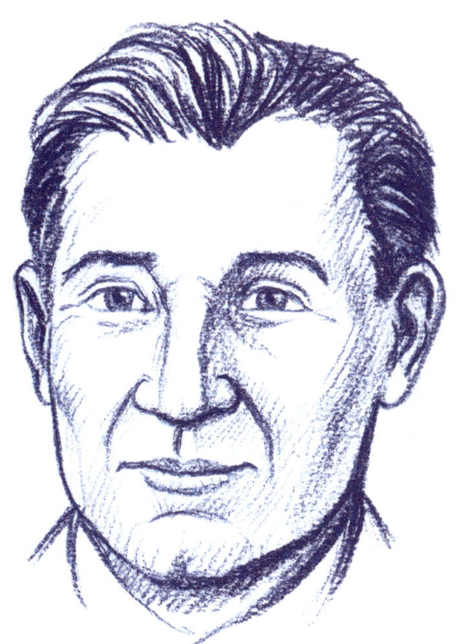

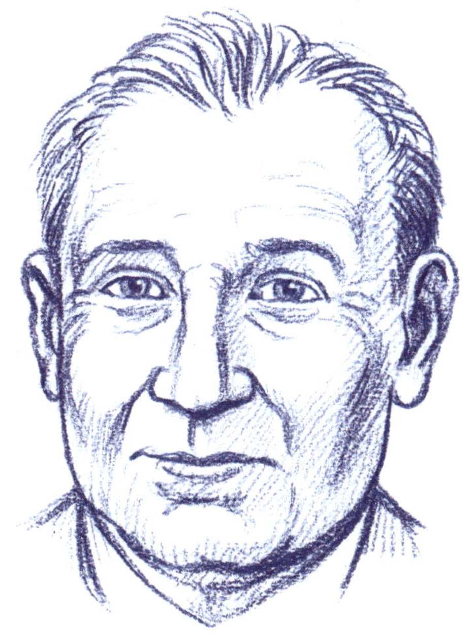

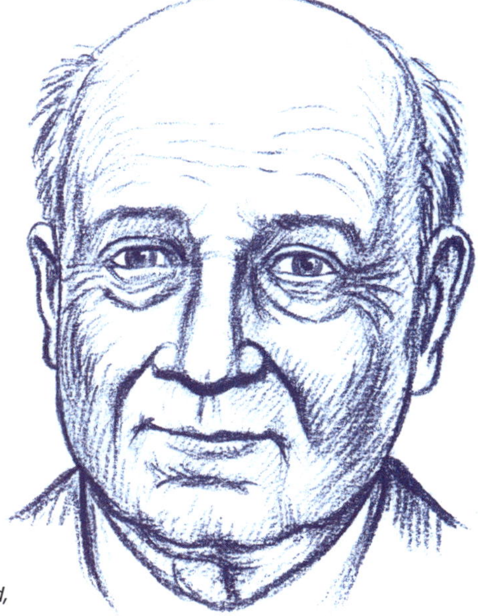

Wrinkles have been added to the forehead, and the hair has become sparse.

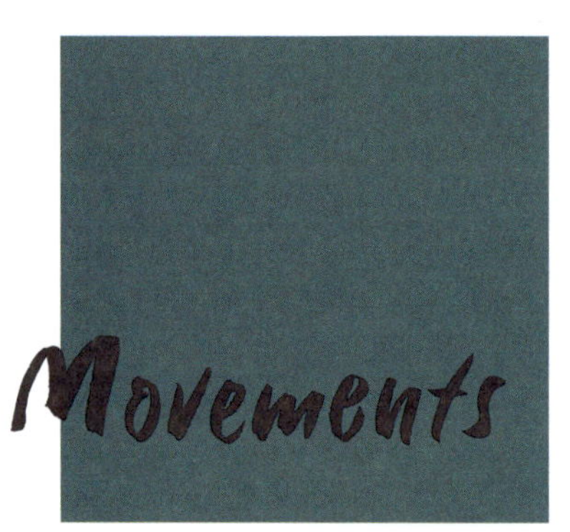

As you move a head around, you will see certain parts of the face beginning to hide other parts. This is how you can put together a three-dimensional view of the face.

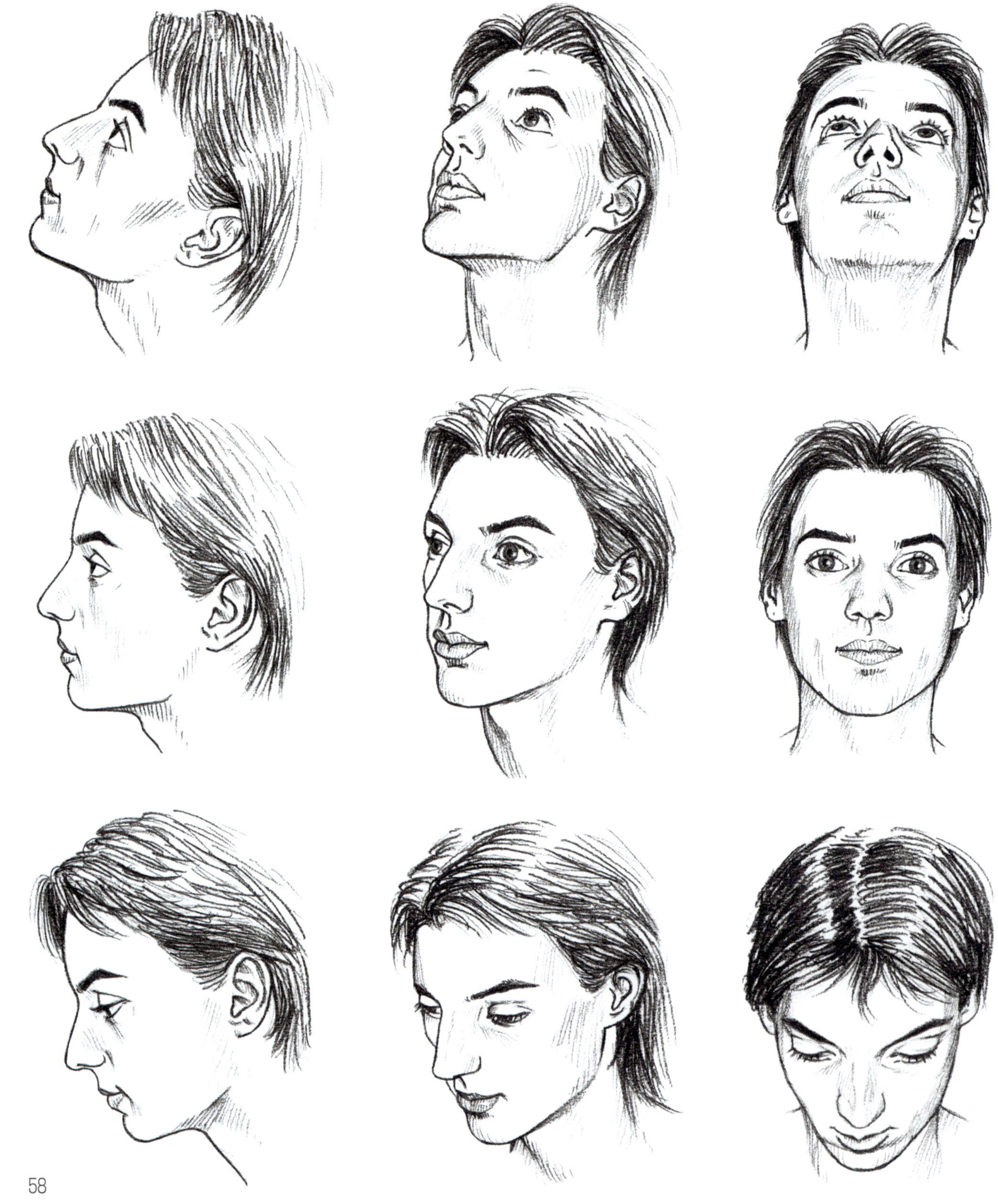

The face shown below has the exact same expression every time: it is only the change in lighting that makes it look different each time. The shadows shape the oval of the face and give it depth.

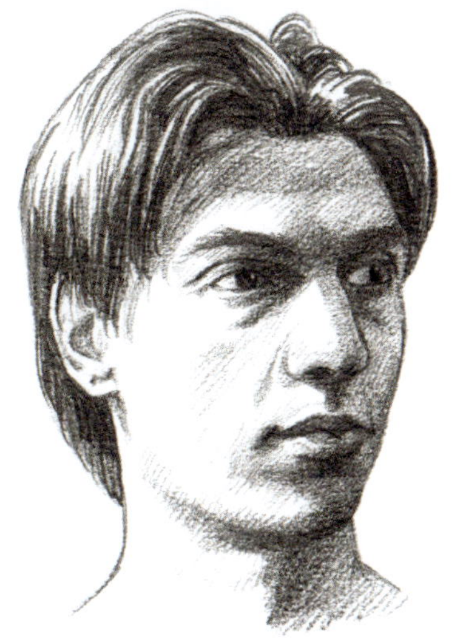

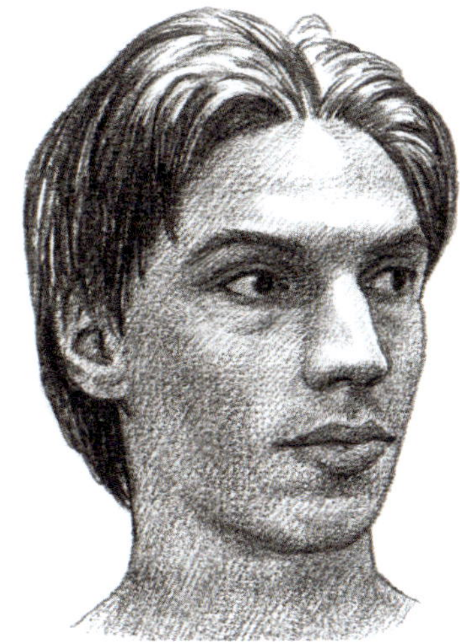

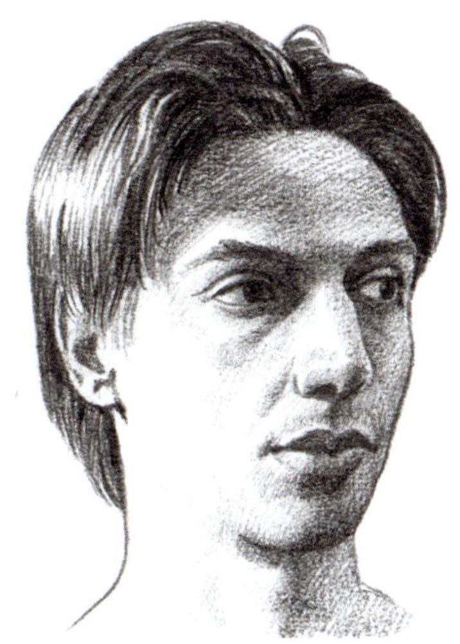

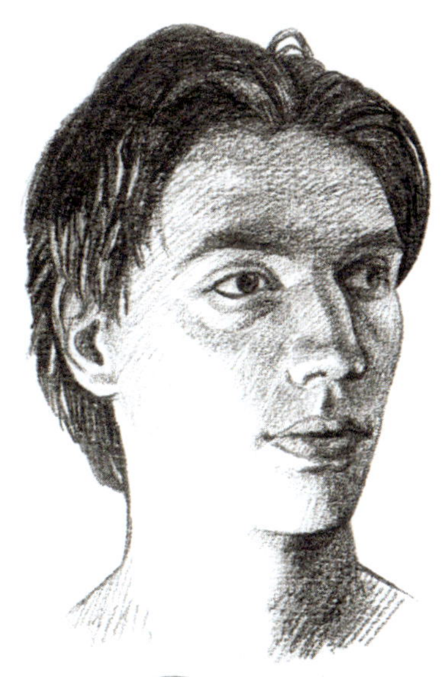

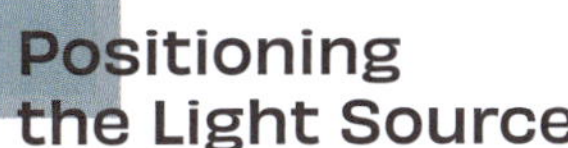

Positioning the Light Source

Whenever you draw a face lit up by a light source, there will be a shadow projected on the side opposite the light source.

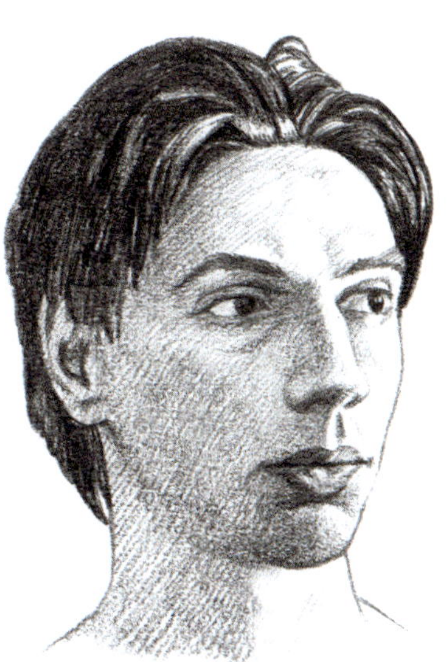

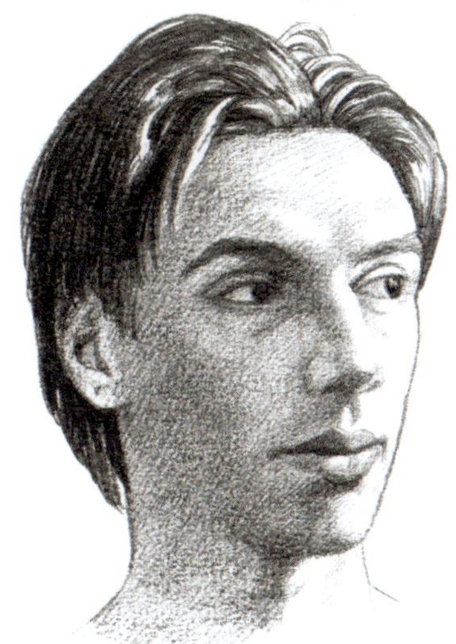

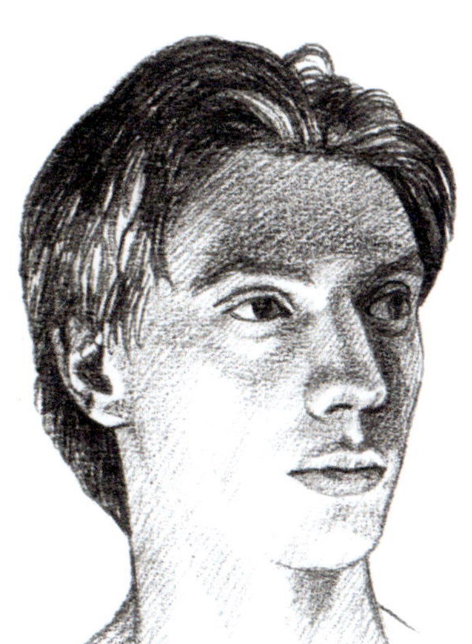

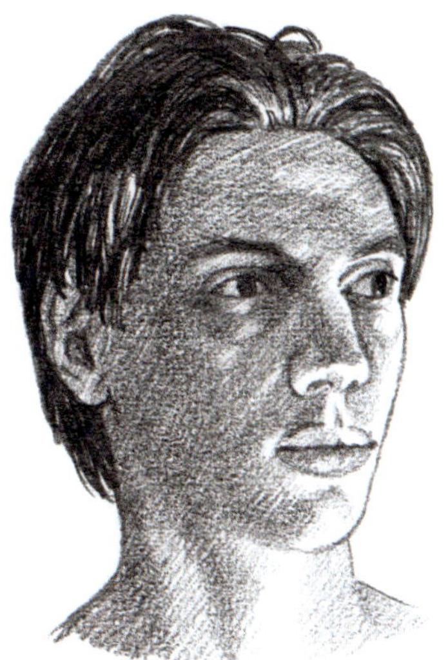

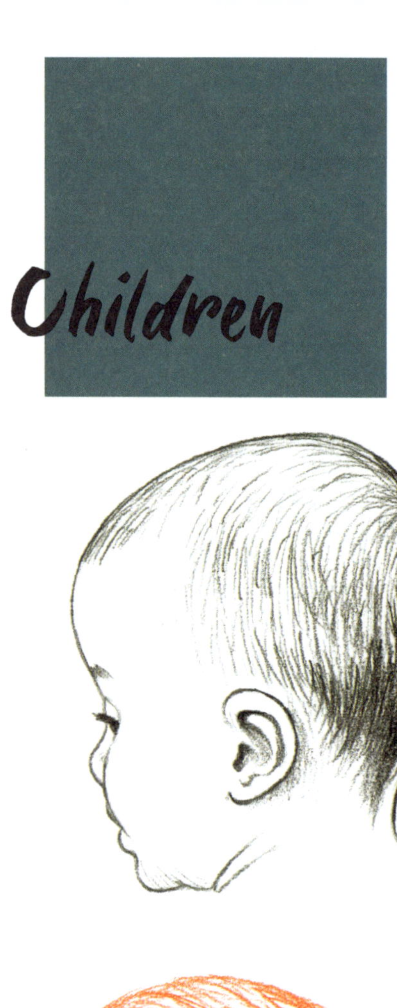

In babies, the facial features are concentrated in a much smaller zone compared to the rest of the head.

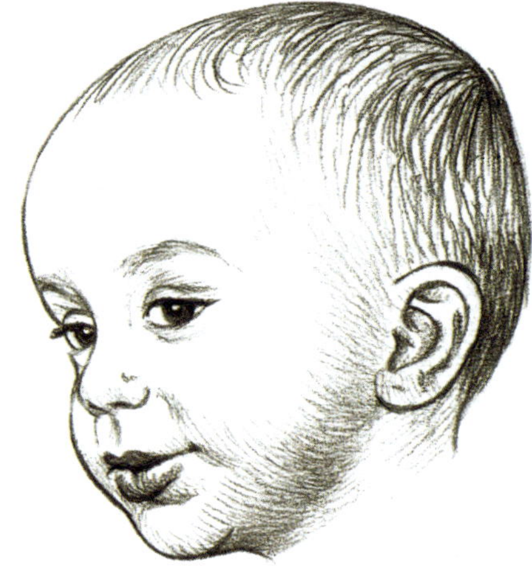

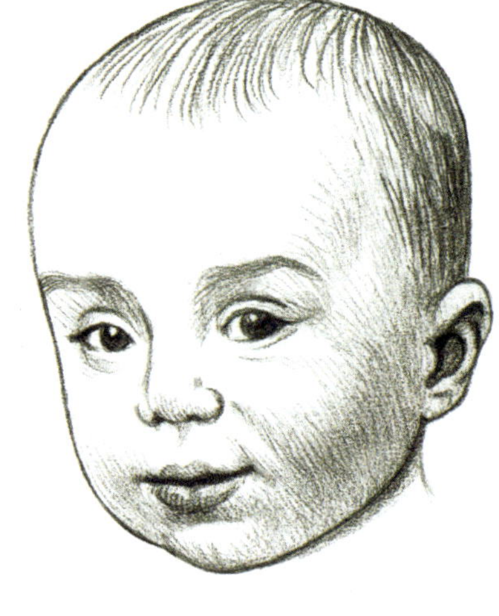

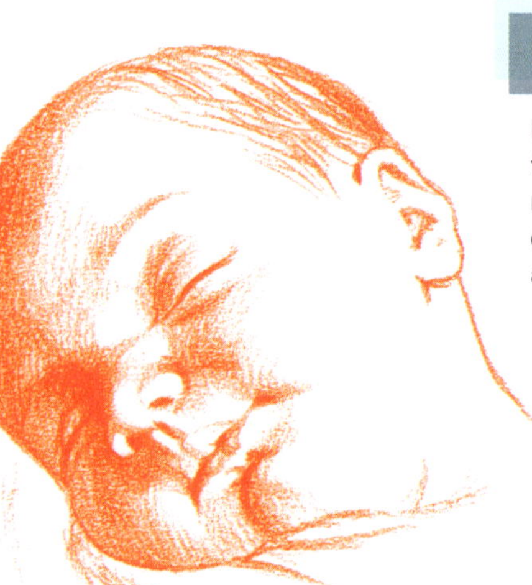

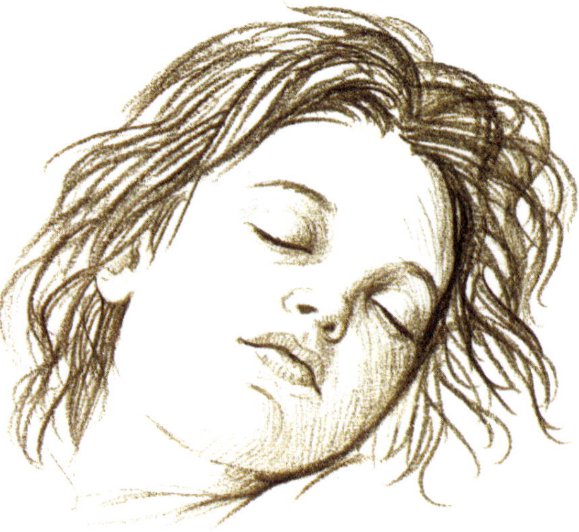

Portraits of children

Drawing children requires a lot of finesse: the noses are small, the mouths have strong borders, their cheeks are round, their eyes are large, and their eyelids are well-defined.

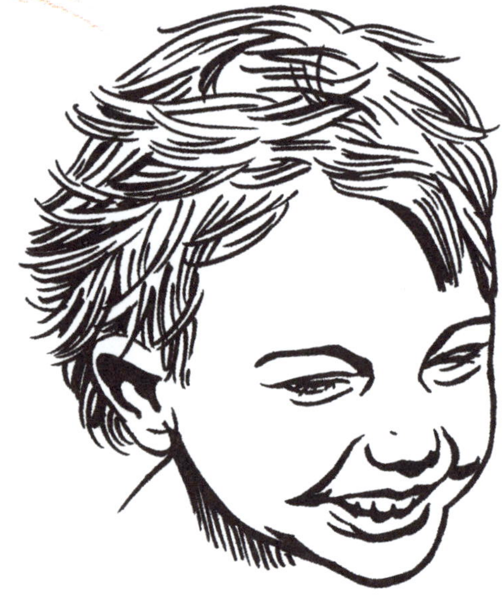

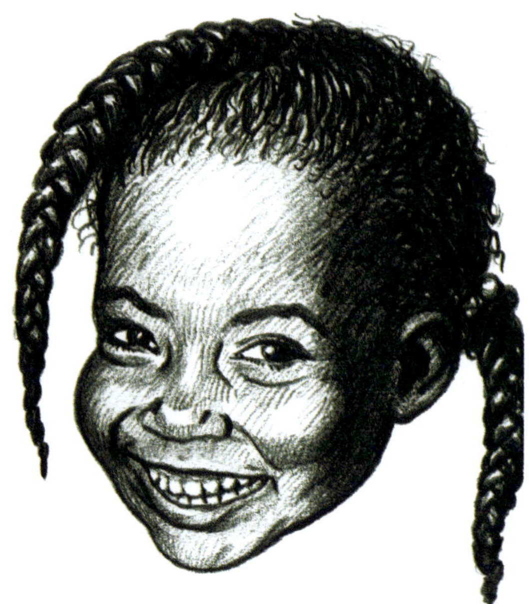

Children shown during their
primary occupations: crying,
laughing, and eating!

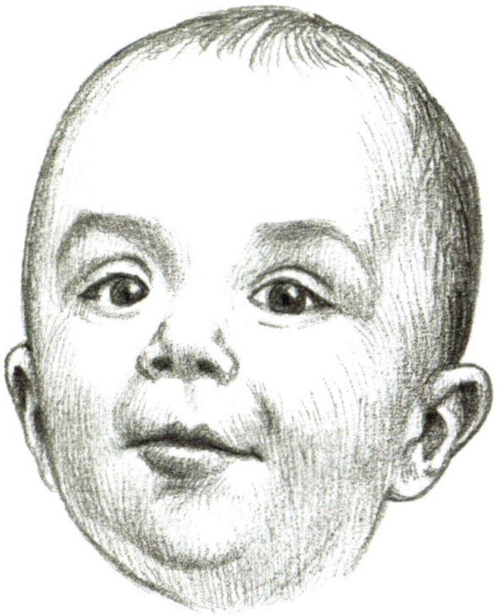

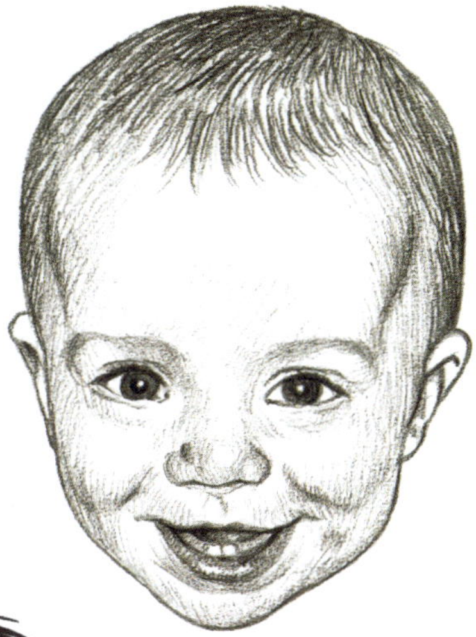

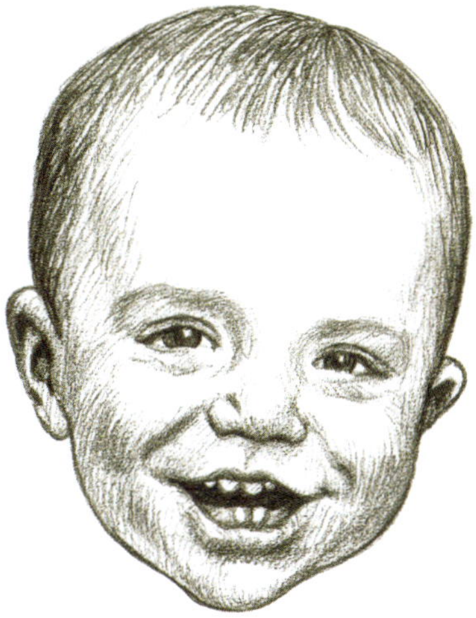

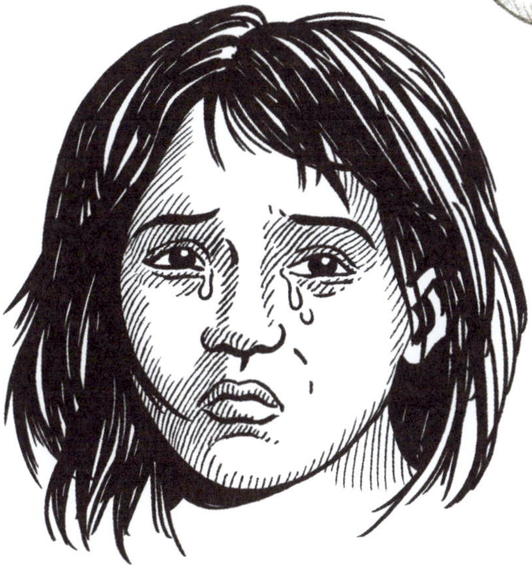

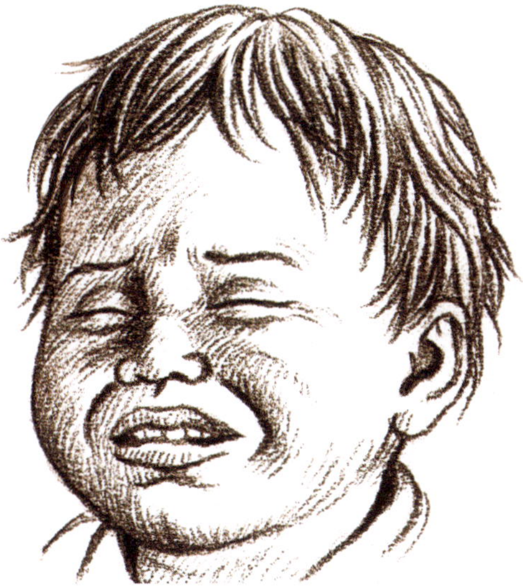

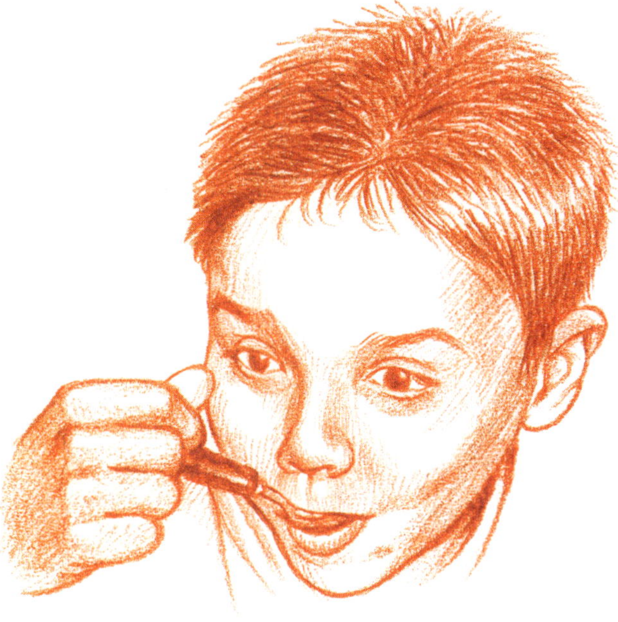

Choose the utensil
that best suits the
model's personality...
and their expression!

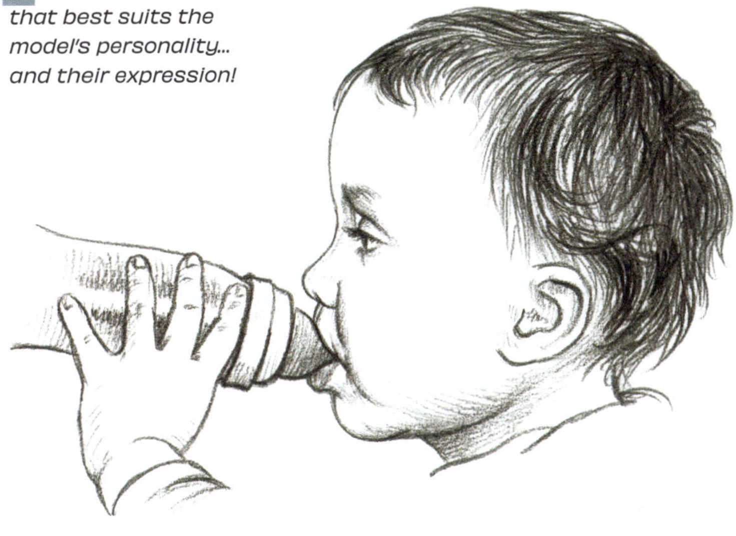

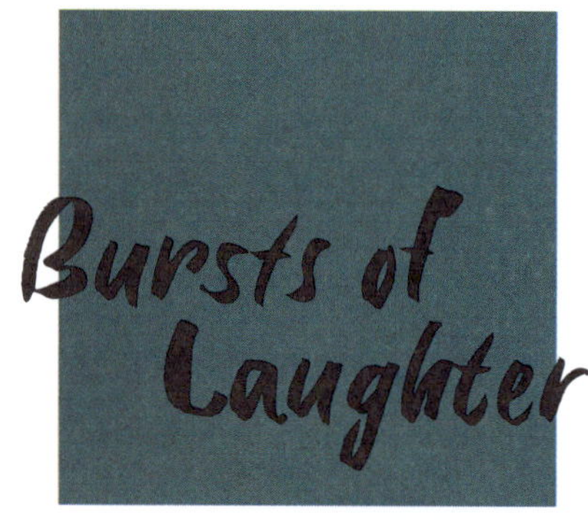

Bursts of Laughter

A laugh is often represented as a kind of croissant:
and yet, on all the laughing faces shown here,
the mouth is, instead, arced in two directions.
The corners of the mouth might go up,
but not necessarily.

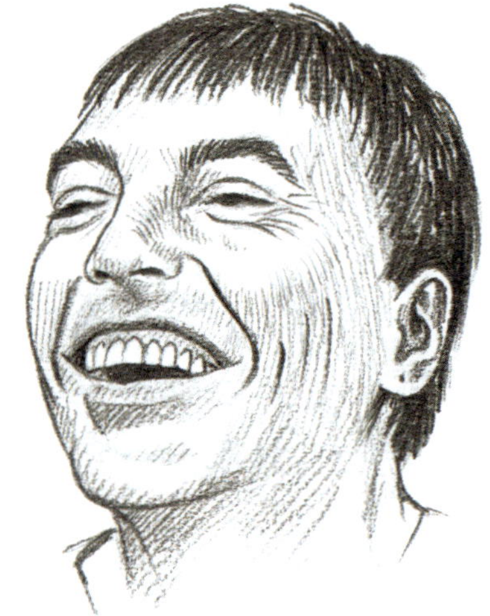

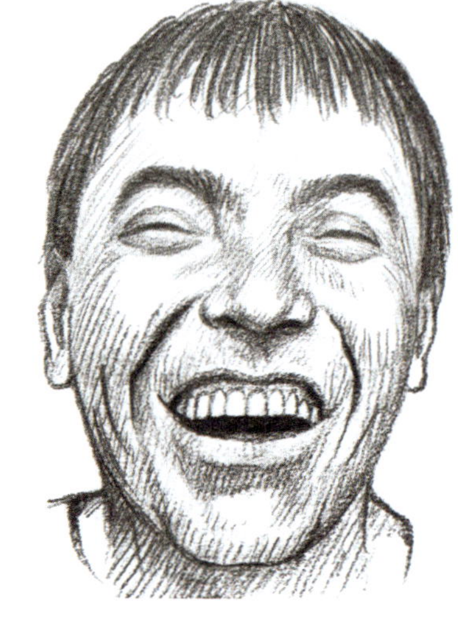

A Wide-Open Mouth

The zygomaticus major muscles always pull the cheeks backwards, in this way putting the mouth in quotation marks, so to speak.

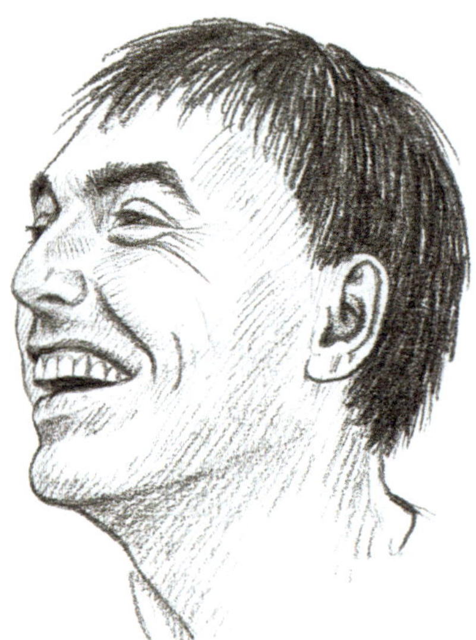

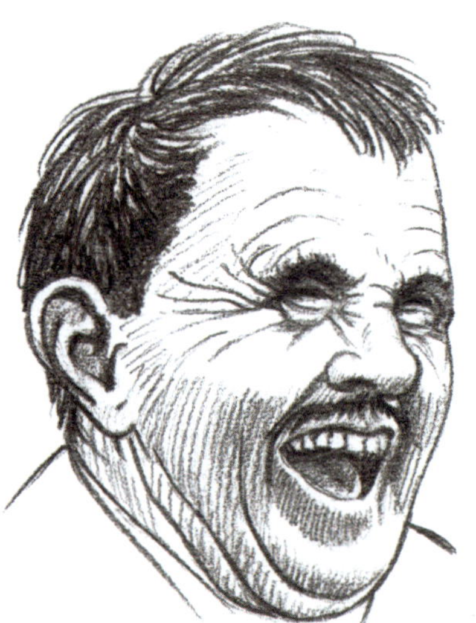

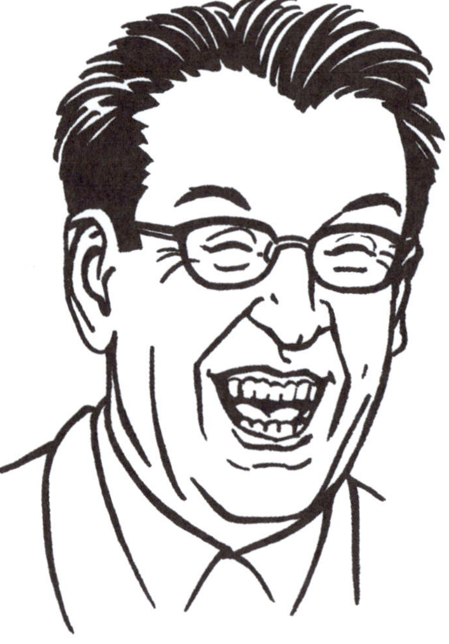

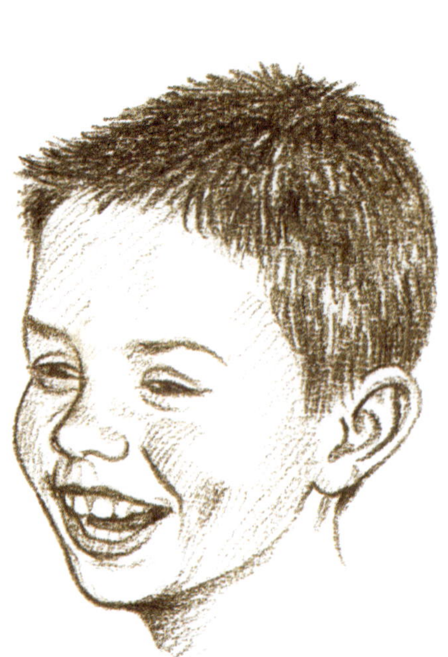

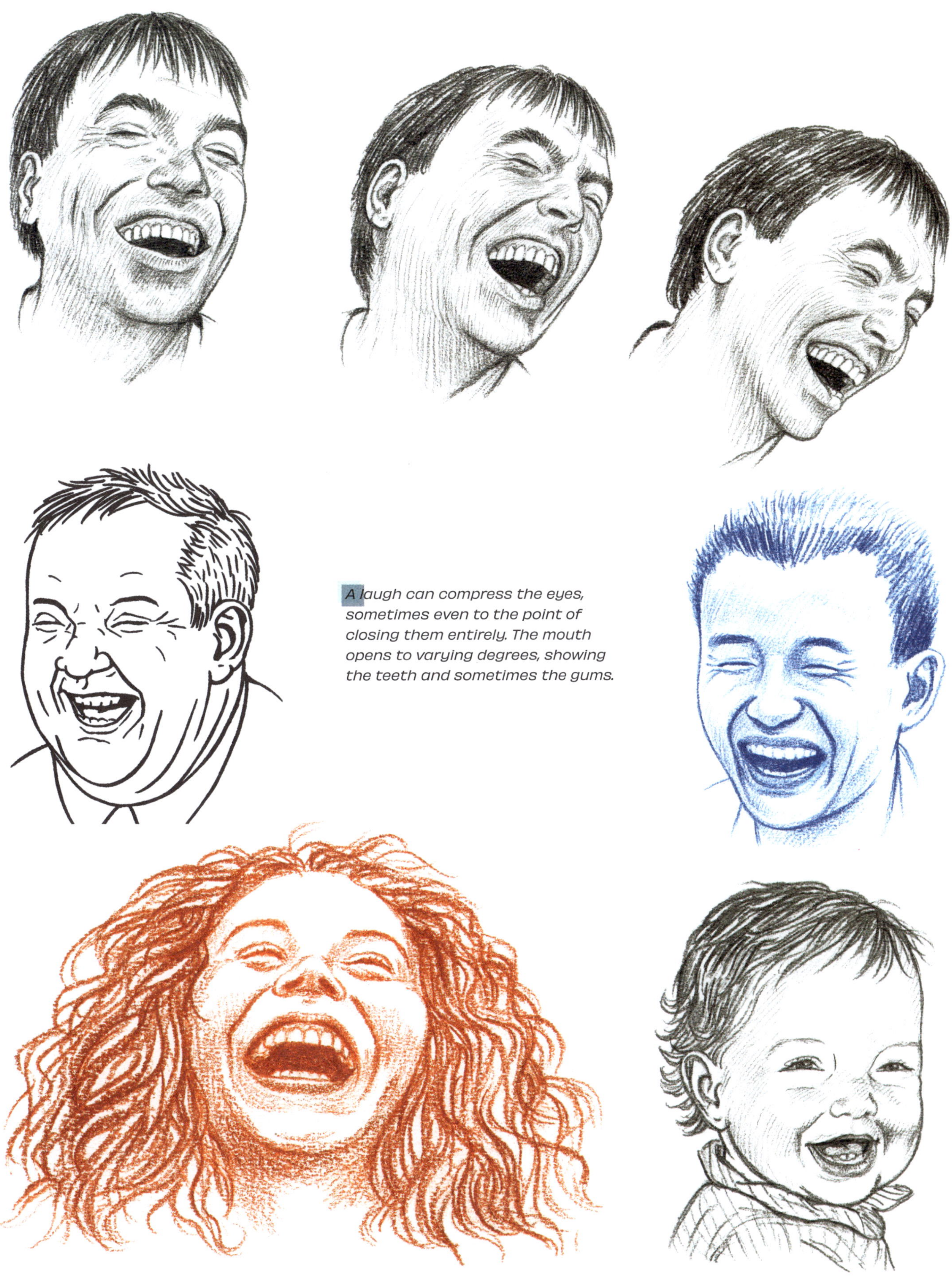

A laugh can compress the eyes, sometimes even to the point of closing them entirely. The mouth opens to varying degrees, showing the teeth and sometimes the gums.

On the Verge of Tears

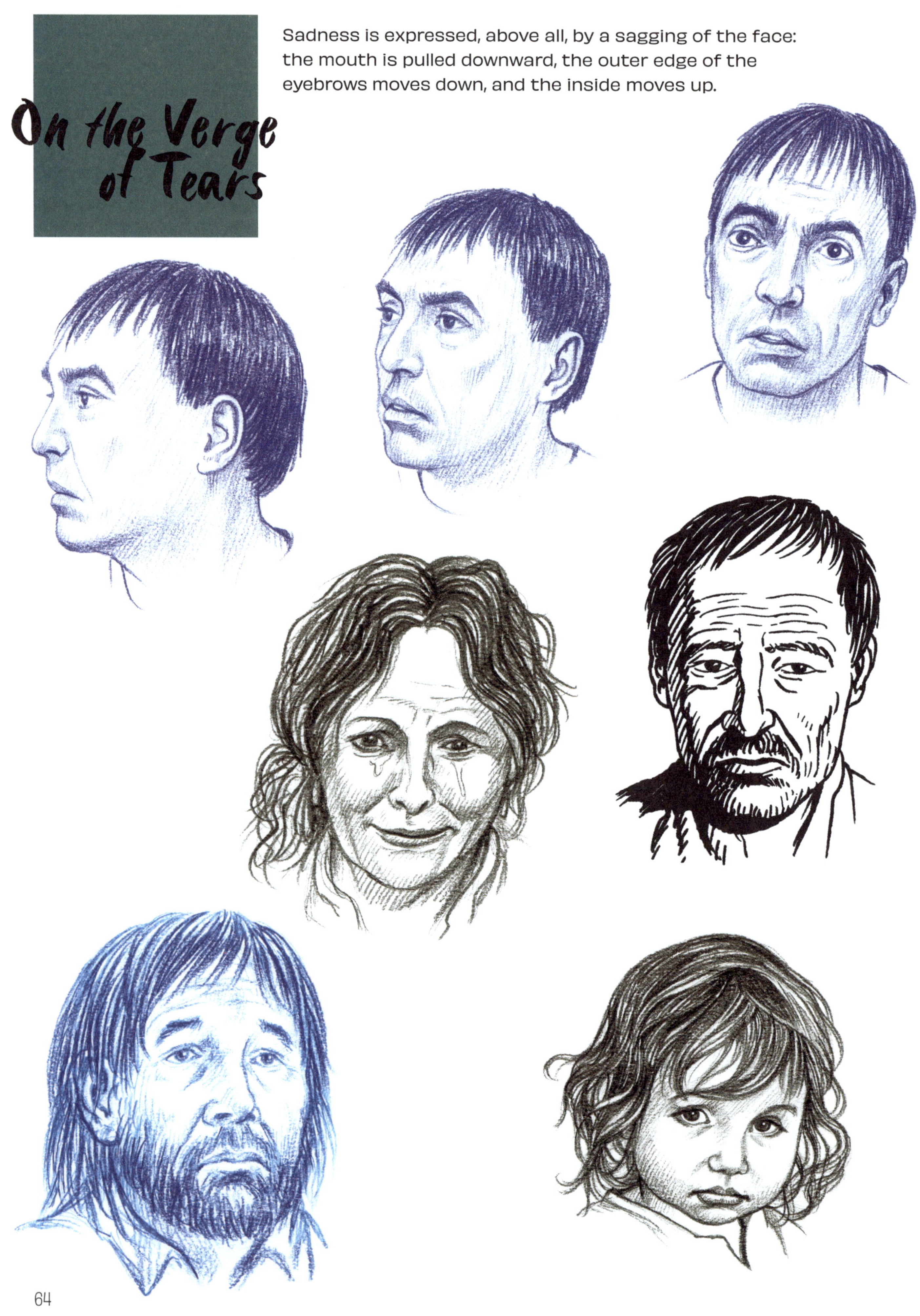

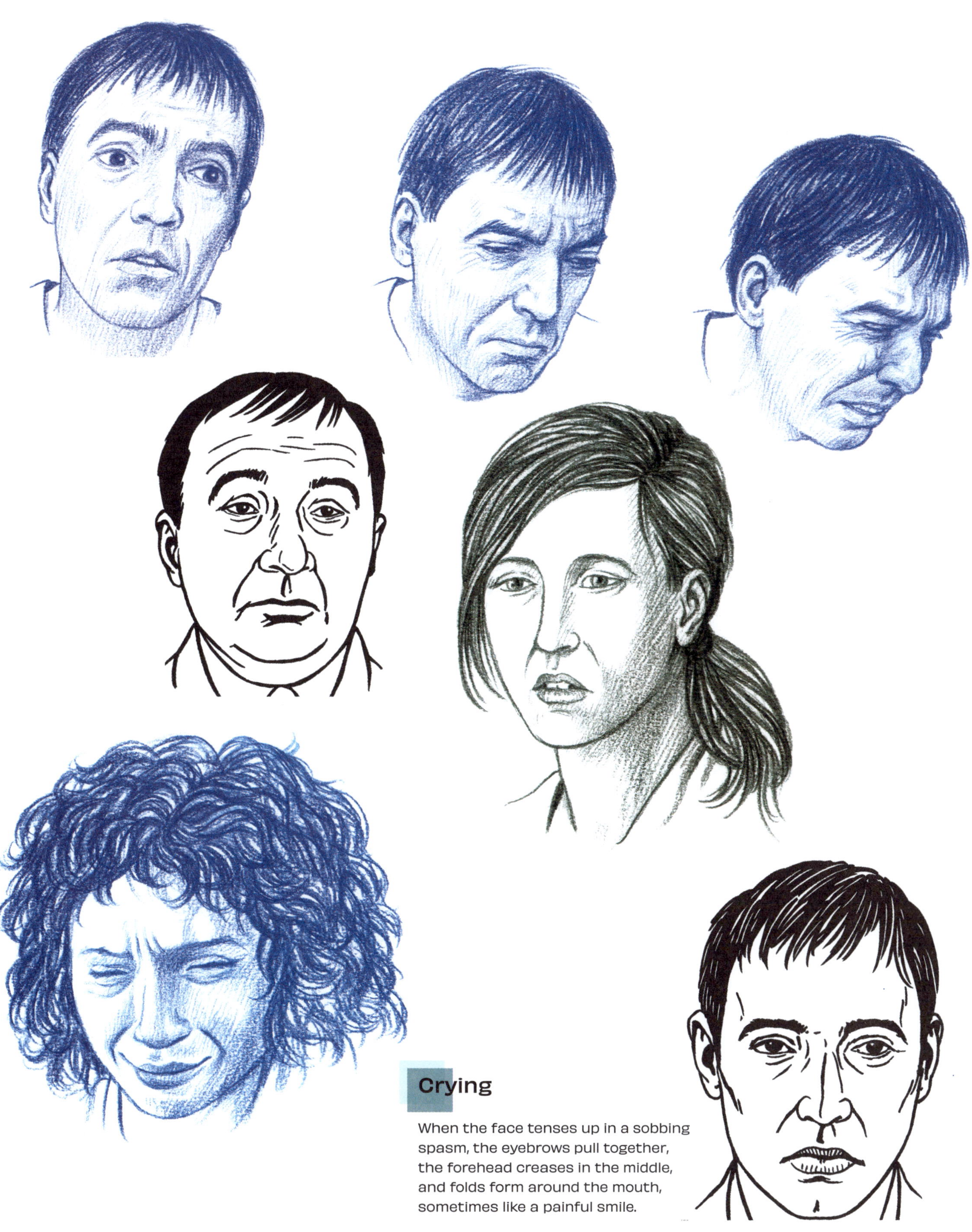

Crying

When the face tenses up in a sobbing spasm, the eyebrows pull together, the forehead creases in the middle, and folds form around the mouth, sometimes like a painful smile.

Fury and Rage

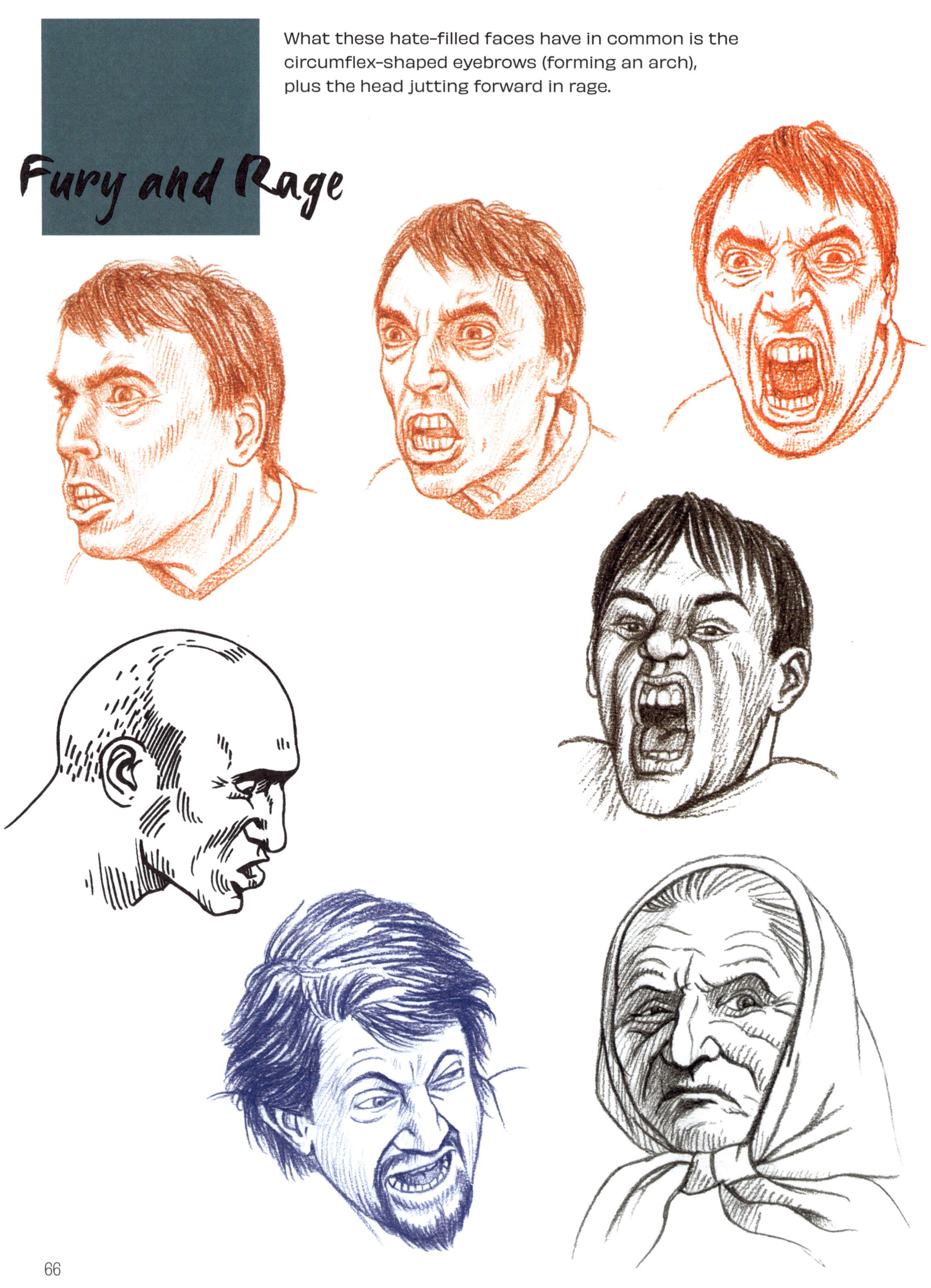

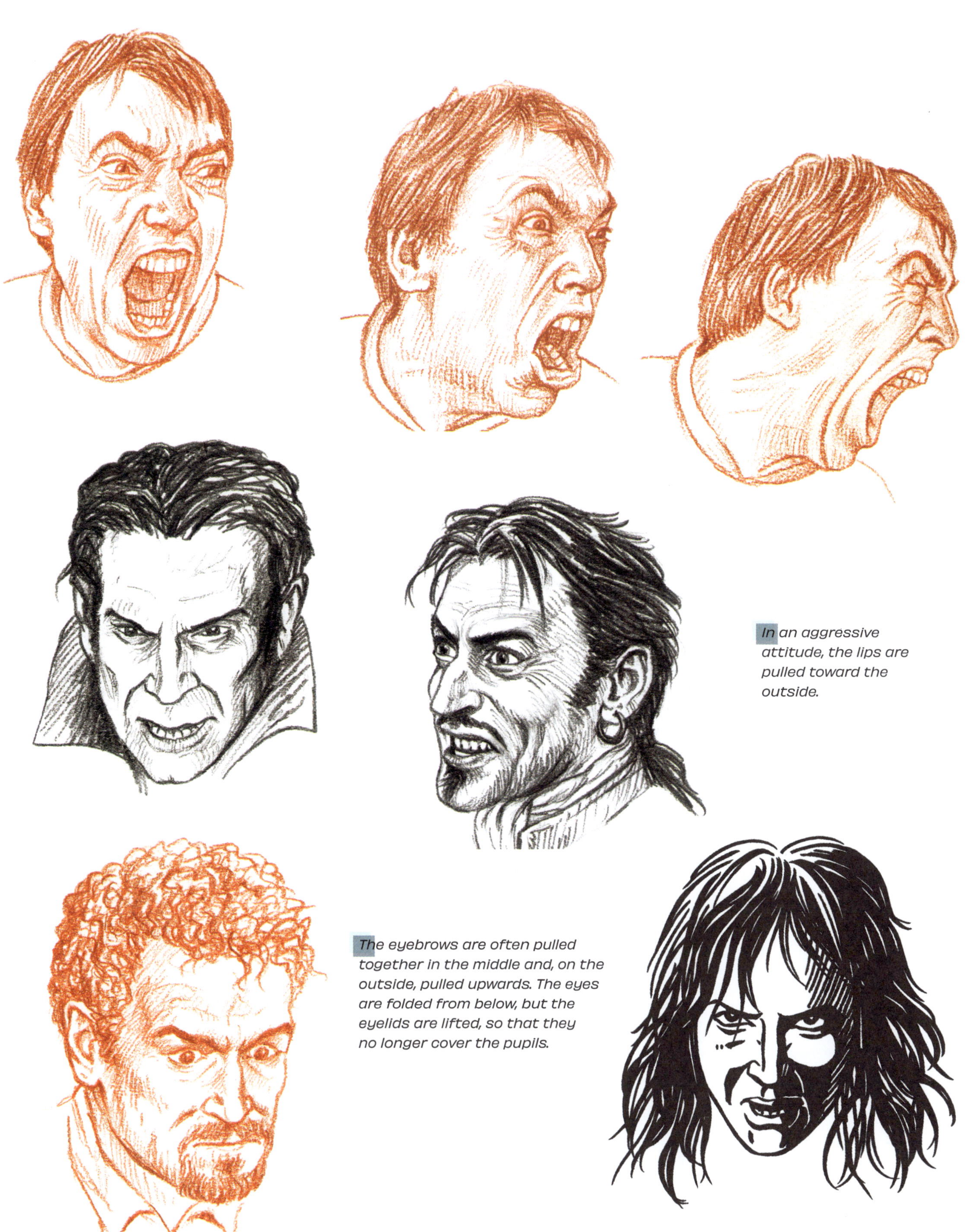

In an aggressive attitude, the lips are pulled toward the outside.

The eyebrows are often pulled together in the middle and, on the outside, pulled upwards. The eyes are folded from below, but the eyelids are lifted, so that they no longer cover the pupils.

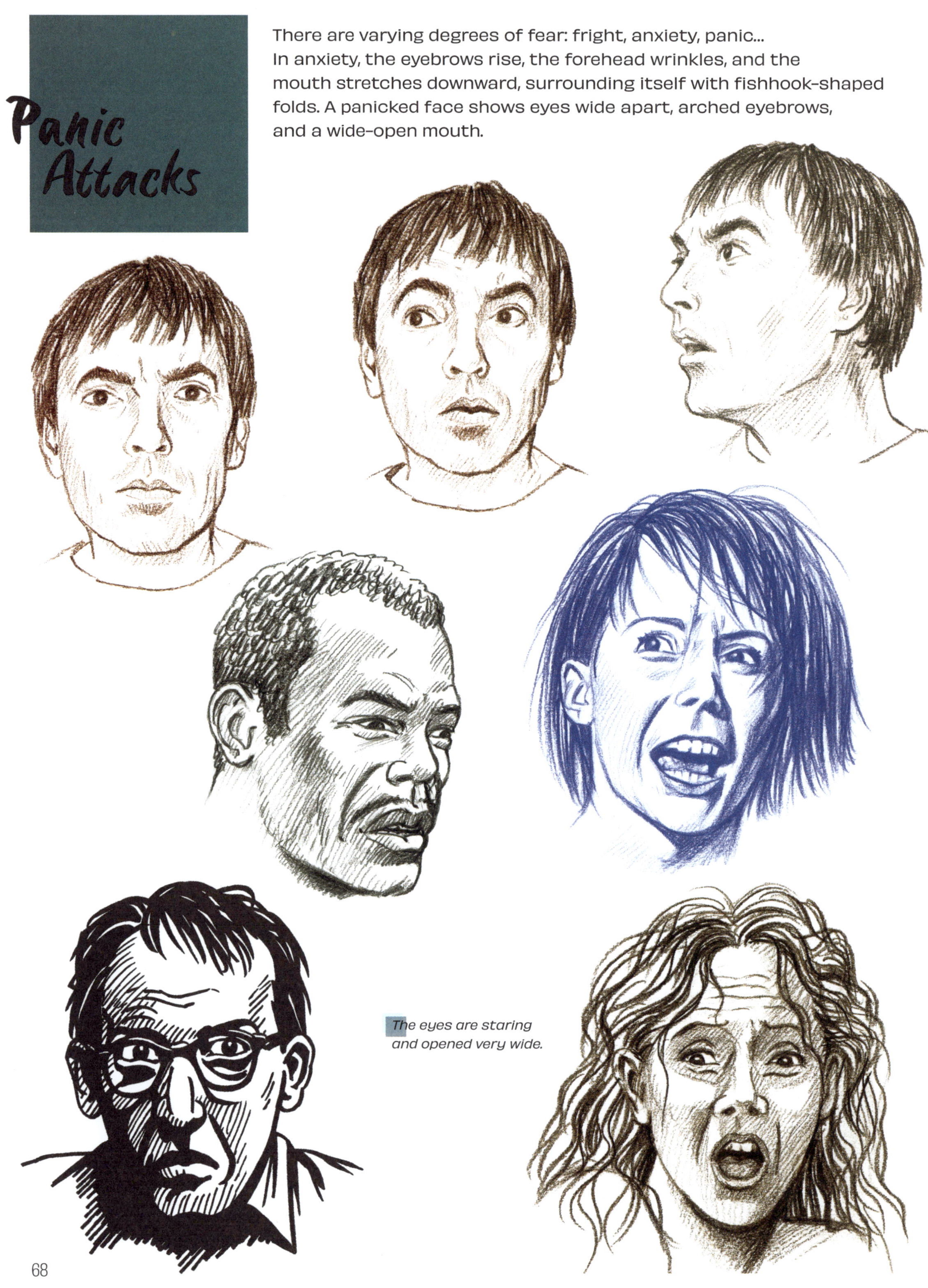

There are varying degrees of fear: fright, anxiety, panic...
In anxiety, the eyebrows rise, the forehead wrinkles, and the
mouth stretches downward, surrounding itself with fishhook-shaped
folds. A panicked face shows eyes wide apart, arched eyebrows,
and a wide–open mouth.

*The eyes are staring
and opened very wide.*

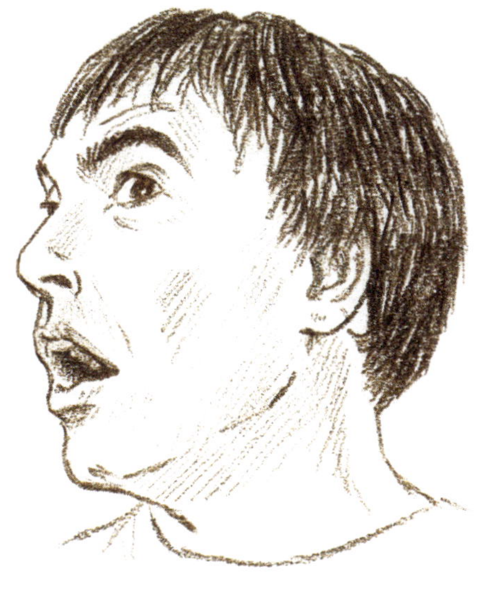

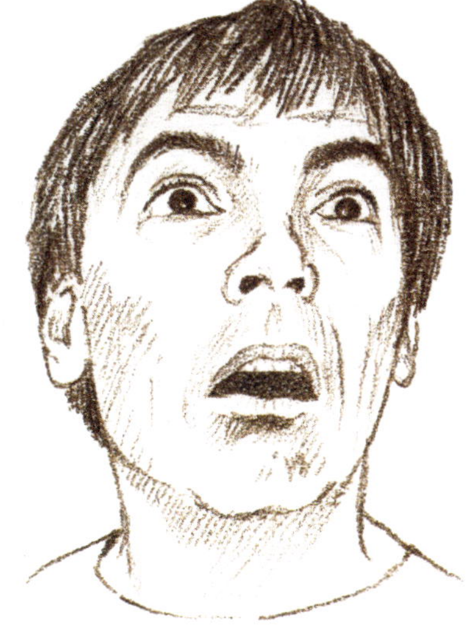

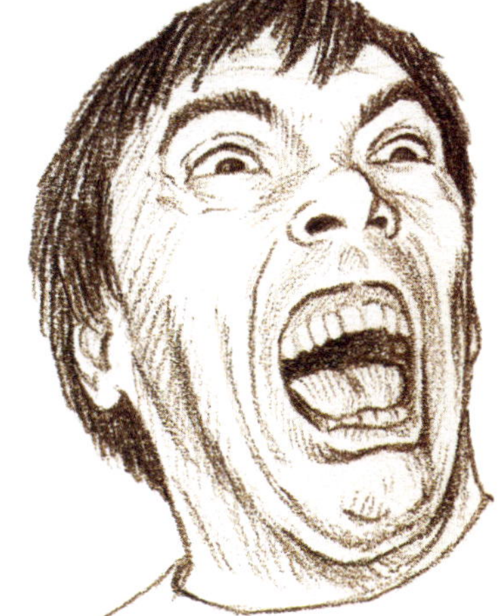

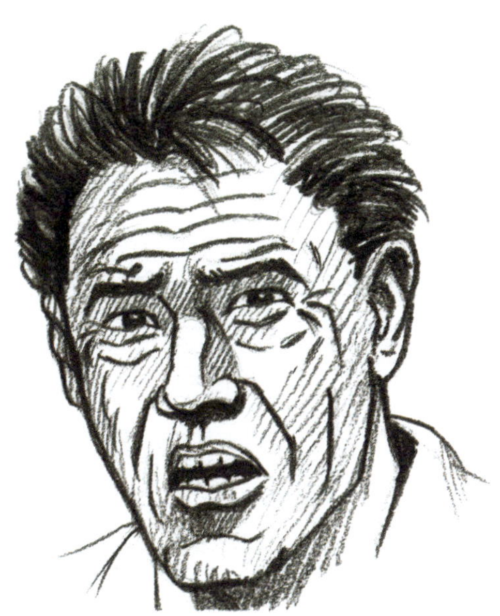

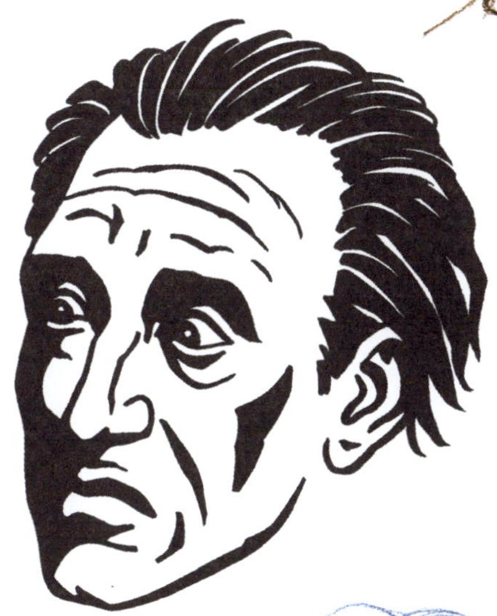

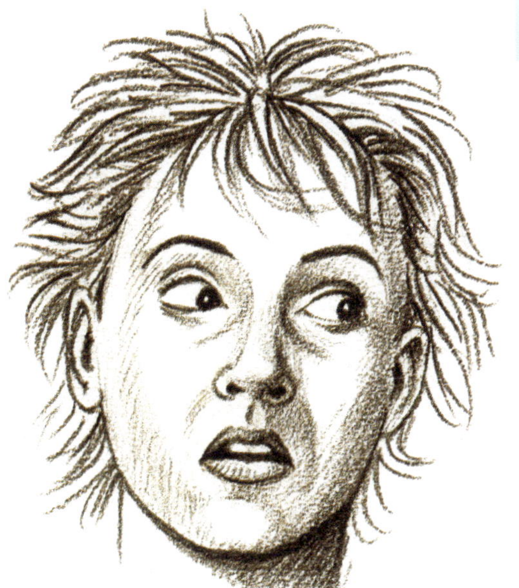

Dread or Fright

A frightened person's face tends to lean backwards. The impression of panic is reinforced by the disheveled hair.

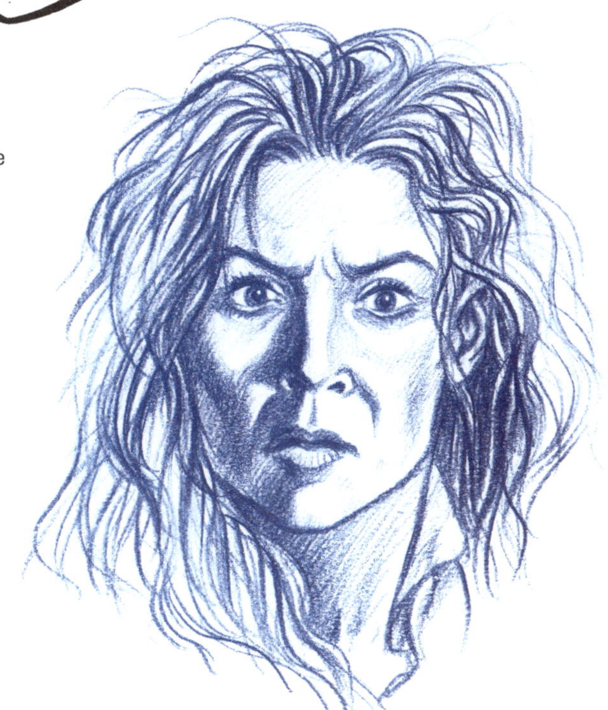

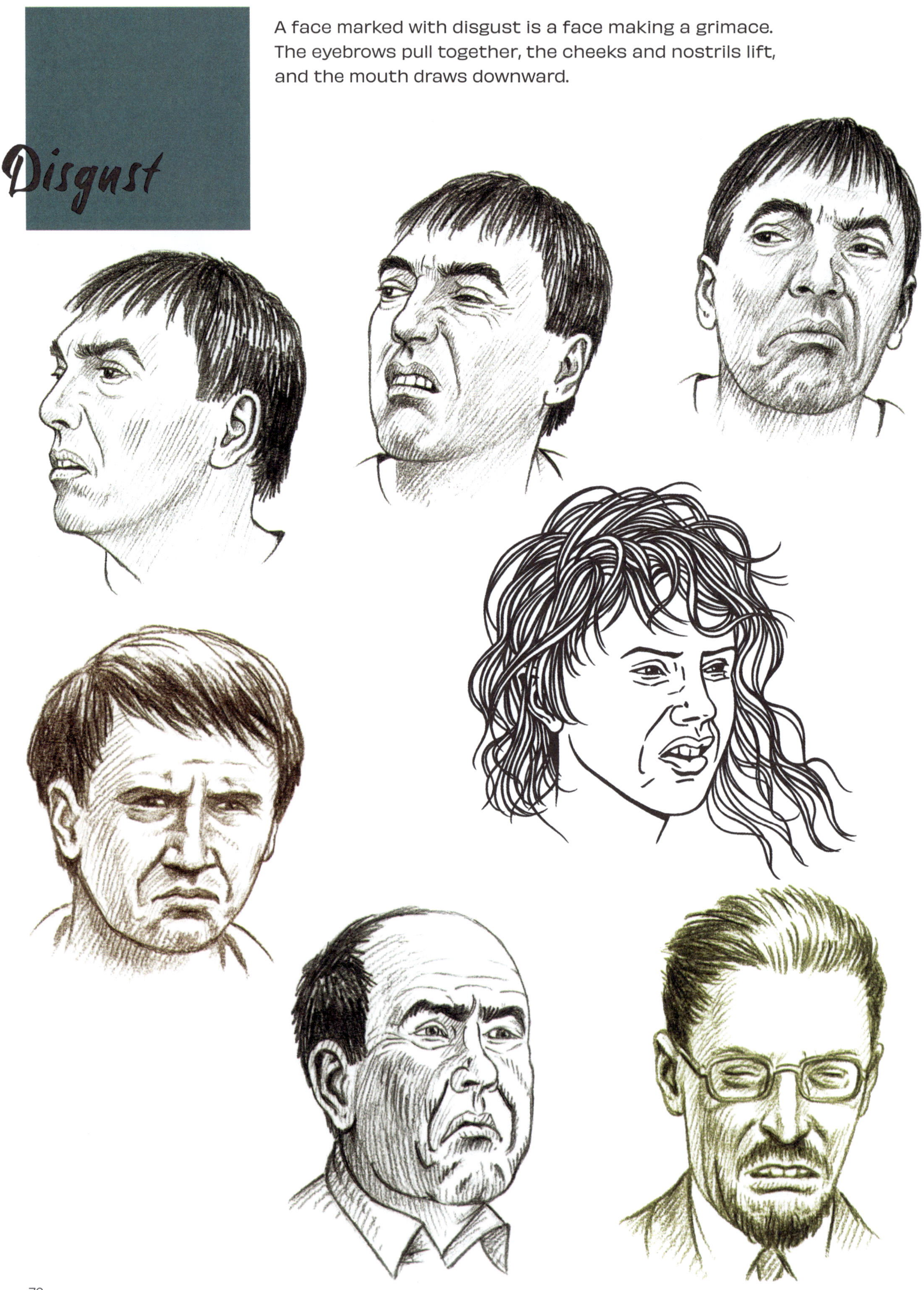

A face marked with disgust is a face making a grimace. The eyebrows pull together, the cheeks and nostrils lift, and the mouth draws downward.

Disgust

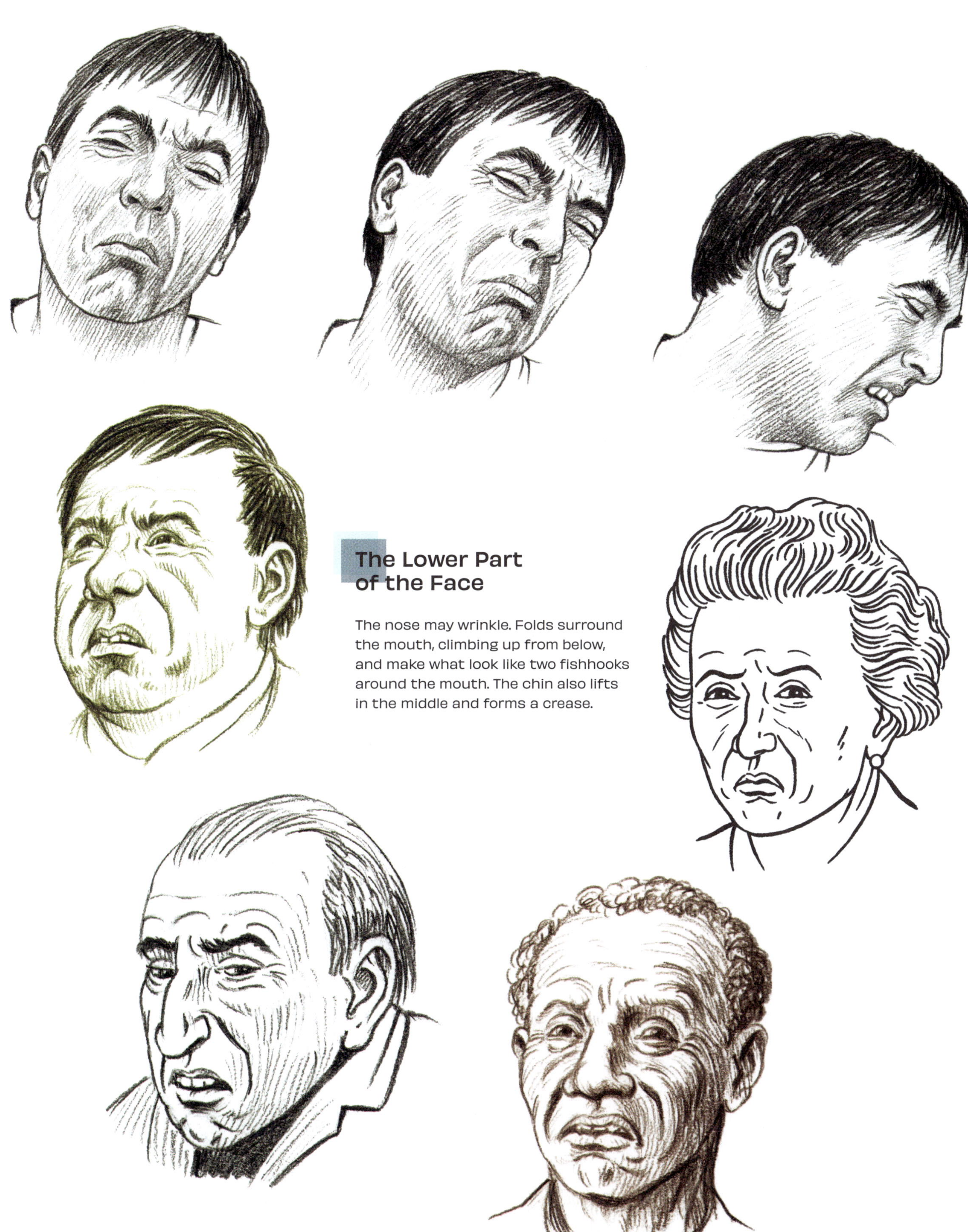

The Lower Part of the Face

The nose may wrinkle. Folds surround the mouth, climbing up from below, and make what look like two fishhooks around the mouth. The chin also lifts in the middle and forms a crease.

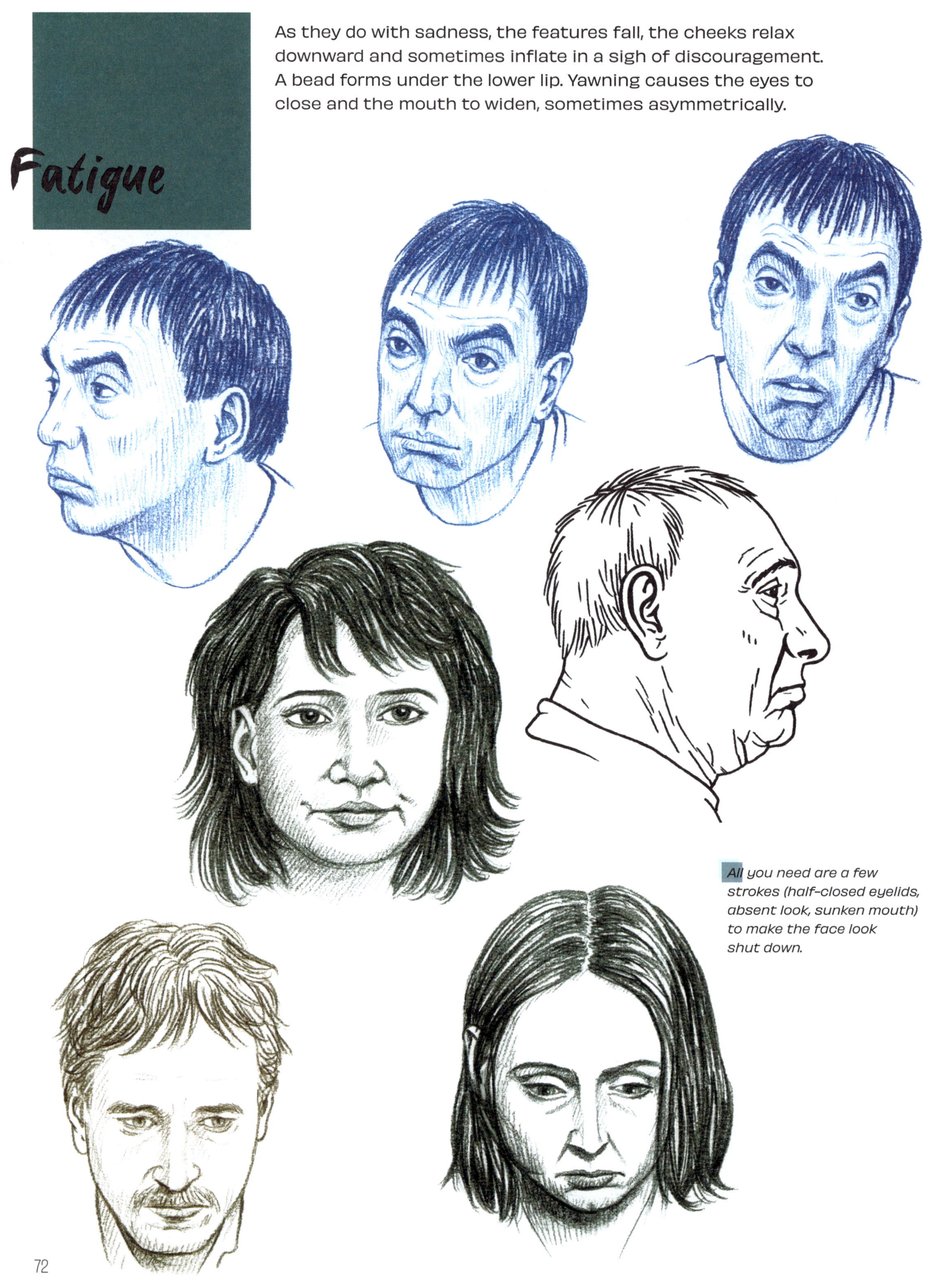

As they do with sadness, the features fall, the cheeks relax downward and sometimes inflate in a sigh of discouragement. A bead forms under the lower lip. Yawning causes the eyes to close and the mouth to widen, sometimes asymmetrically.

Fatigue

All you need are a few strokes (half-closed eyelids, absent look, sunken mouth) to make the face look shut down.

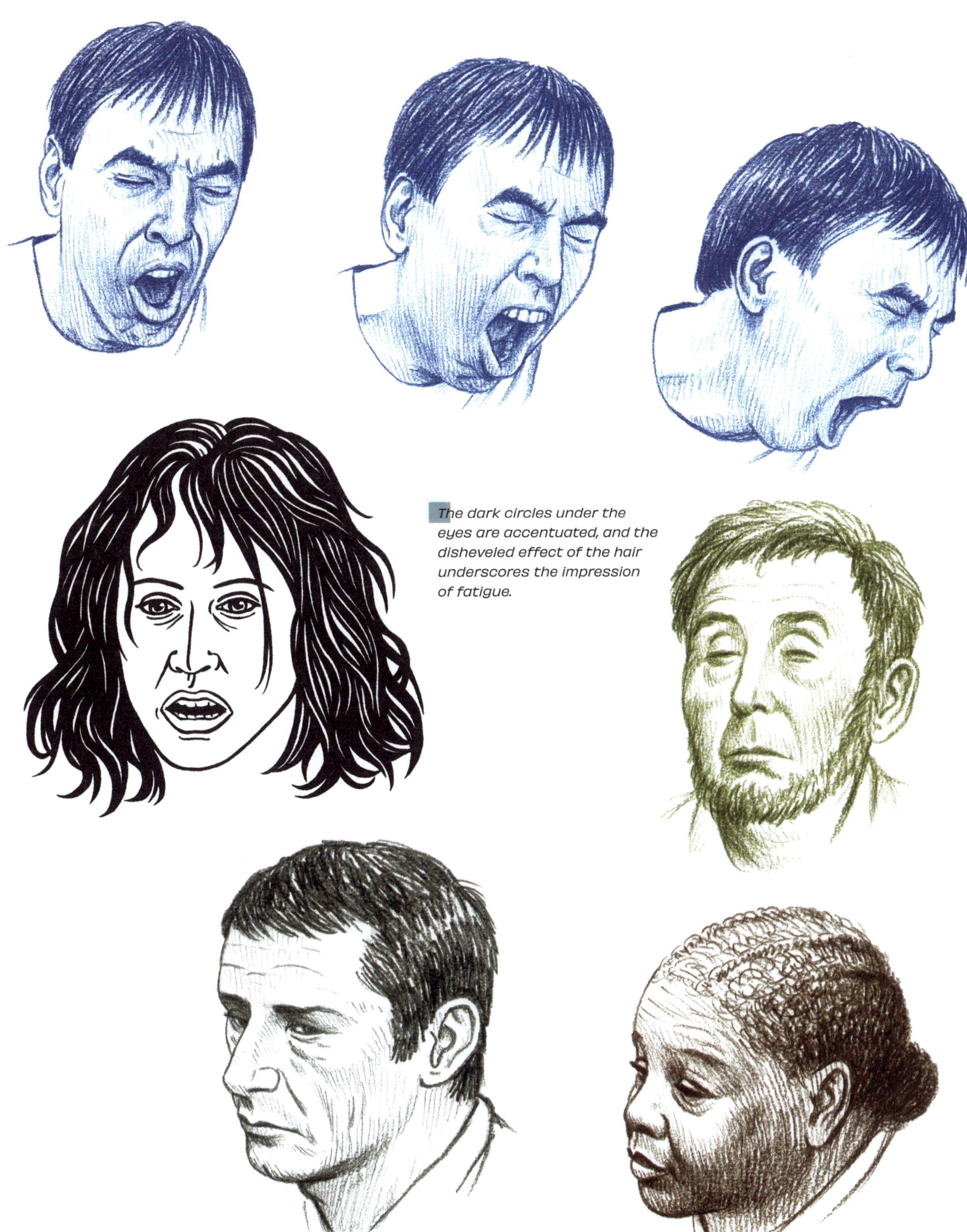

The dark circles under the eyes are accentuated, and the disheveled effect of the hair underscores the impression of fatigue.

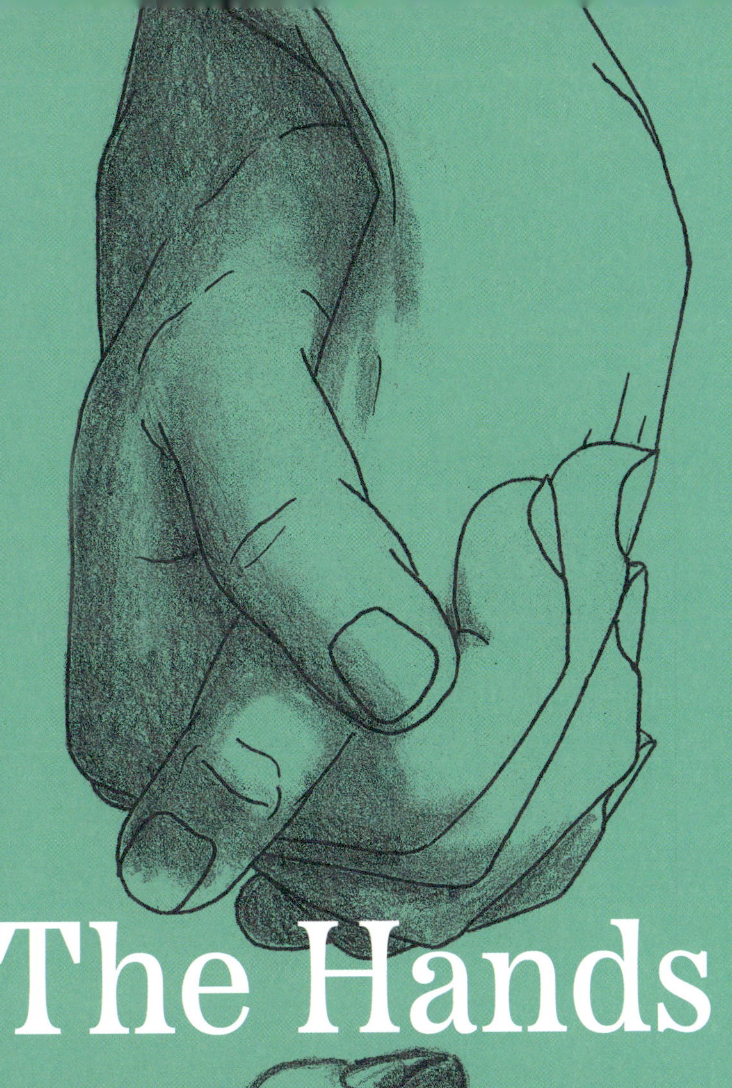

The Hands

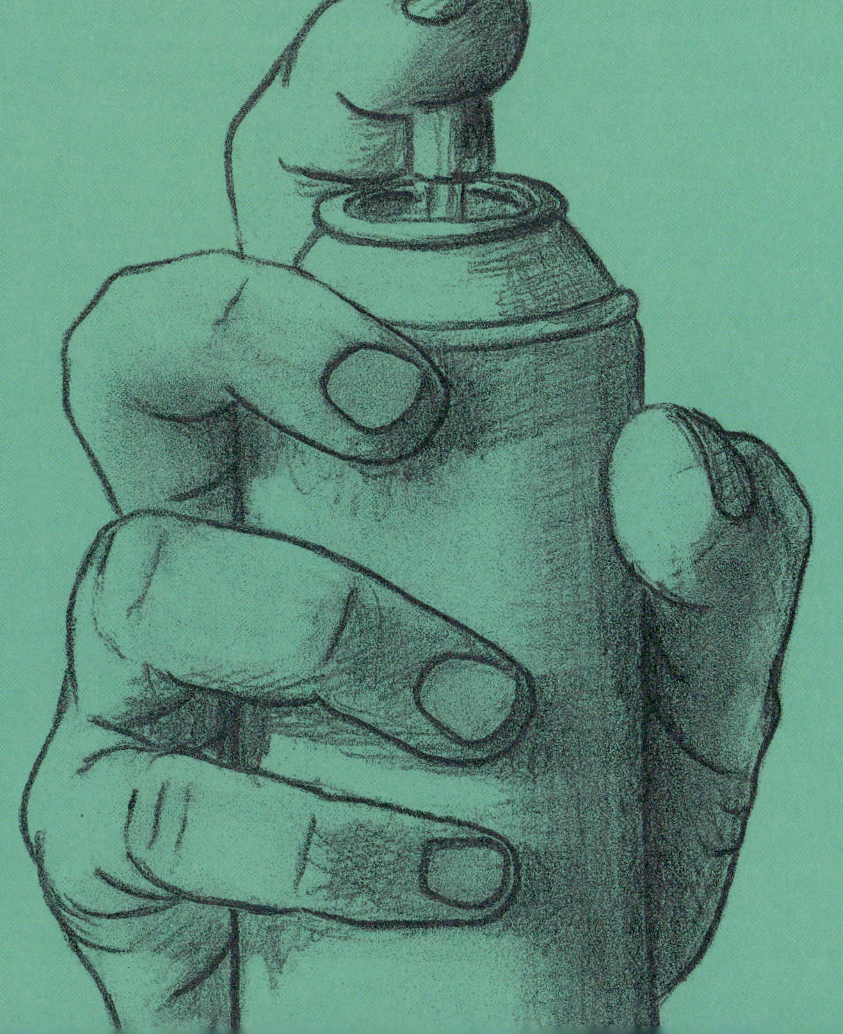

Unlike the other parts of the body, the proportions of the hand vary from one individual to the next. Similarly, there is no perfect symmetry between the right and left hands.

Proportions and Anatomy

Back of the Hand

The rules suggested here are based on average proportions. Thus, we can posit that:

The middle of the hand (**O**) is underneath the first knuckle of the middle finger.

The first section (or phalange) of each finger (except for the thumb) is as long as the other two phalanges together (**A = B+C**).

For each finger, the last two phalanges are of equal length (**B=C** and **J=K**).

The thin skin connection linking each two fingers is positioned halfway up the first phalange of each of the four fingers (**H = I**).

The base of the fingernail is positioned halfway up the last phalange on each of the five fingers (including the thumb) (**F = G**).

The tip of the thumb, if you pull it back to lie alongside the palm, comes to just below the second knuckle on the index finger.

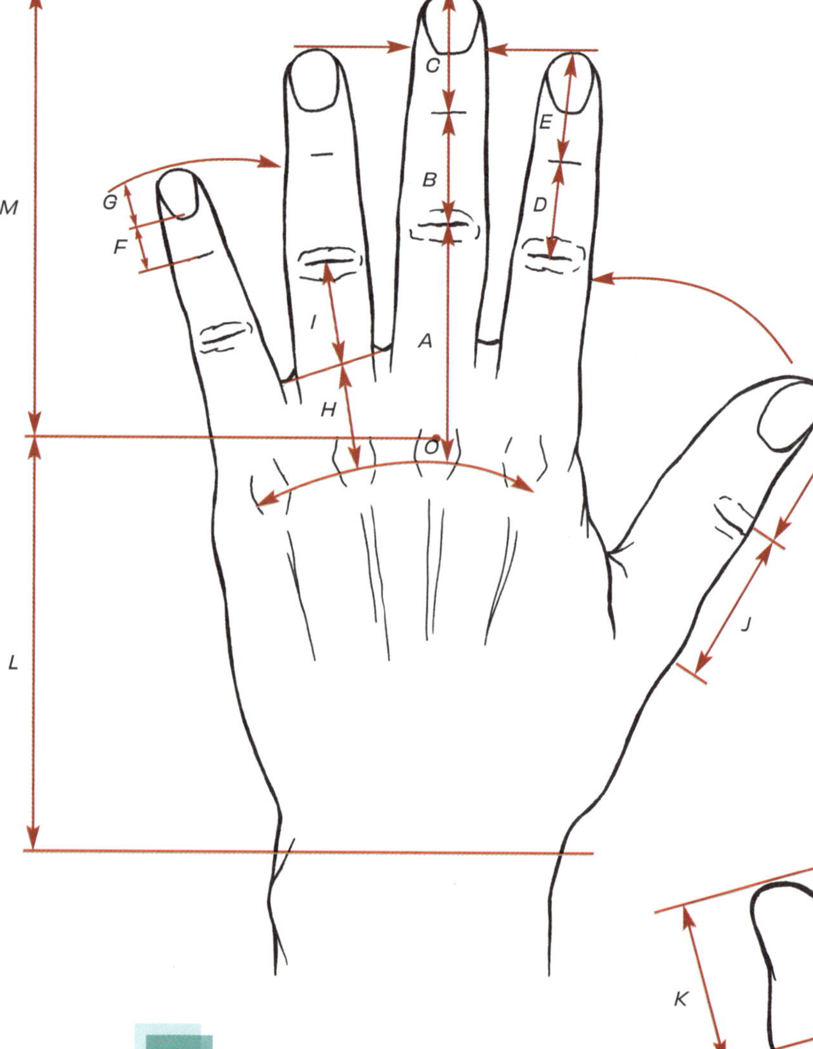

Front of the Hand (Palm Side)

Three folds divide the interior of each of the fingers (not including the thumb)

Segments **P** and **Q** are of equal length.

The tip of the finger (**R**) is thinner and slightly longer.

The thenar and hypothenar eminences (fleshy parts of the palm, see diagram) are positioned on either side of an imaginary line that bisects the axis of the wrist (**S = T**).

The wrist creates a depression just before the thenar and hypothenar eminences.

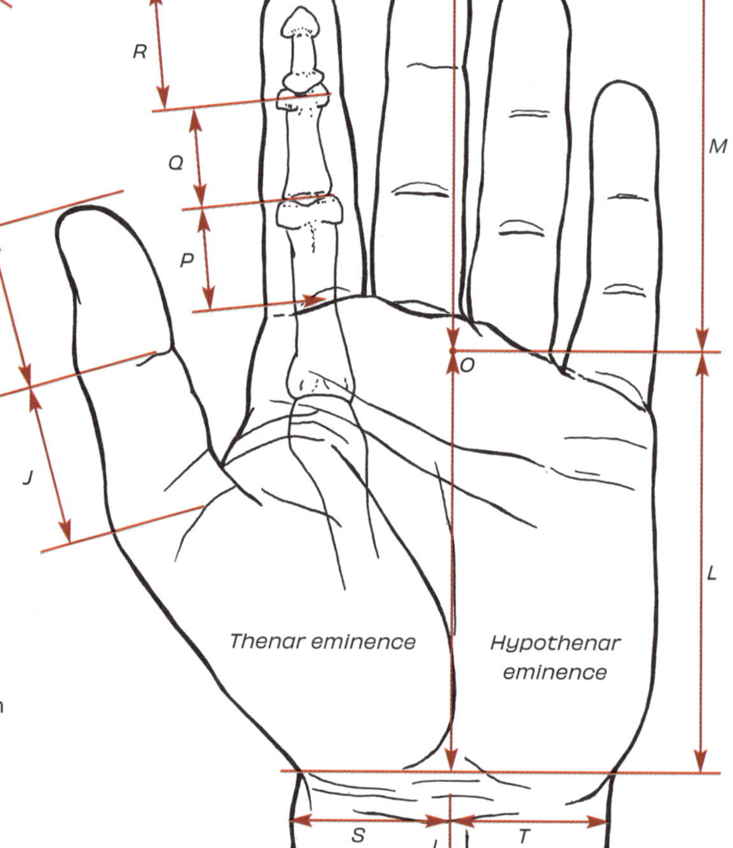

Superficial Muscles and Tendons

These two anatomical plates only represent the superficial muscles and tendons. The fatty tissues and nervous and veinous systems are abstracted away here.

Back of the Hand

The striated muscles, which are contracting organs, make possible the voluntary movements of the joints that connect the bones. Most muscles are attached to the skeleton at their two extremities, which pull closer together in muscular contractions. The muscle's fixed anchor point is called the "origin," while the mobile part, generally a tendon, is called the "insertion."

The index, middle, ring, and little fingers share their extensor muscles, which is why it is hard— especially for the middle and ring fingers, which have no extensors of their own— to bend or unbend them without causing other fingers to flex or extend at the same time.

The tendons of the index, middle, and ring fingers converge towards the same point on the axis of the wrist. The tendons of the thumb and of the little finger lie on either side of this axis.

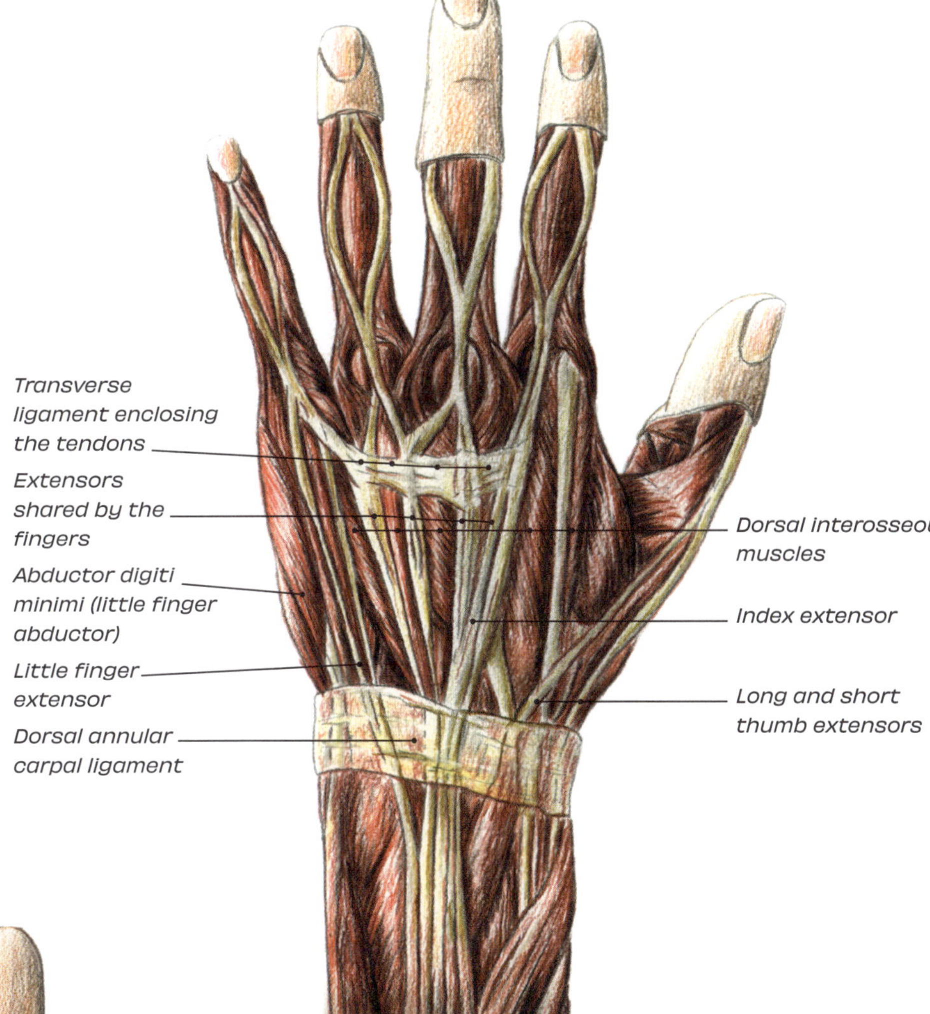

Front of the Hand (Palm Side)

The hand is home to many joints, but with very few muscles with which to activate them, for lack of space.

The large and powerful muscles of the fingers and wrist are situated in the forearm; they are inserted onto the bones of the fingers by long tendons.

The hand's own muscles are primarily the interosseous, the lumbrical, and, especially, the abductors and adductors of the thumb and little finger, located in the thenar and hypothenar eminences of the palm. The adductors serve to bring the fingers towards each other, laterally; the abductors spread them apart.

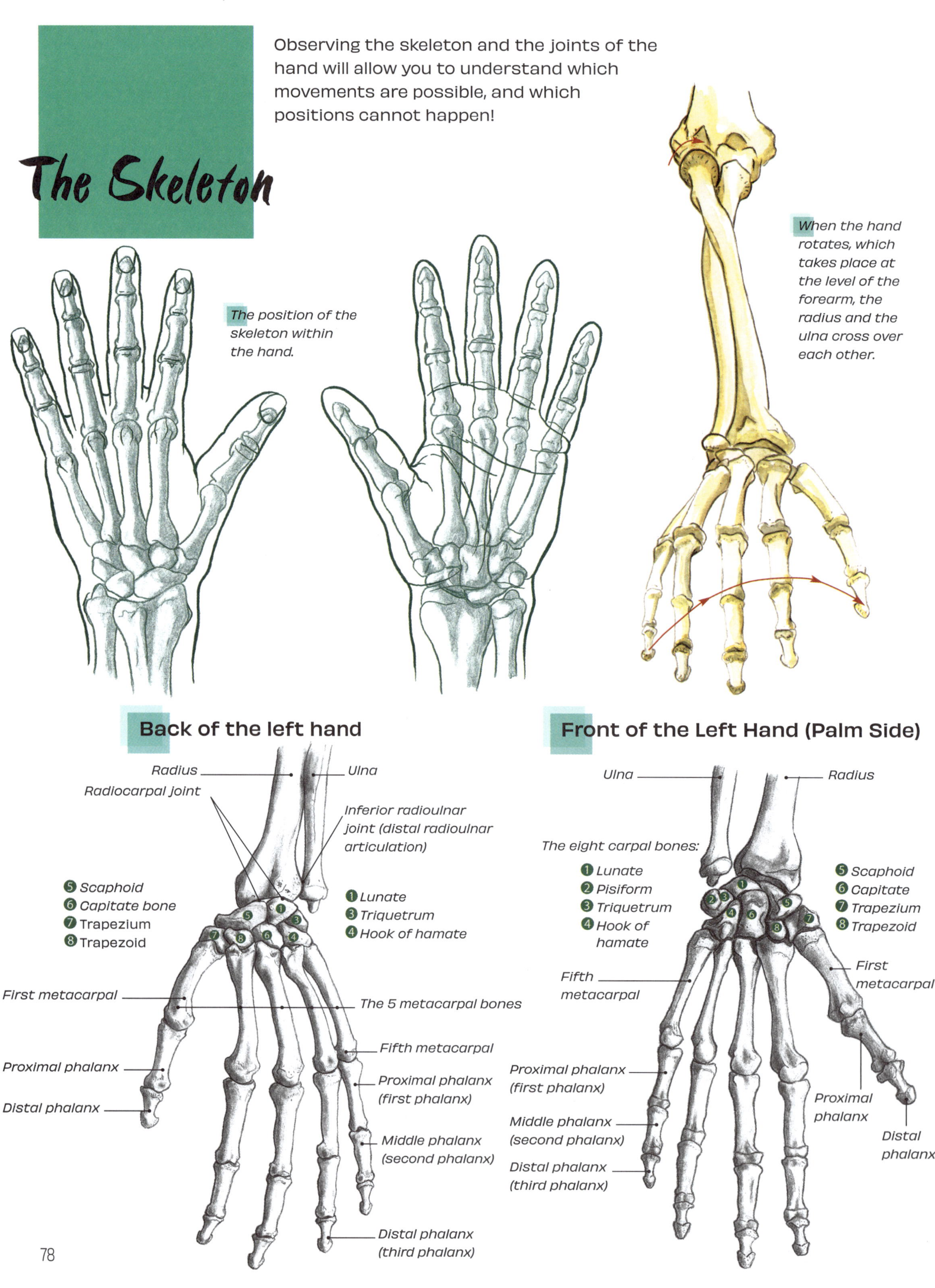

Back of the left hand

Front of the Left Hand (Palm Side)

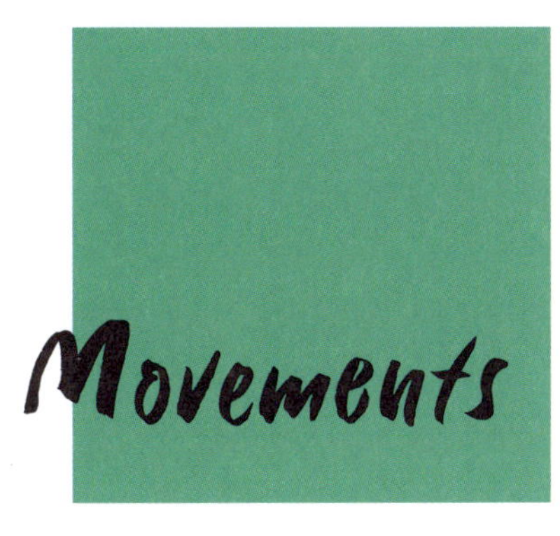

Movements

Flexion, extension, and side-to-side movement... the wrist allows the hand to move with ease. The skeletal structure of the forearm allows the entire hand to rotate.

The "circumduction" of the hand (in other words extension, flexion, and side-to-side movement) takes place within an oval.

Rotation

The hand can be rotated no matter what position it is in relative to the body. It is, however, limited in certain cases (when the hand is at shoulder level, or behind the back, etc.).

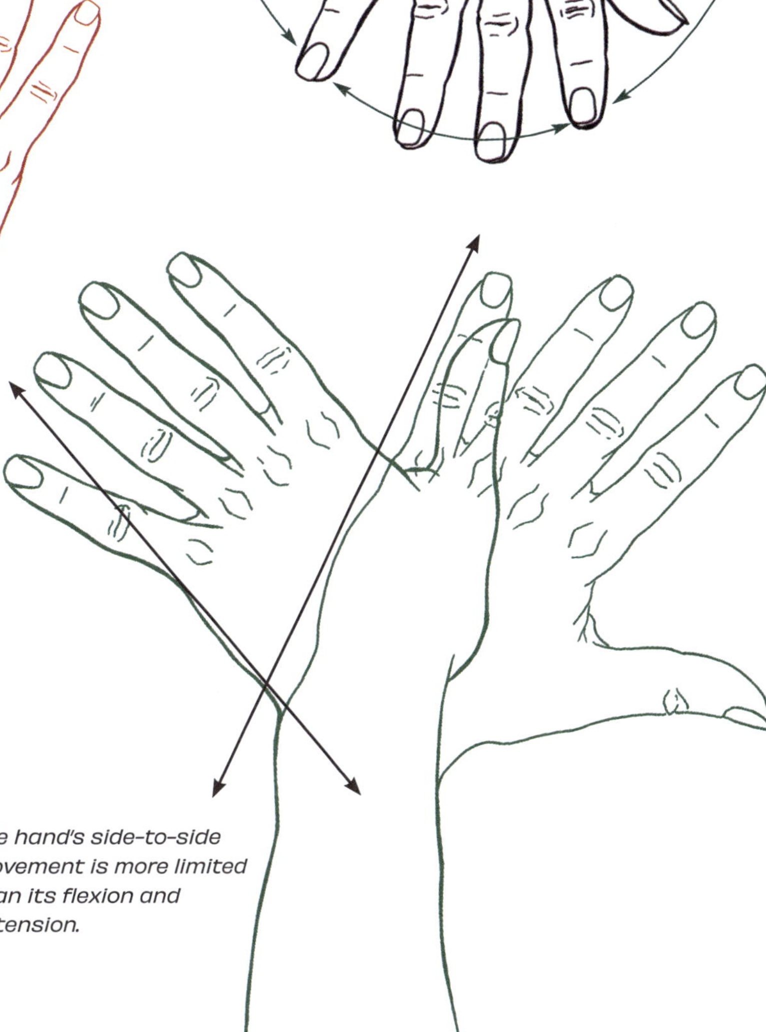

The hand's side-to-side movement is more limited than its flexion and extension.

The Geometry of the Fingers

You may find it useful to simplify your subject by reducing it to some elementary forms. Here are a few pieces of information you should always keep in mind to draw hands coherently.

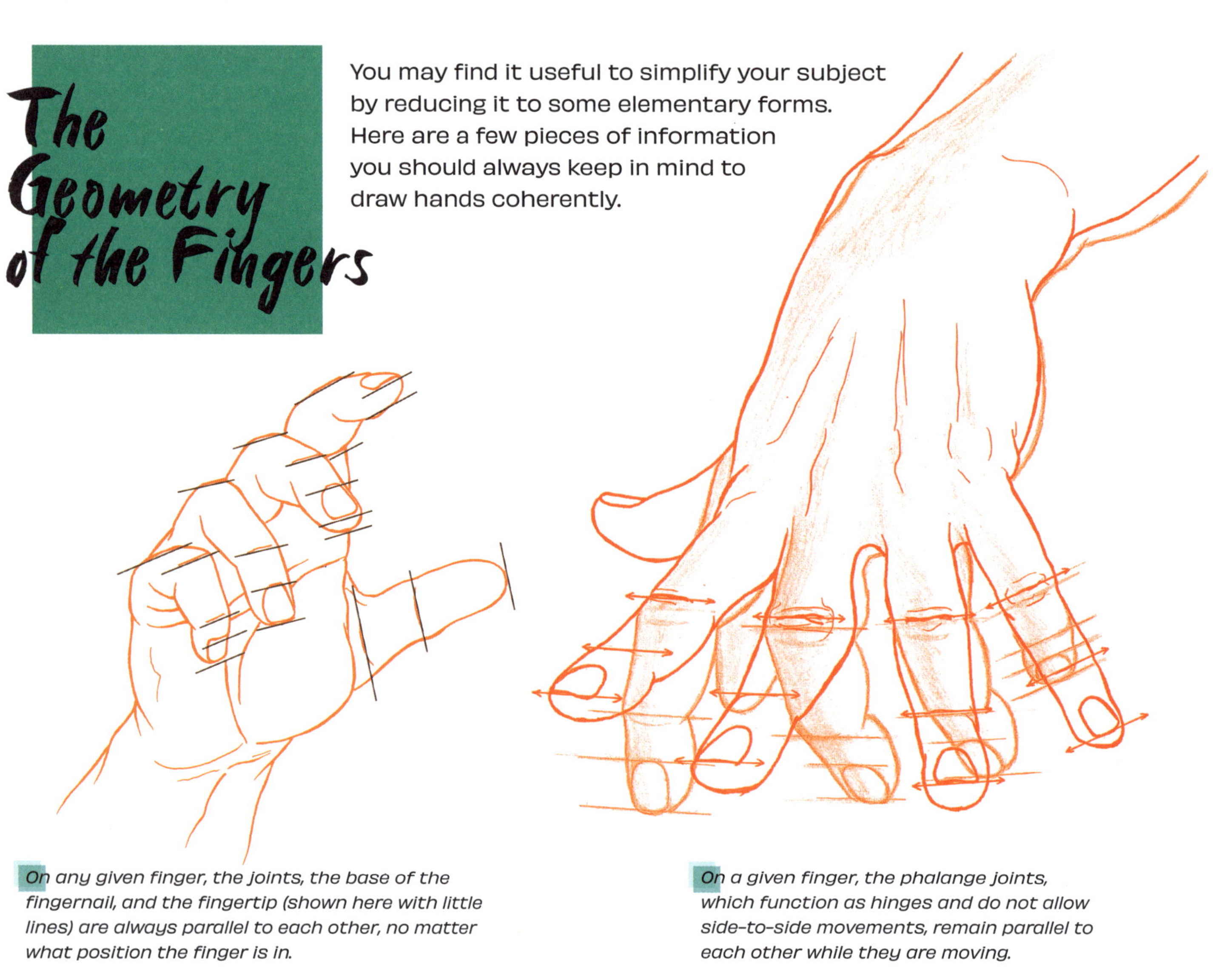

On any given finger, the joints, the base of the fingernail, and the fingertip (shown here with little lines) are always parallel to each other, no matter what position the finger is in.

On a given finger, the phalange joints, which function as hinges and do not allow side-to-side movements, remain parallel to each other while they are moving.

...From a geometrical point of view, this makes logical sense: these lines are all perpendicular to the plane in which the finger moves.

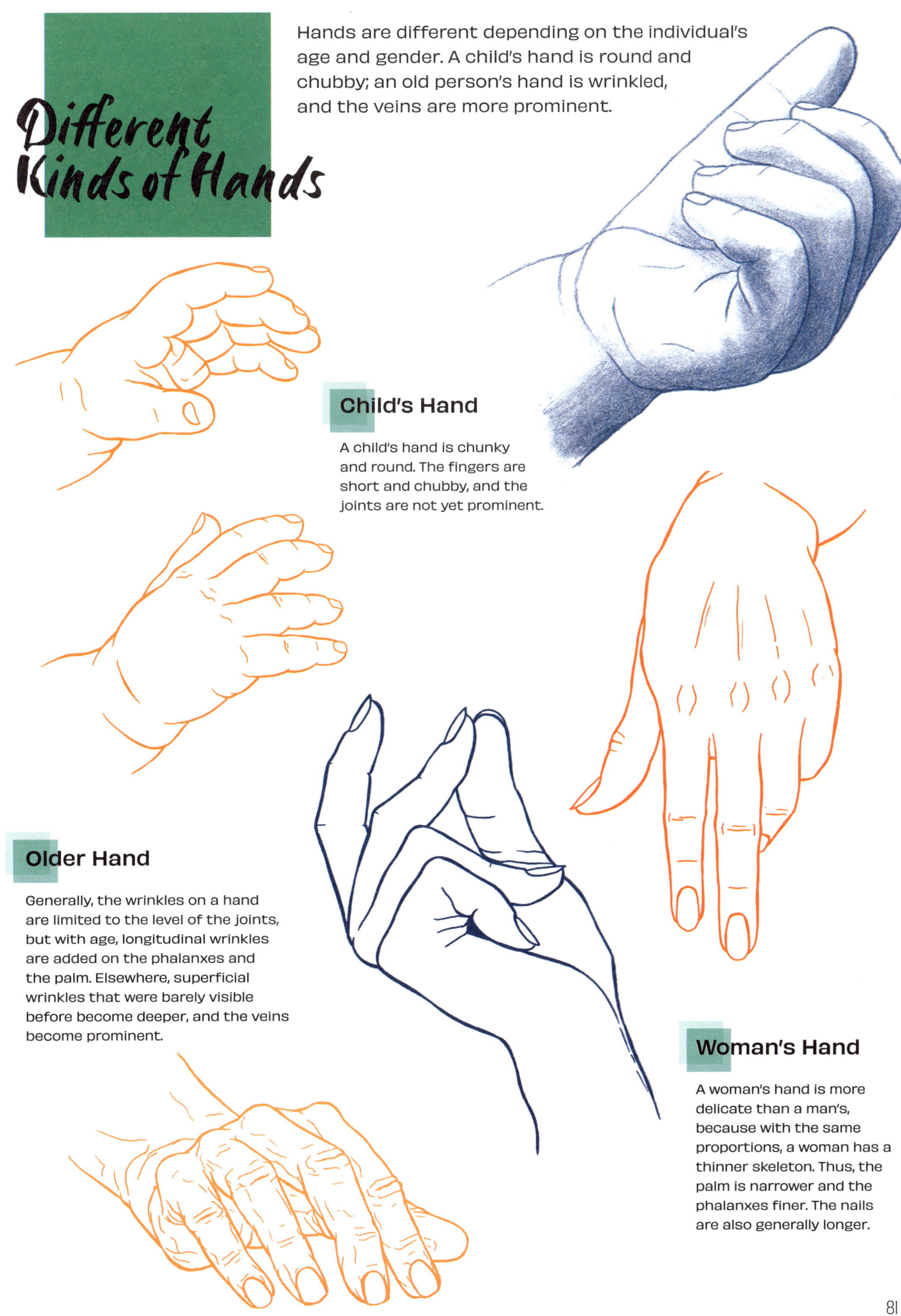

Different Kinds of Hands

Hands are different depending on the individual's age and gender. A child's hand is round and chubby; an old person's hand is wrinkled, and the veins are more prominent.

Child's Hand

A child's hand is chunky and round. The fingers are short and chubby, and the joints are not yet prominent.

Older Hand

Generally, the wrinkles on a hand are limited to the level of the joints, but with age, longitudinal wrinkles are added on the phalanxes and the palm. Elsewhere, superficial wrinkles that were barely visible before become deeper, and the veins become prominent.

Woman's Hand

A woman's hand is more delicate than a man's, because with the same proportions, a woman has a thinner skeleton. Thus, the palm is narrower and the phalanxes finer. The nails are also generally longer.

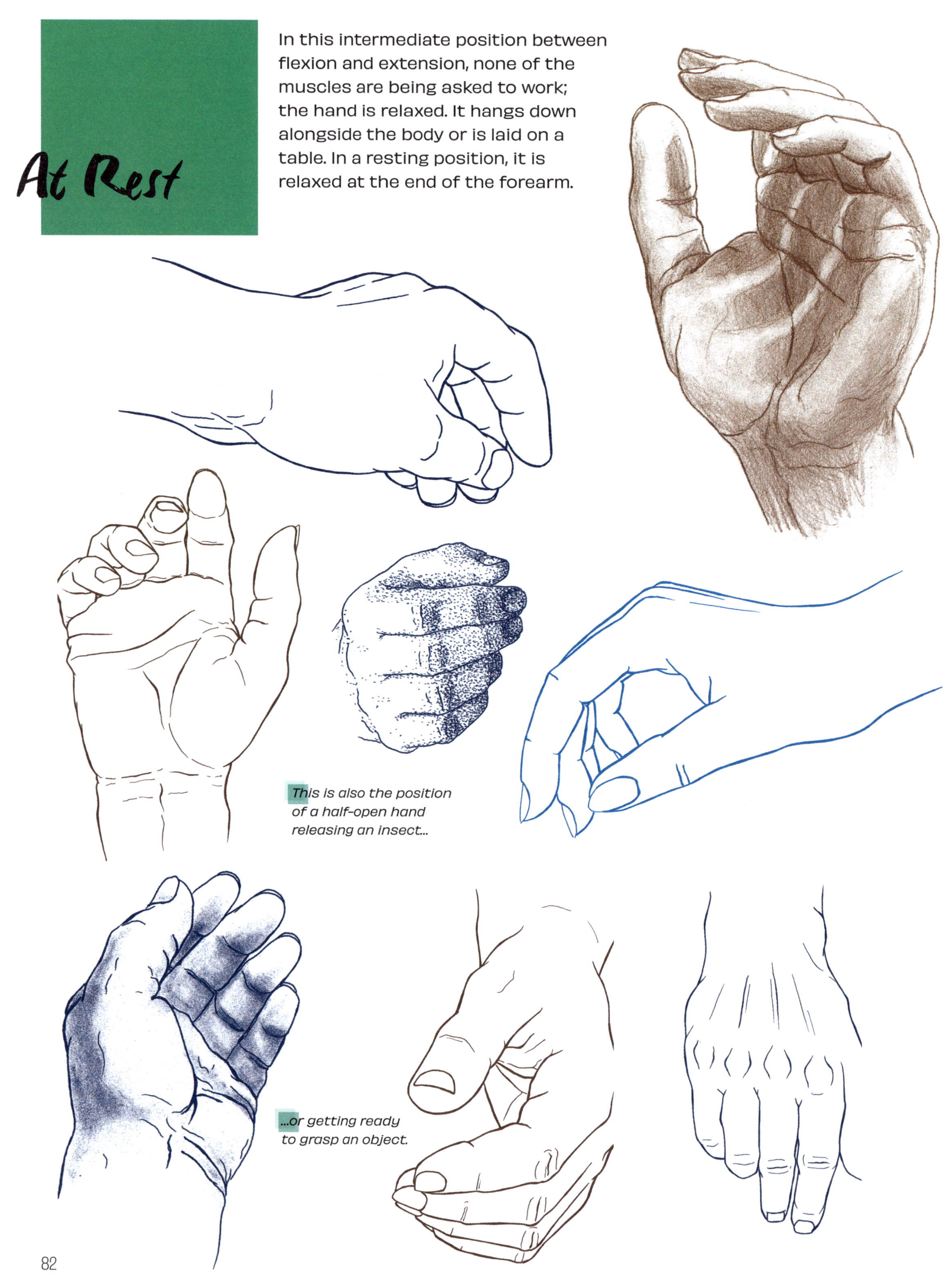

At Rest

In this intermediate position between flexion and extension, none of the muscles are being asked to work; the hand is relaxed. It hangs down alongside the body or is laid on a table. In a resting position, it is relaxed at the end of the forearm.

This is also the position of a half-open hand releasing an insect...

...or getting ready to grasp an object.

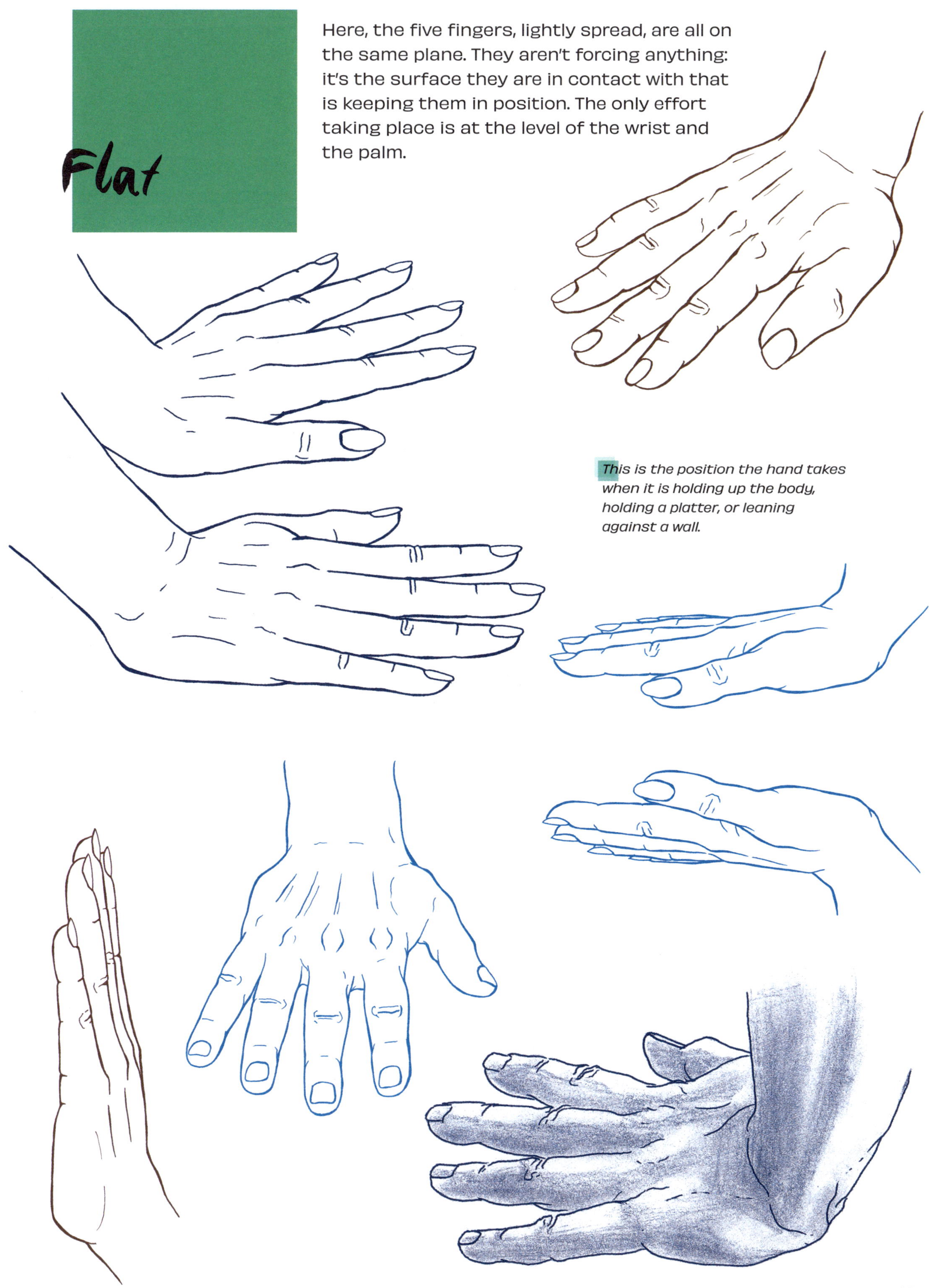

Flat

Here, the five fingers, lightly spread, are all on the same plane. They aren't forcing anything: it's the surface they are in contact with that is keeping them in position. The only effort taking place is at the level of the wrist and the palm.

This is the position the hand takes when it is holding up the body, holding a platter, or leaning against a wall.

Outstretched Hand

"Watch out!"? Or an attack using the edge of the hand? When it is brought back along the palm, the thumb is more strained than the other fingers. When it is released, the gesture is like a hand signal for "good-bye."

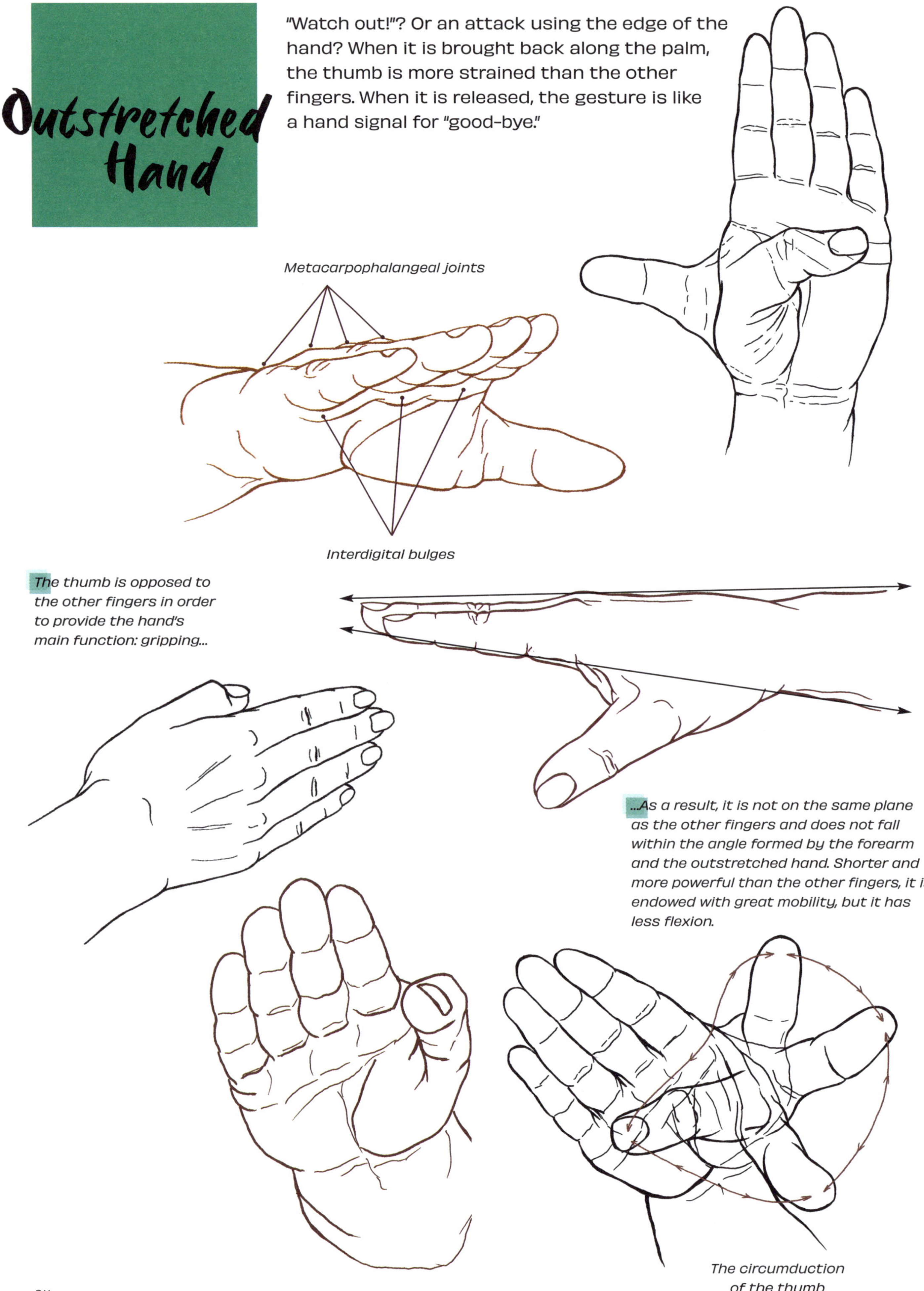

The thumb is opposed to the other fingers in order to provide the hand's main function: gripping...

...As a result, it is not on the same plane as the other fingers and does not fall within the angle formed by the forearm and the outstretched hand. Shorter and more powerful than the other fingers, it is endowed with great mobility, but it has less flexion.

The circumduction of the thumb

Clenched Fist

The closed fist expresses violence: we clench our fists in anger, we bang our fists on the table, we use them to strike an opponent... In this position, the index is usually more prominent than the other fingers, because its tip pushes against the thenar eminence.

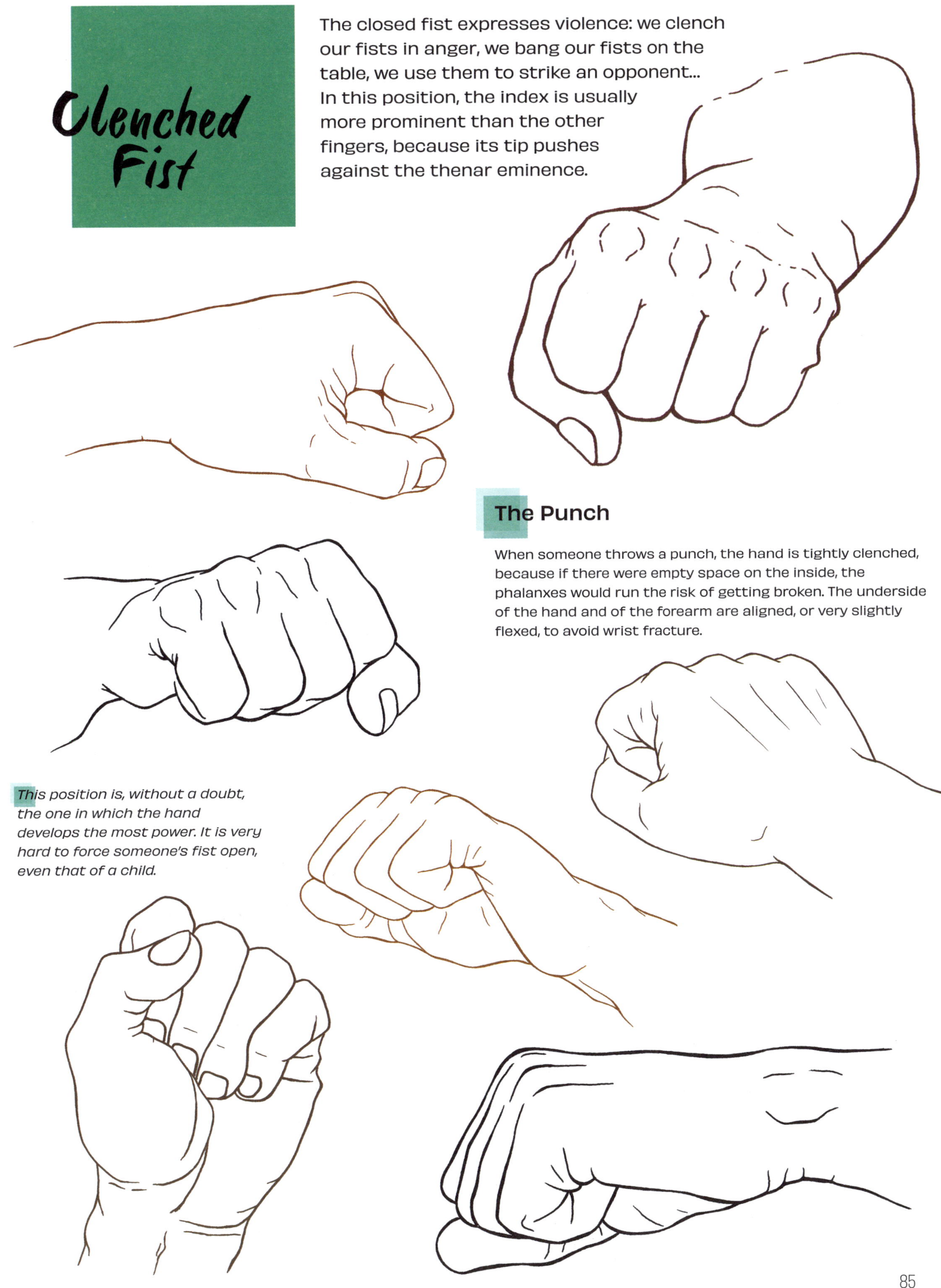

The Punch

When someone throws a punch, the hand is tightly clenched, because if there were empty space on the inside, the phalanxes would run the risk of getting broken. The underside of the hand and of the forearm are aligned, or very slightly flexed, to avoid wrist fracture.

This position is, without a doubt, the one in which the hand develops the most power. It is very hard to force someone's fist open, even that of a child.

Outstretched Fingers

An outstretched hand is prepared to grasp an object that is offered to it or to catch something thrown to it. It uses large gestures to punctuate a lively conversation. Or, more dramatically, it implores, or it freezes in surprise, in pain, or in fright.

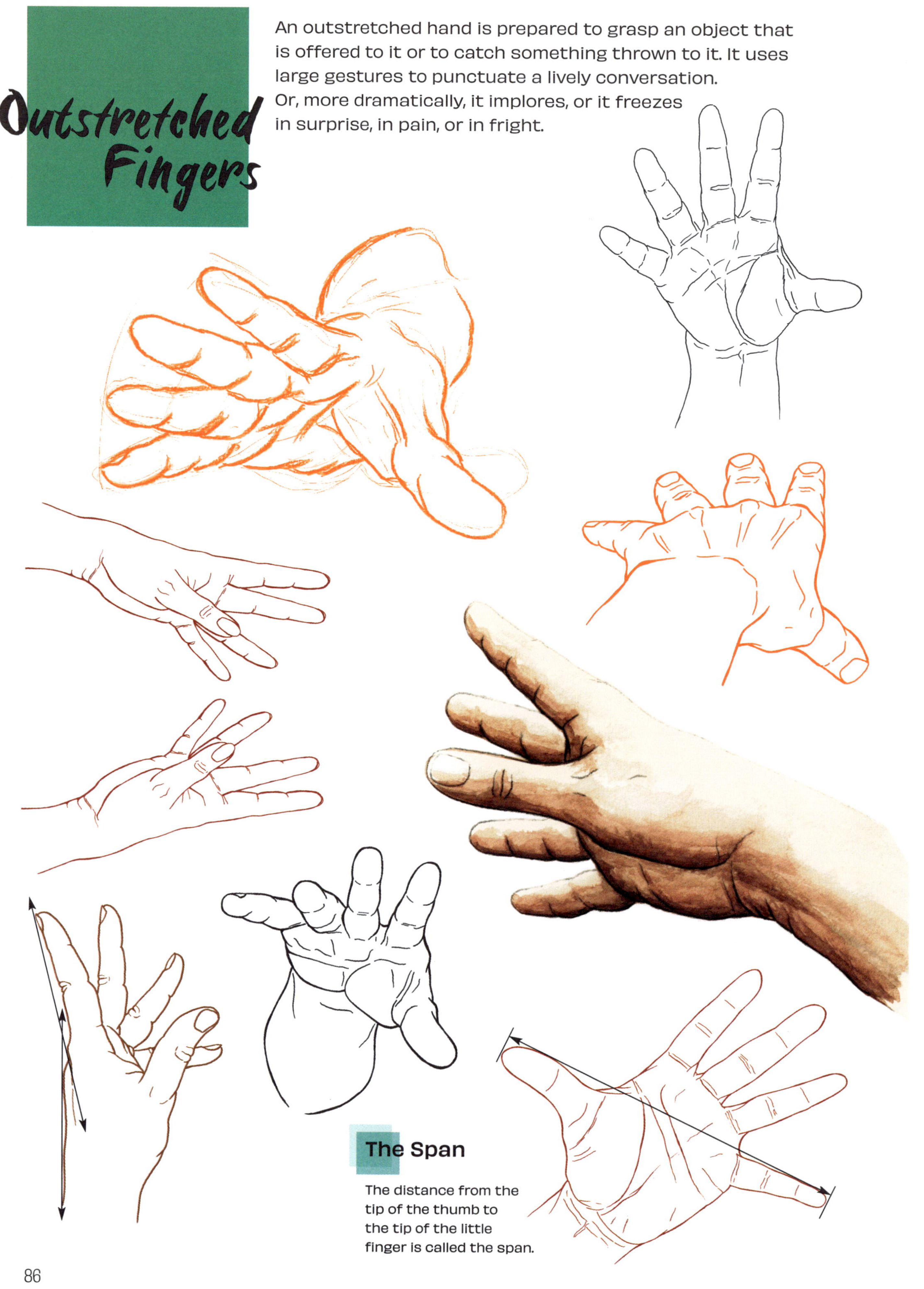

The Span

The distance from the tip of the thumb to the tip of the little finger is called the span.

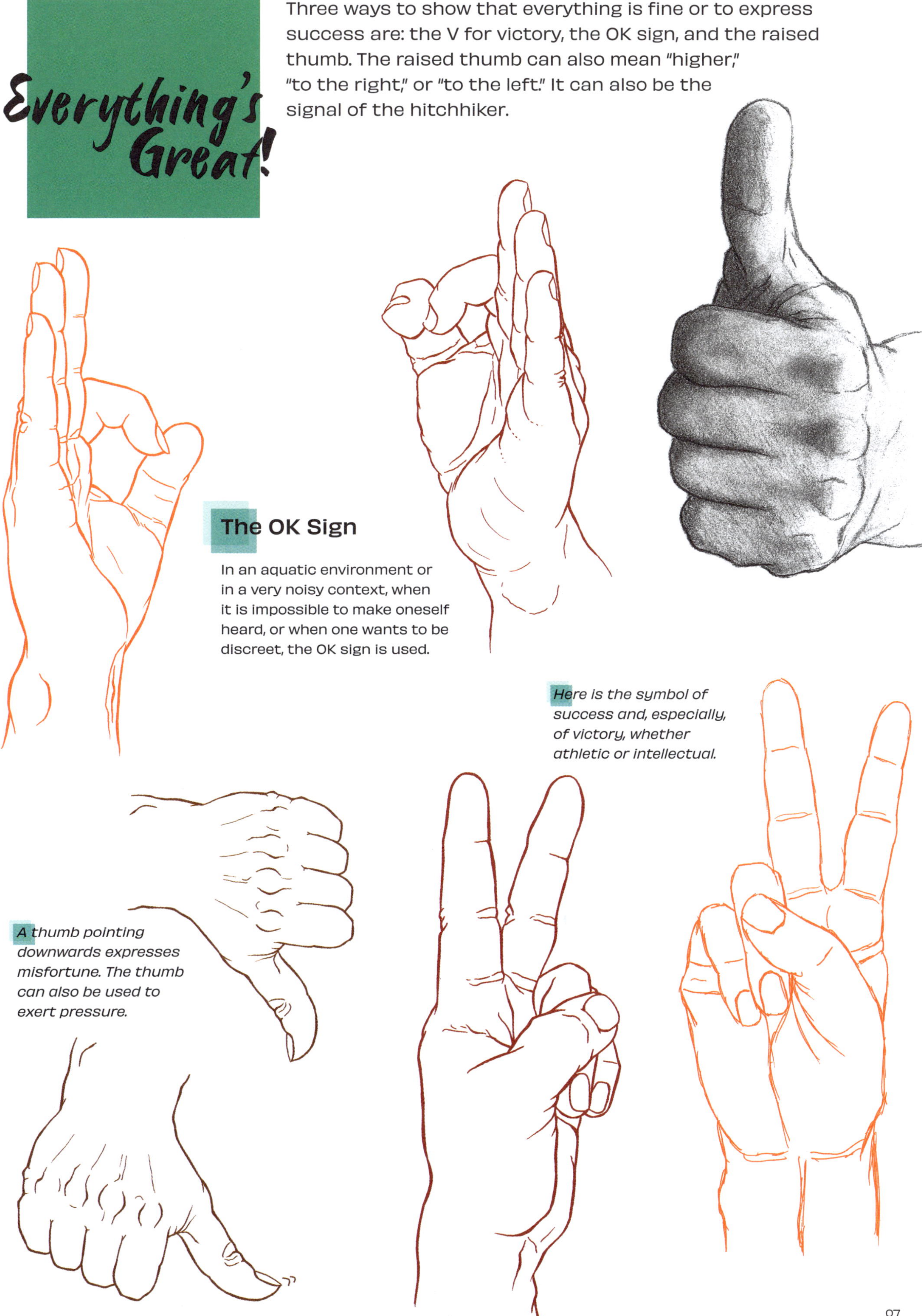

Three ways to show that everything is fine or to express success are: the V for victory, the OK sign, and the raised thumb. The raised thumb can also mean "higher," "to the right," or "to the left." It can also be the signal of the hitchhiker.

The OK Sign

In an aquatic environment or in a very noisy context, when it is impossible to make oneself heard, or when one wants to be discreet, the OK sign is used.

Here is the symbol of success and, especially, of victory, whether athletic or intellectual.

A thumb pointing downwards expresses misfortune. The thumb can also be used to exert pressure.

Joined Hands

Whether the fingers are extended or crossed, joined hands are an invitation to prayer. We rub our hands in extreme cold; we make them into a cup to collect liquid or to protect a small precious object.

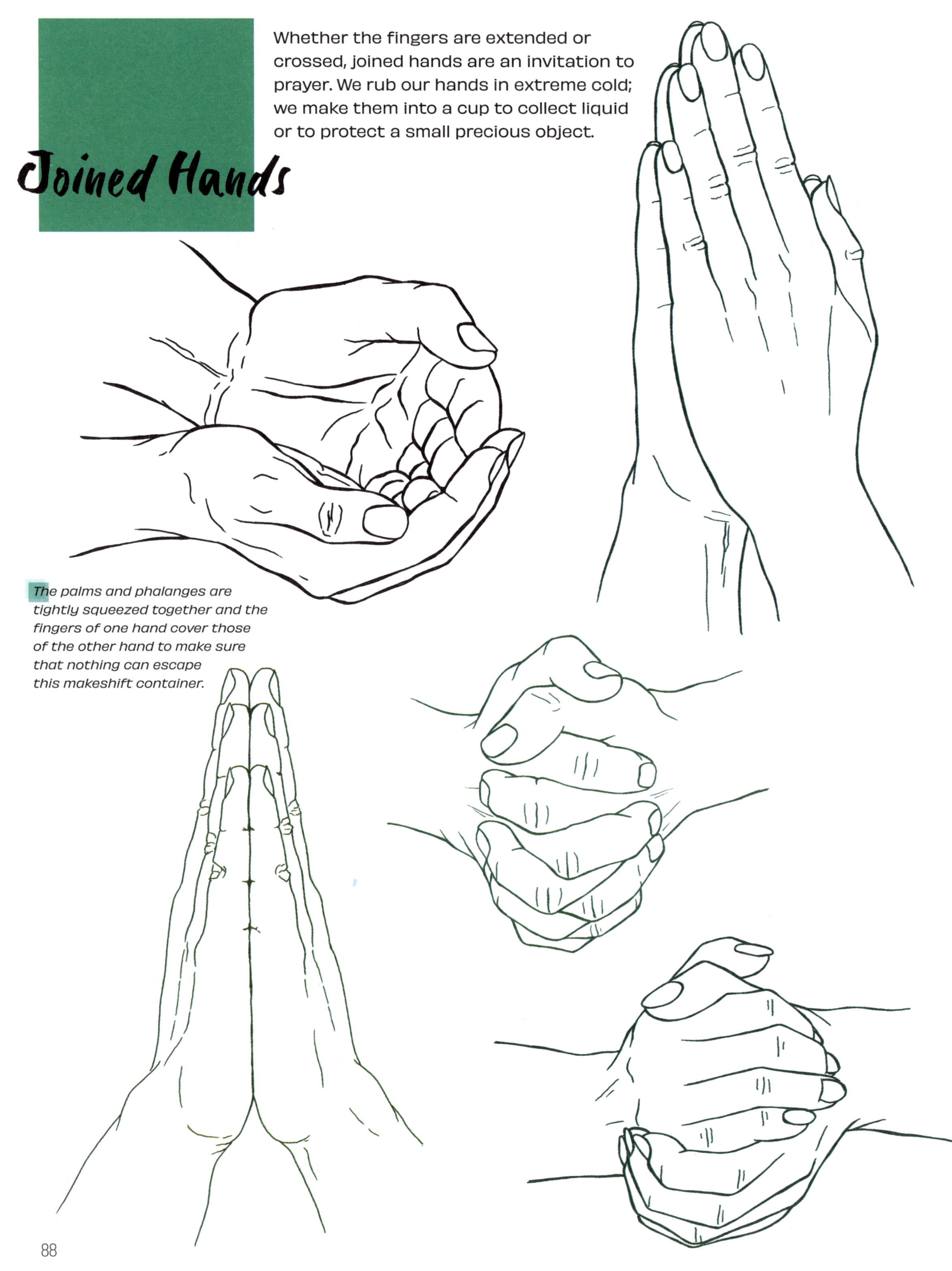

The palms and phalanges are tightly squeezed together and the fingers of one hand cover those of the other hand to make sure that nothing can escape this makeshift container.

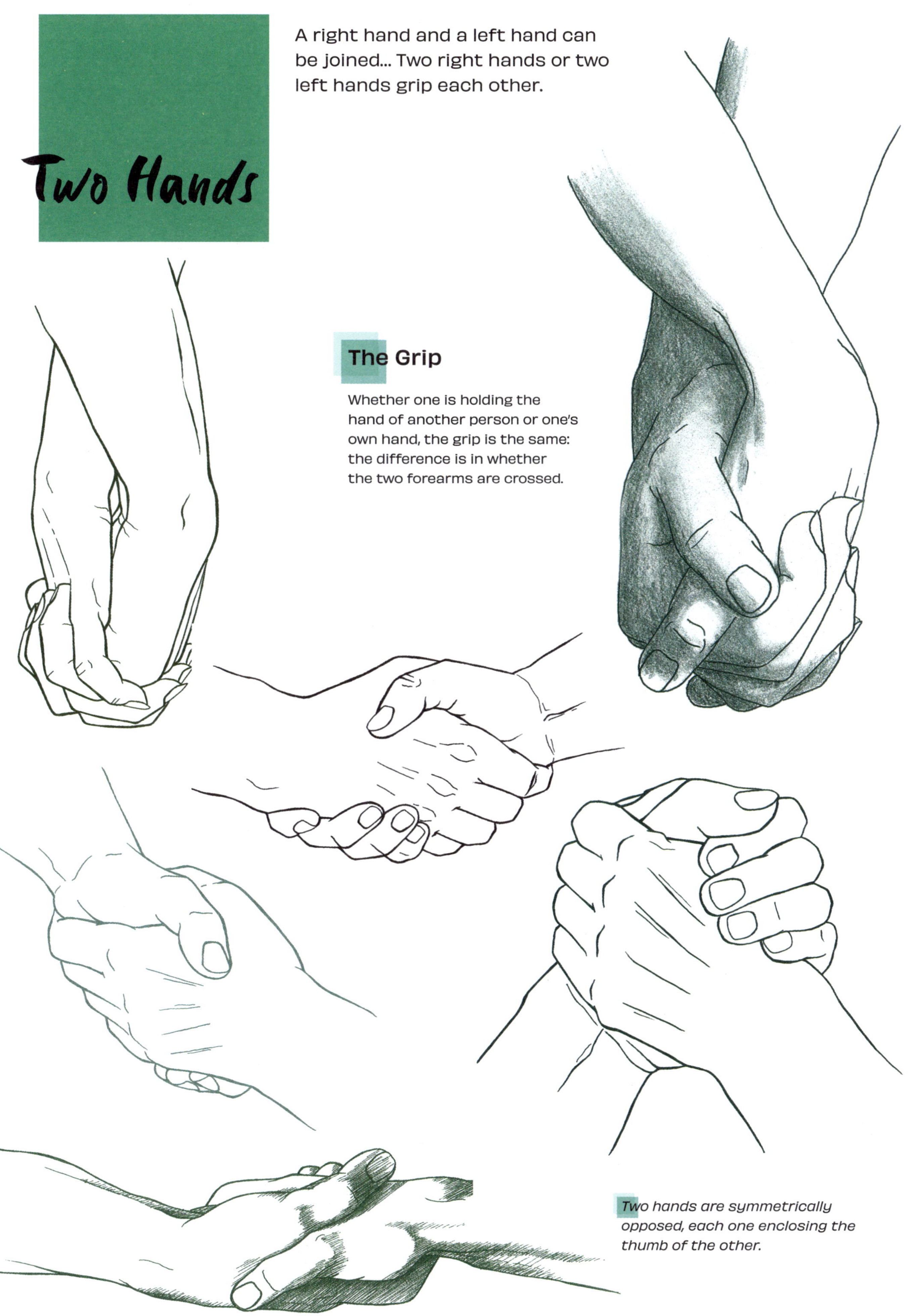

Two Hands

The Grip

Whether one is holding the
hand of another person or one's
own hand, the grip is the same:
the difference is in whether
the two forearms are crossed.

*Two hands are symmetrically
opposed, each one enclosing the
thumb of the other.*

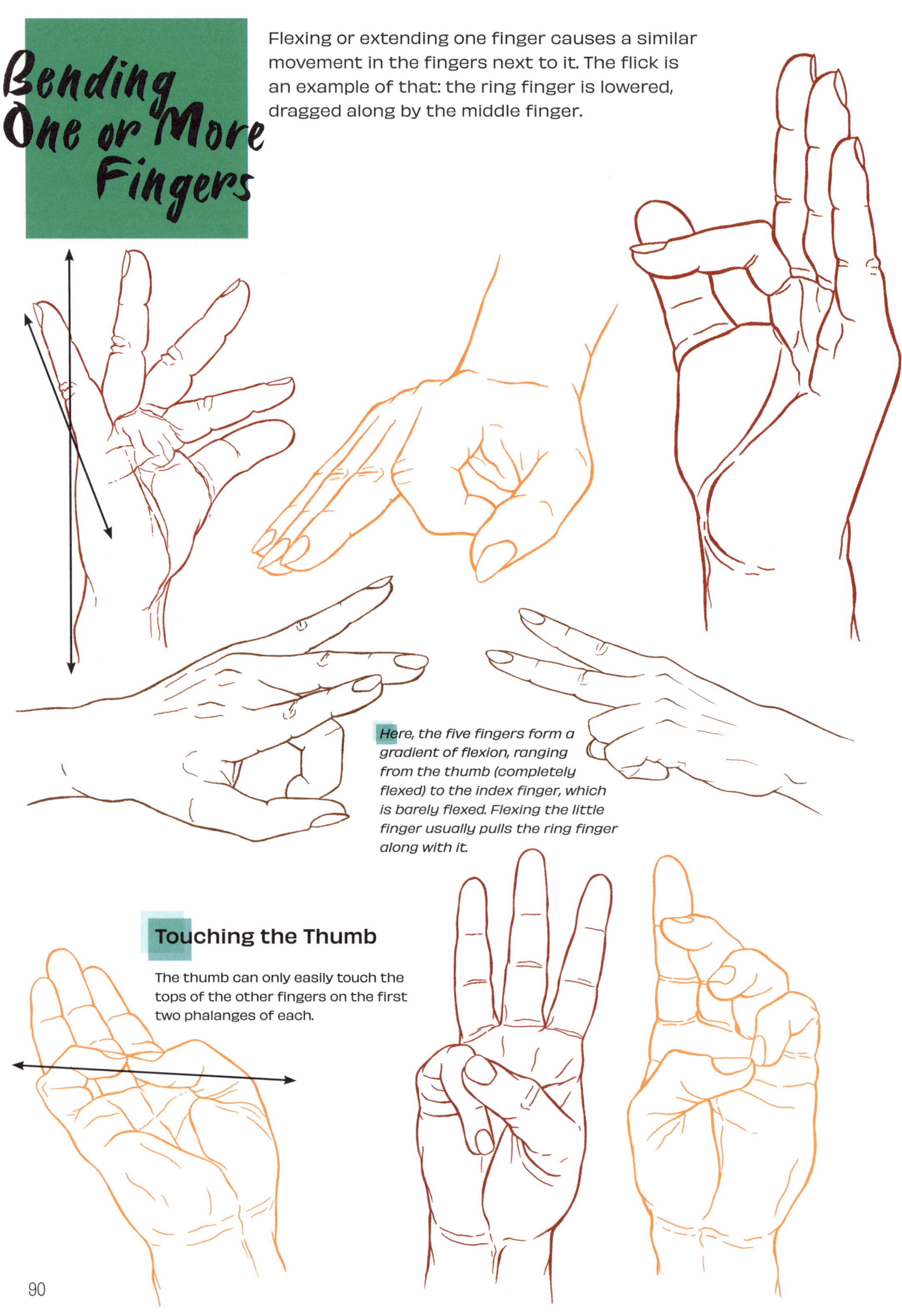

Bending One or More Fingers

Flexing or extending one finger causes a similar movement in the fingers next to it. The flick is an example of that: the ring finger is lowered, dragged along by the middle finger.

Here, the five fingers form a gradient of flexion, ranging from the thumb (completely flexed) to the index finger, which is barely flexed. Flexing the little finger usually pulls the ring finger along with it.

Touching the Thumb

The thumb can only easily touch the tops of the other fingers on the first two phalanges of each.

The index finger extending from a clenched fist implies vigor and tension. It is accusatory, severe, or commanding. When the other fingers are not so tightly clenched, the gesture is more relaxed. Now it is an explorer discovering a new country or a guide showing the way.

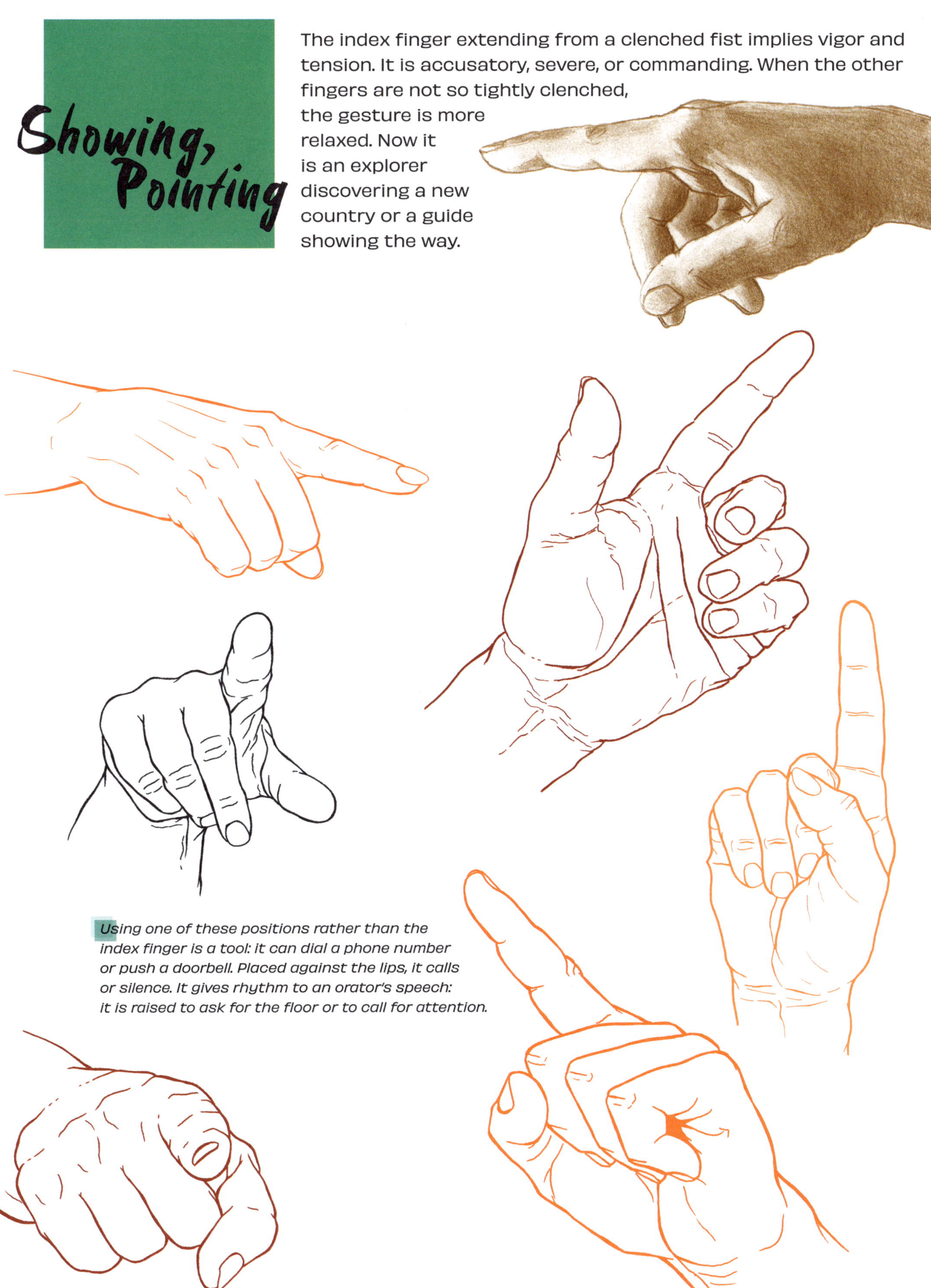

Using one of these positions rather than the index finger is a tool: it can dial a phone number or push a doorbell. Placed against the lips, it calls or silence. It gives rhythm to an orator's speech: it is raised to ask for the floor or to call for attention.

A Full Hand

In this kind of grip, the fingers mold themselves to the contours of the object. Unlike for the other fingers, it is the side and not the fleshy pad of the little finger that opposes the thumb.

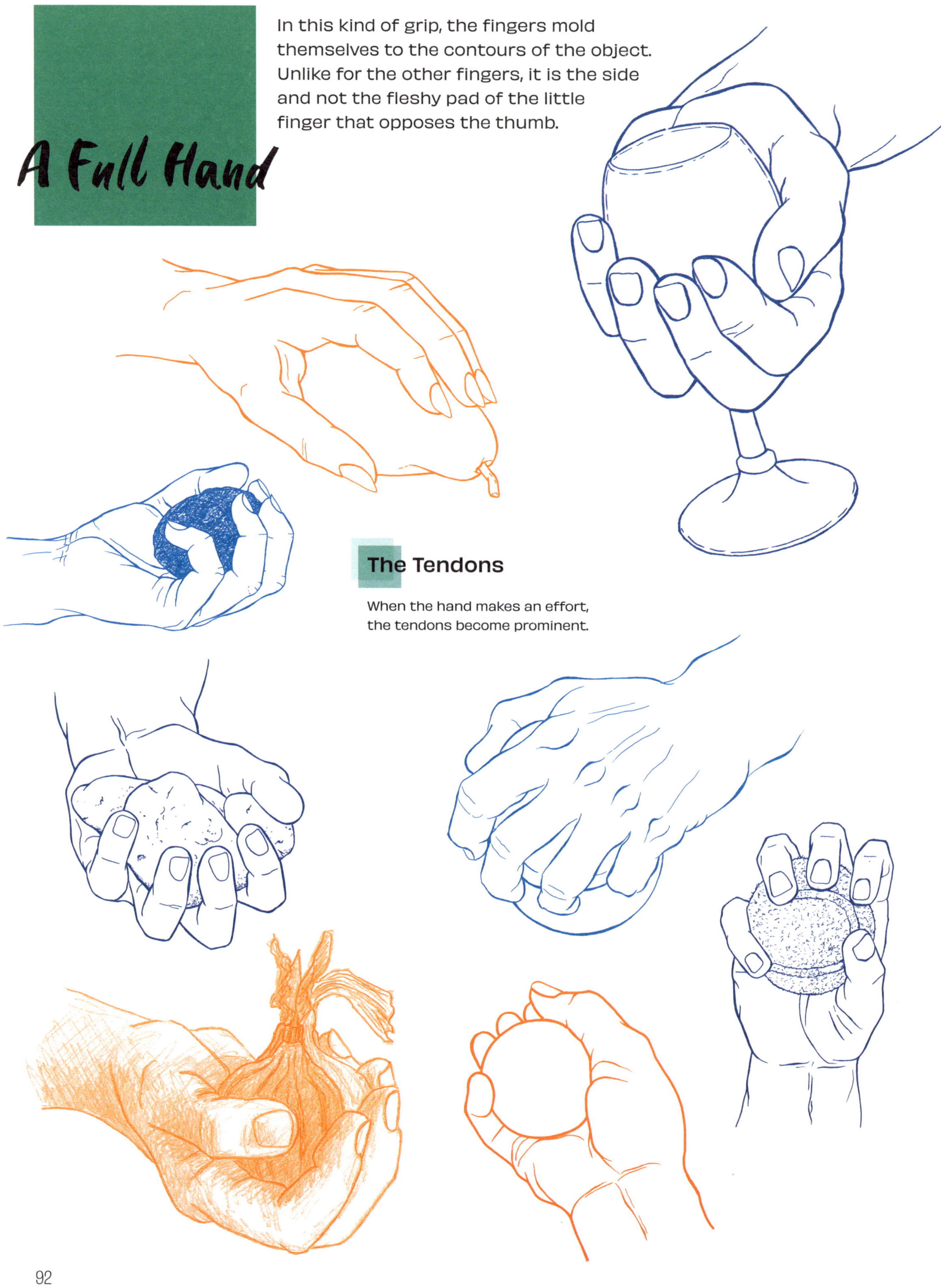

The Tendons

When the hand makes an effort, the tendons become prominent.

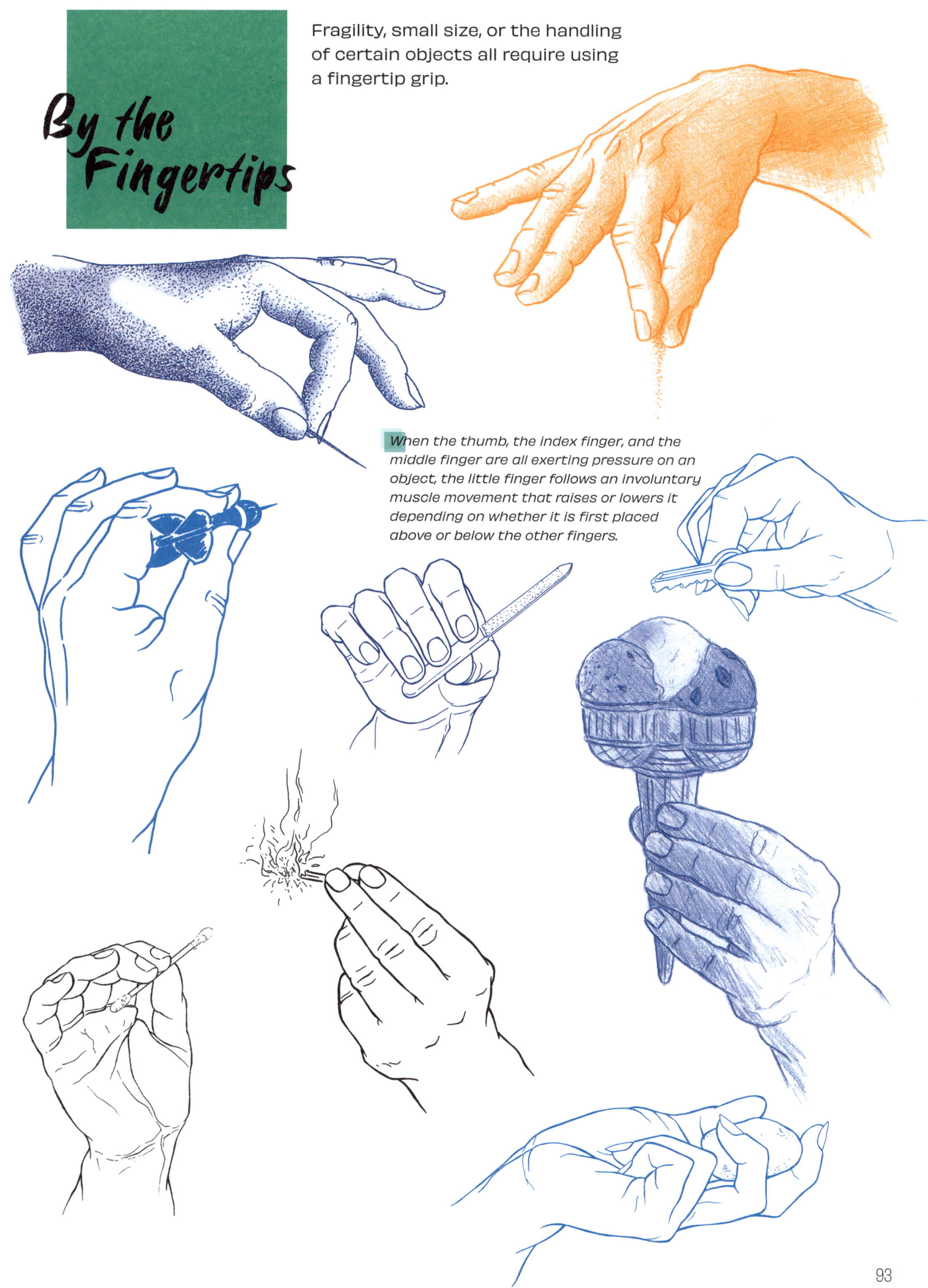

By the Fingertips

Fragility, small size, or the handling of certain objects all require using a fingertip grip.

When the thumb, the index finger, and the middle finger are all exerting pressure on an object, the little finger follows an involuntary muscle movement that raises or lowers it depending on whether it is first placed above or below the other fingers.

The firmest—and therefore the safest—way to grip several different objects (a bowl, a piece of paper, etc.) is by pinching them between the fingers.

Curved Fingers

In this position, all fingers (except for the thumb) are curled inward.

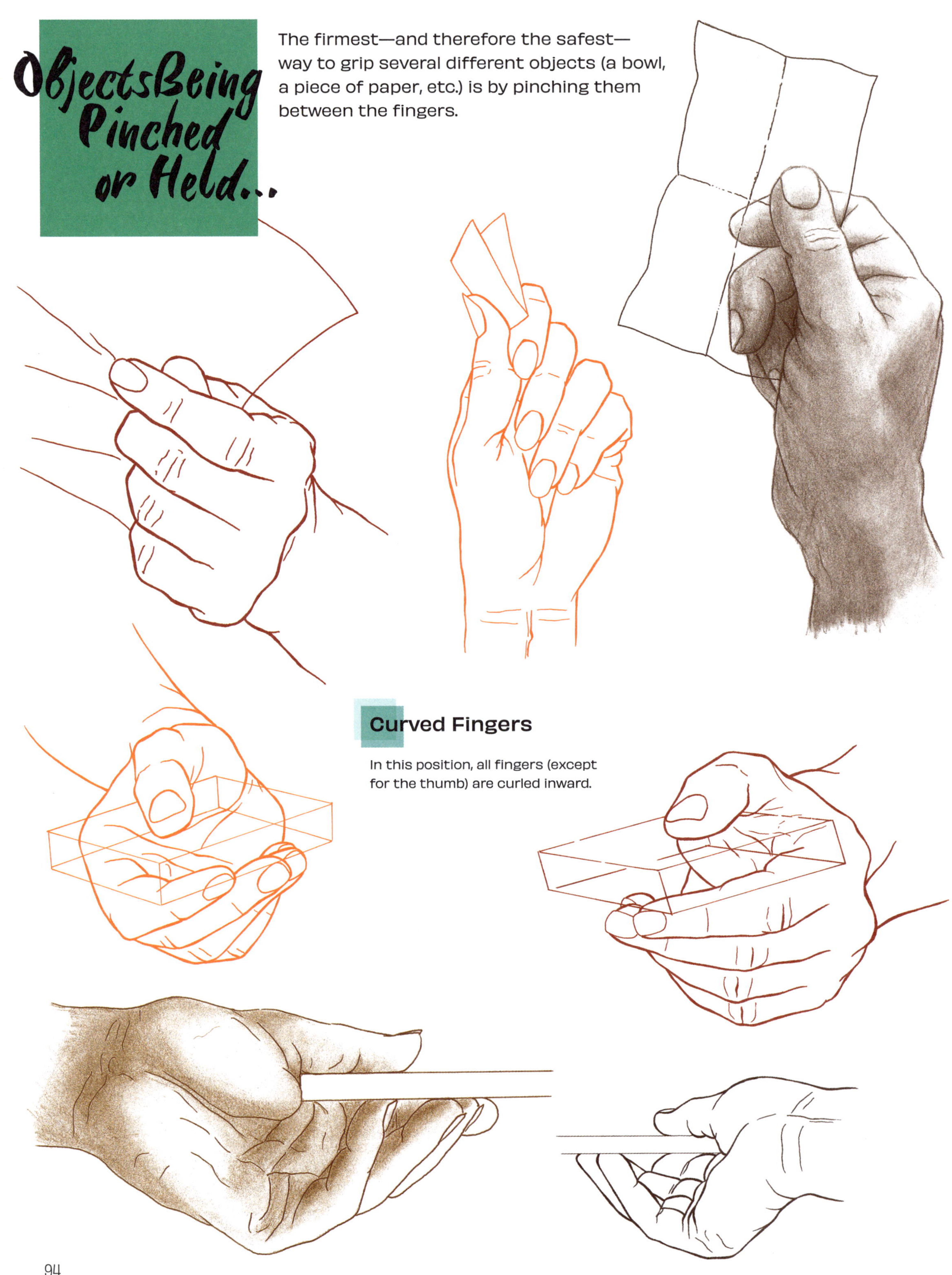

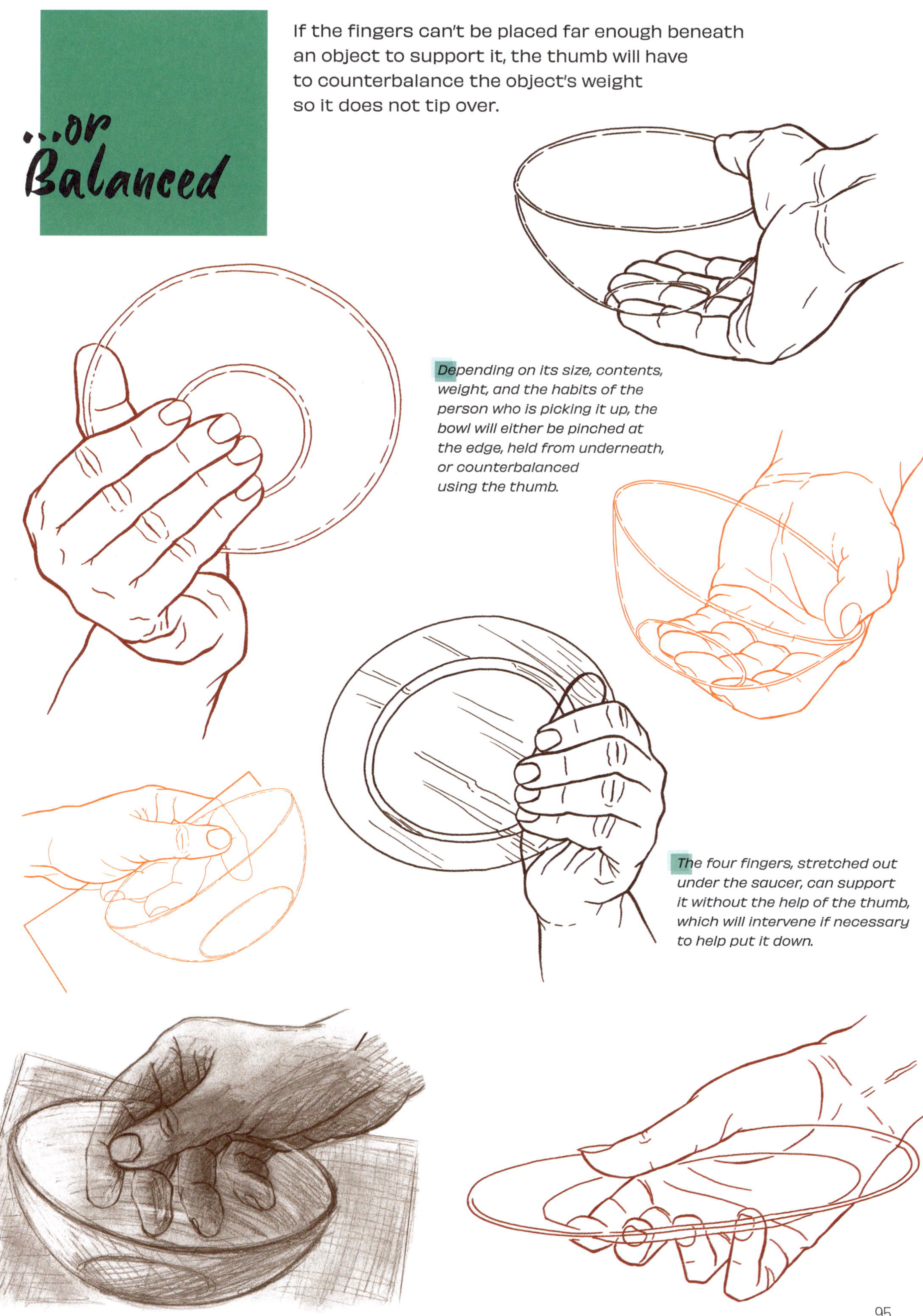

...or Balanced

If the fingers can't be placed far enough beneath an object to support it, the thumb will have to counterbalance the object's weight so it does not tip over.

Depending on its size, contents, weight, and the habits of the person who is picking it up, the bowl will either be pinched at the edge, held from underneath, or counterbalanced using the thumb.

The four fingers, stretched out under the saucer, can support it without the help of the thumb, which will intervene if necessary to help put it down.

Drinking

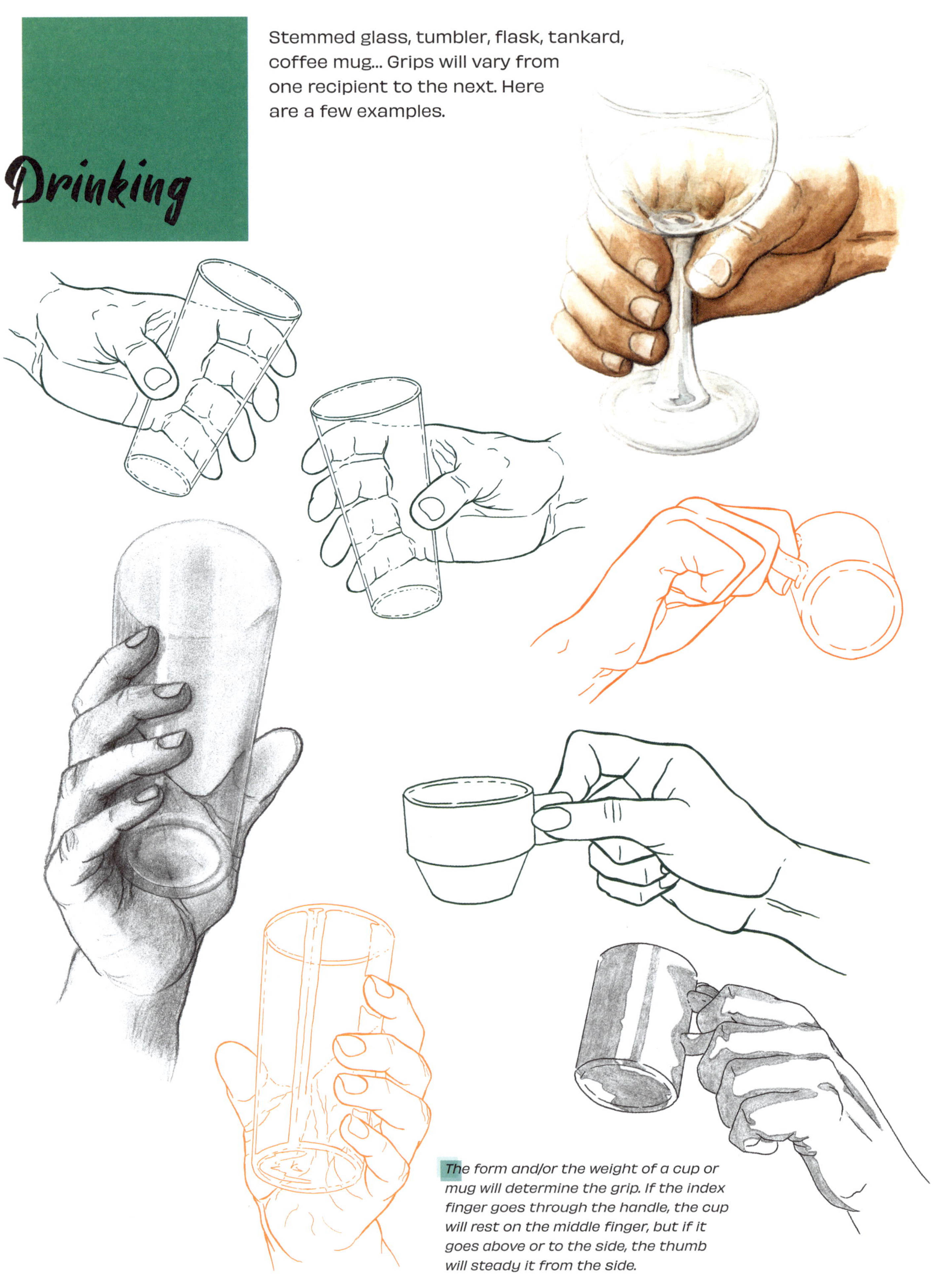

The form and/or the weight of a cup or mug will determine the grip. If the index finger goes through the handle, the cup will rest on the middle finger, but if it goes above or to the side, the thumb will steady it from the side.

Eating

Chopsticks, knives, forks, etc. There are many kinds of cutlery and kitchen utensils, and they take all sorts of forms. The way they are held can also change from one individual to the next.

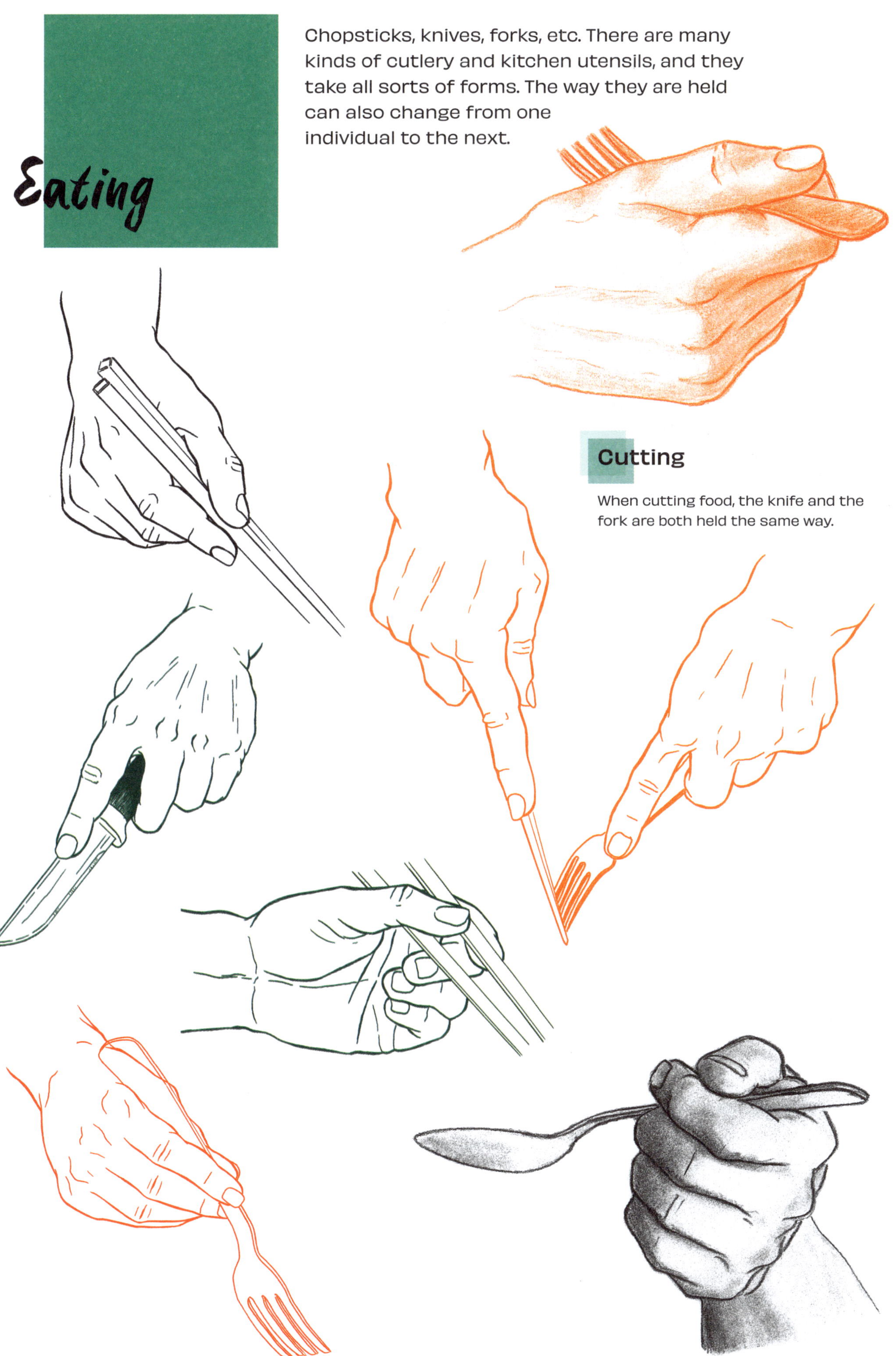

Cutting

When cutting food, the knife and the fork are both held the same way.

Writing, Drawing

A hand holding a writing instrument in the middle, flexible and mobile, evokes nonchalance or relaxation. On the other hand, a hand that is tensed near the tip of the writing utensil will indicate hard work or concentration. Paintbrushes used for delicate work are held like a pen or pencil.

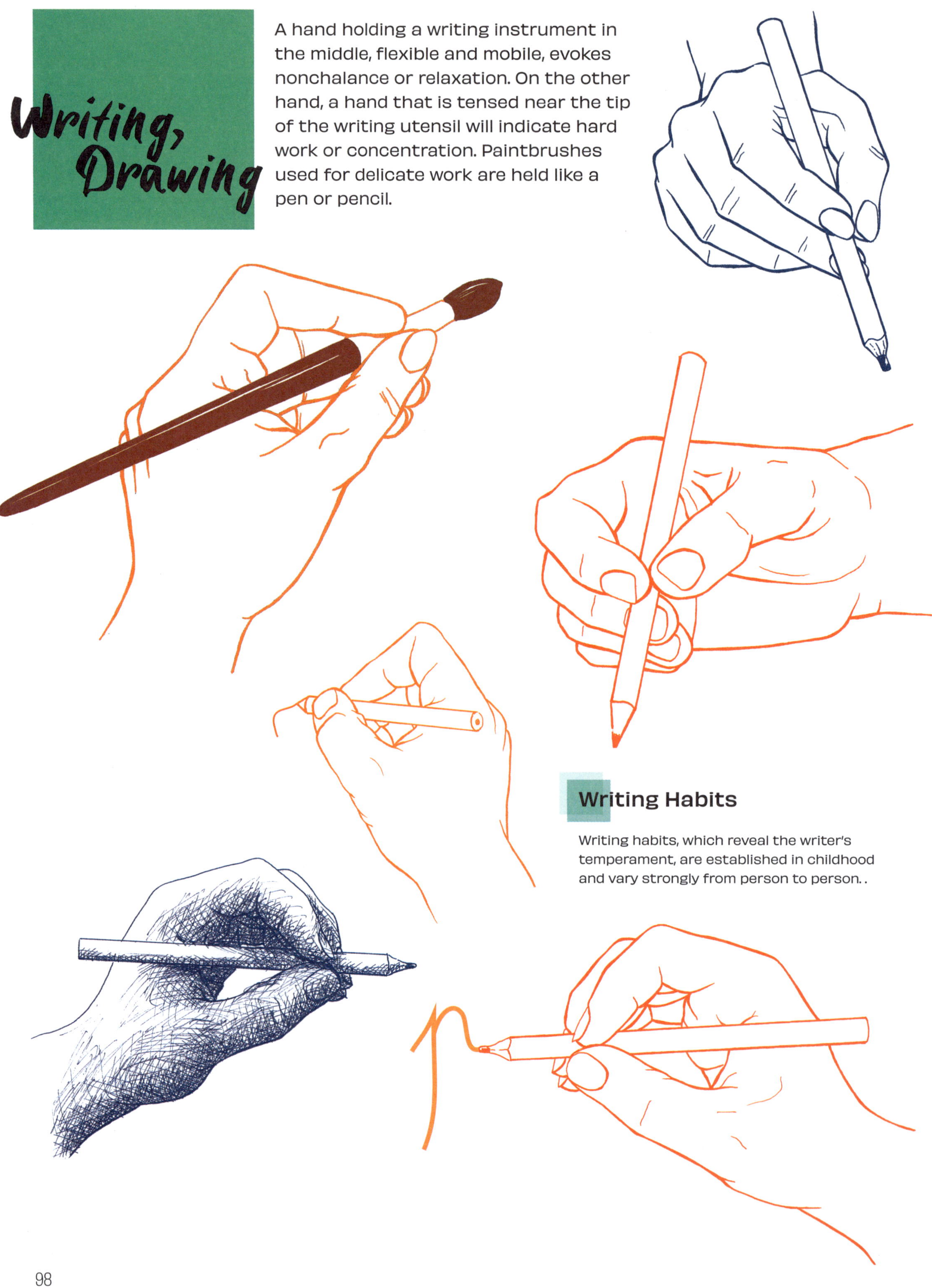

Writing Habits

Writing habits, which reveal the writer's temperament, are established in childhood and vary strongly from person to person. .

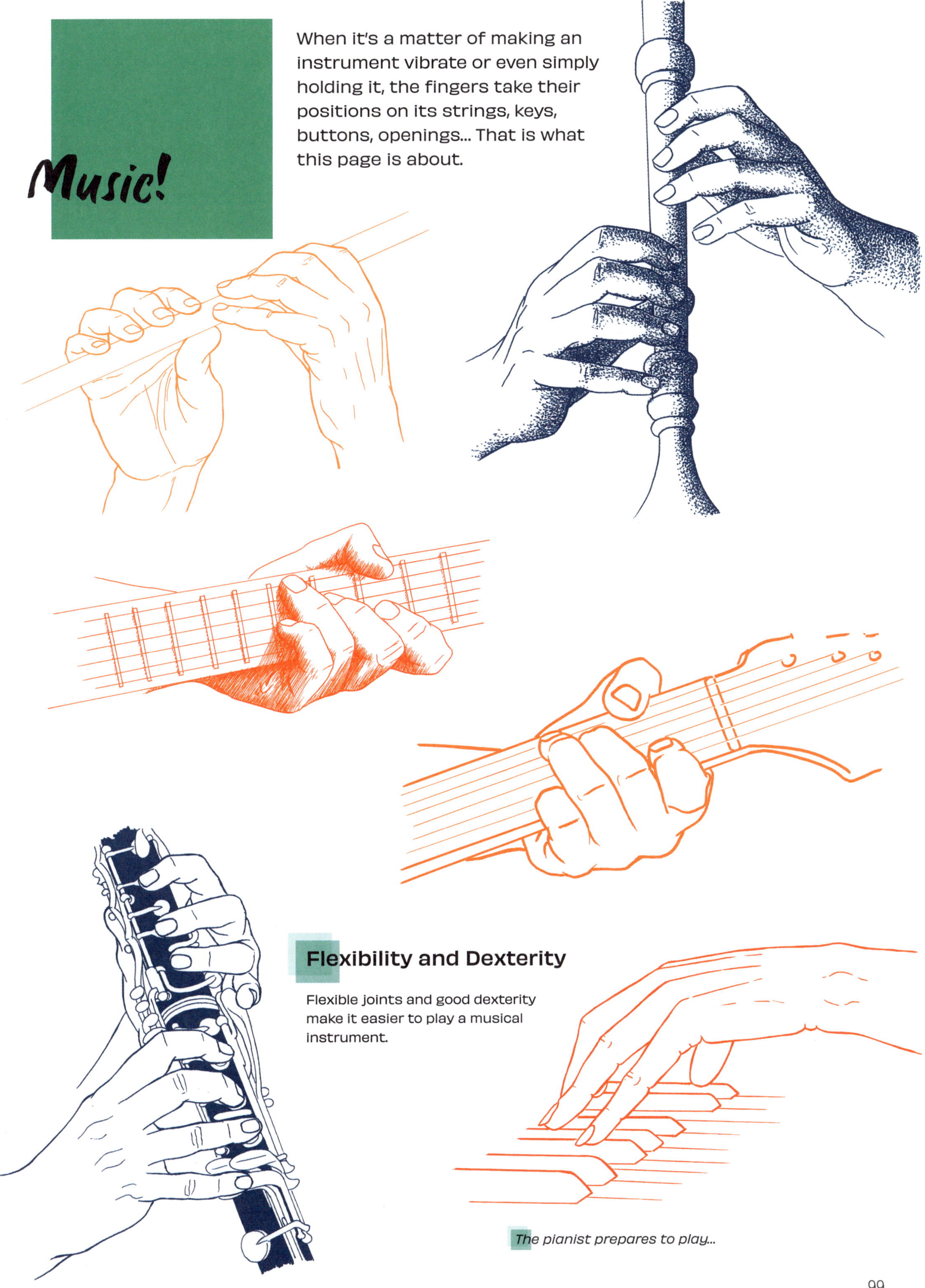

When it's a matter of making an instrument vibrate or even simply holding it, the fingers take their positions on its strings, keys, buttons, openings... That is what this page is about.

Flexibility and Dexterity

Flexible joints and good dexterity make it easier to play a musical instrument.

The pianist prepares to play...

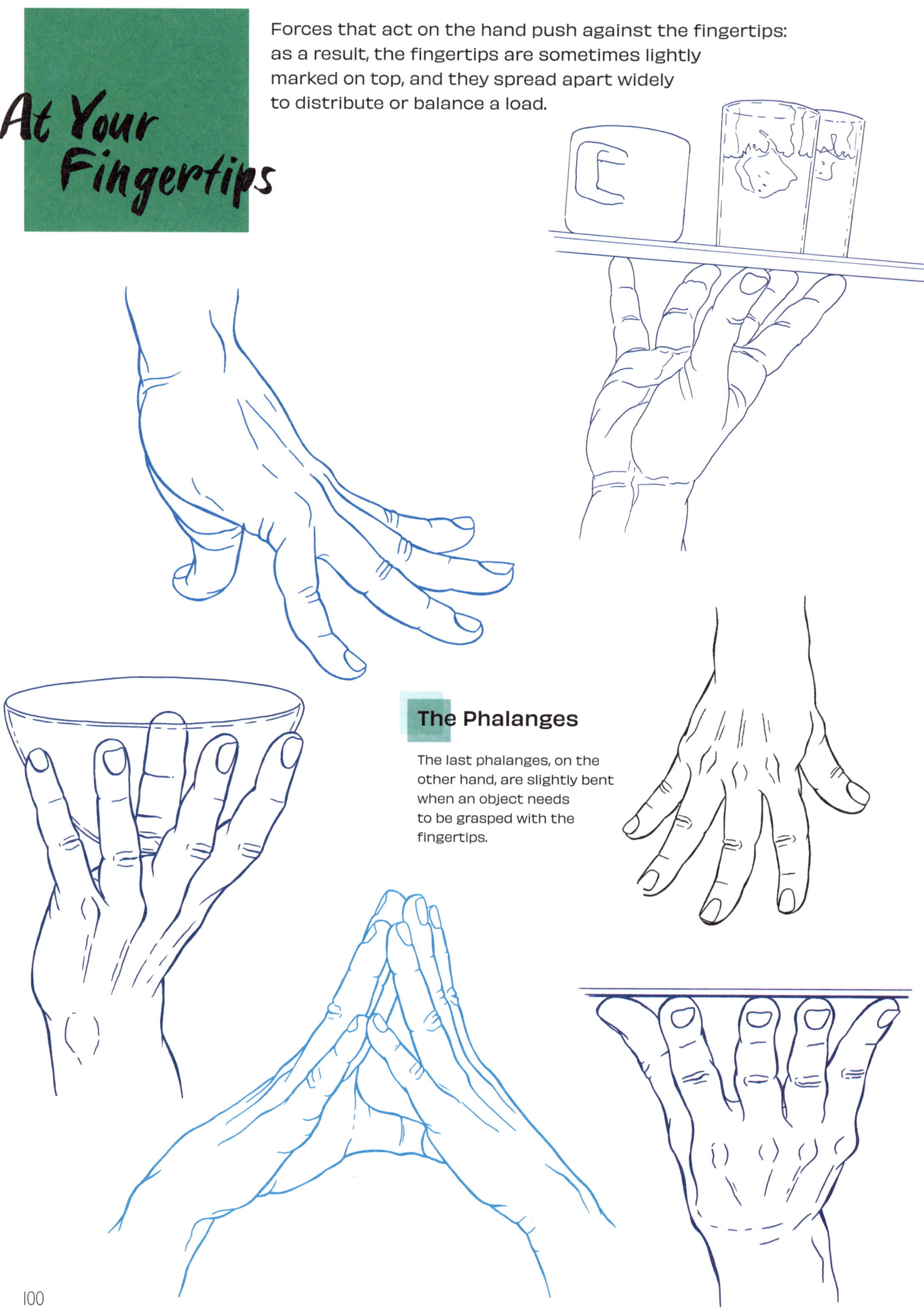

Forces that act on the hand push against the fingertips: as a result, the fingertips are sometimes lightly marked on top, and they spread apart widely to distribute or balance a load.

The Phalanges

The last phalanges, on the other hand, are slightly bent when an object needs to be grasped with the fingertips.

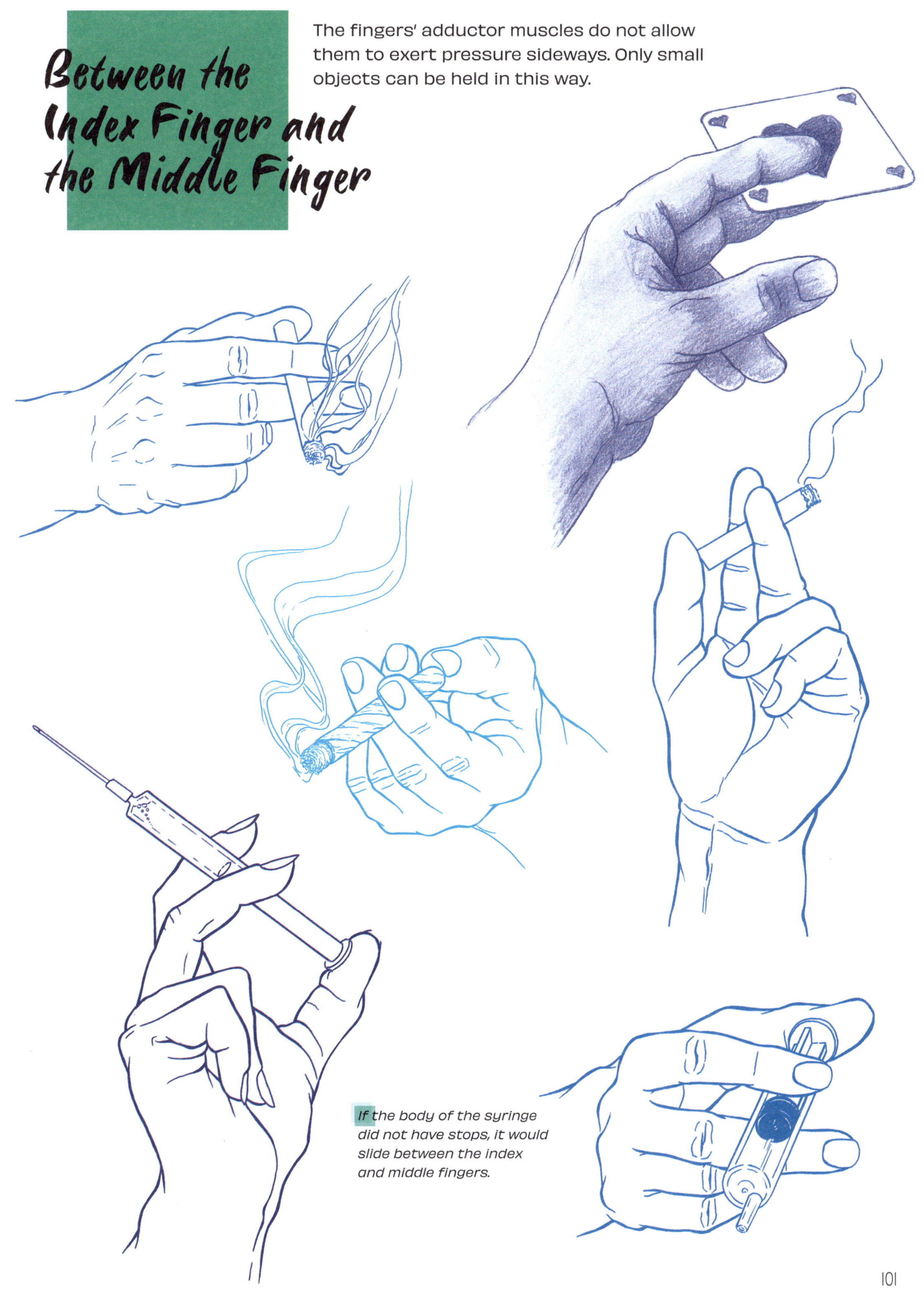

The fingers' adductor muscles do not allow them to exert pressure sideways. Only small objects can be held in this way.

If the body of the syringe did not have stops, it would slide between the index and middle fingers.

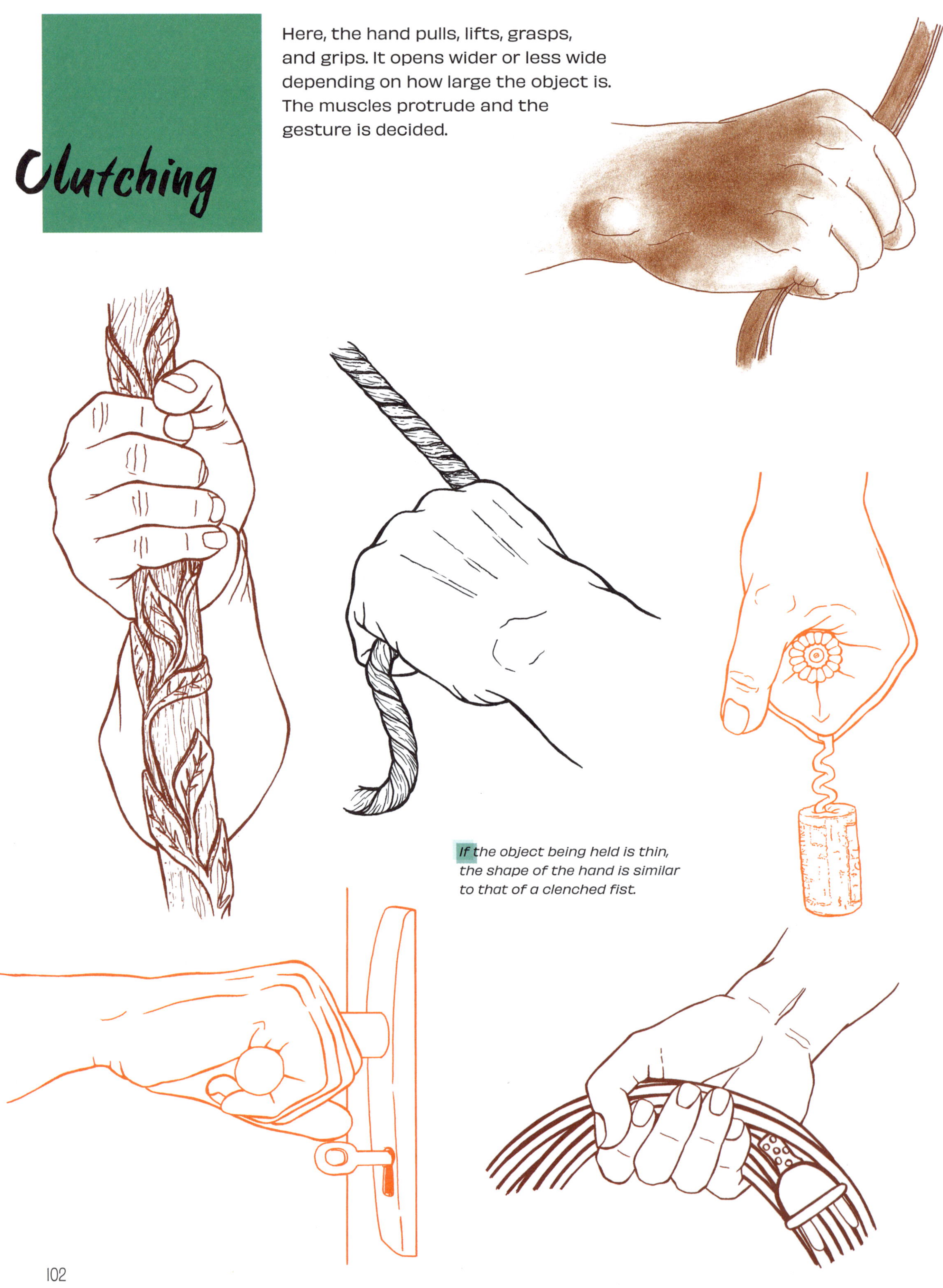

Clutching

Here, the hand pulls, lifts, grasps, and grips. It opens wider or less wide depending on how large the object is. The muscles protrude and the gesture is decided.

If the object being held is thin, the shape of the hand is similar to that of a clenched fist.

The fingertips curl up and form a hook into which the handle of a piece of luggage or of a basket can nestle

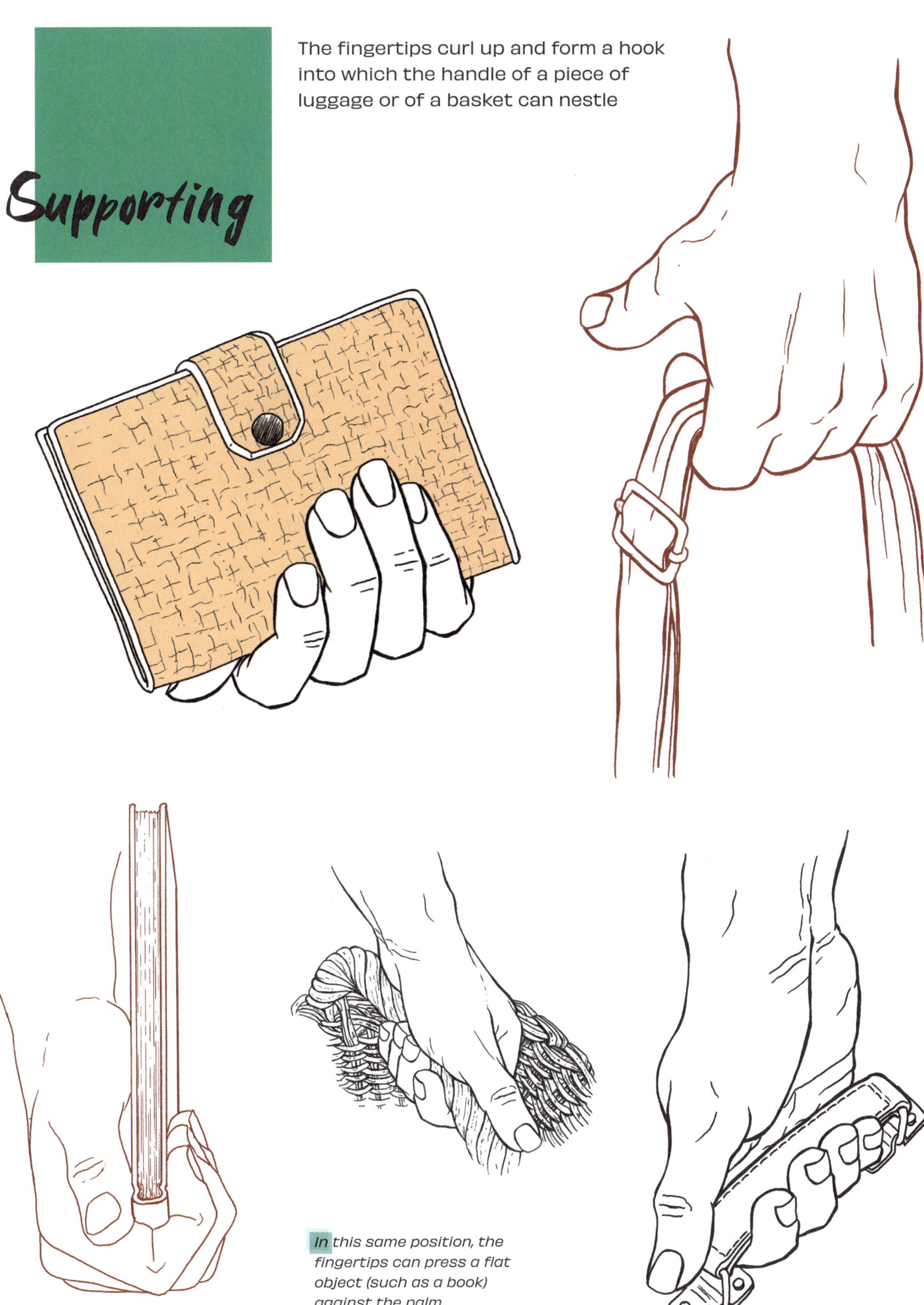

In this same position, the fingertips can press a flat object (such as a book) against the palm.

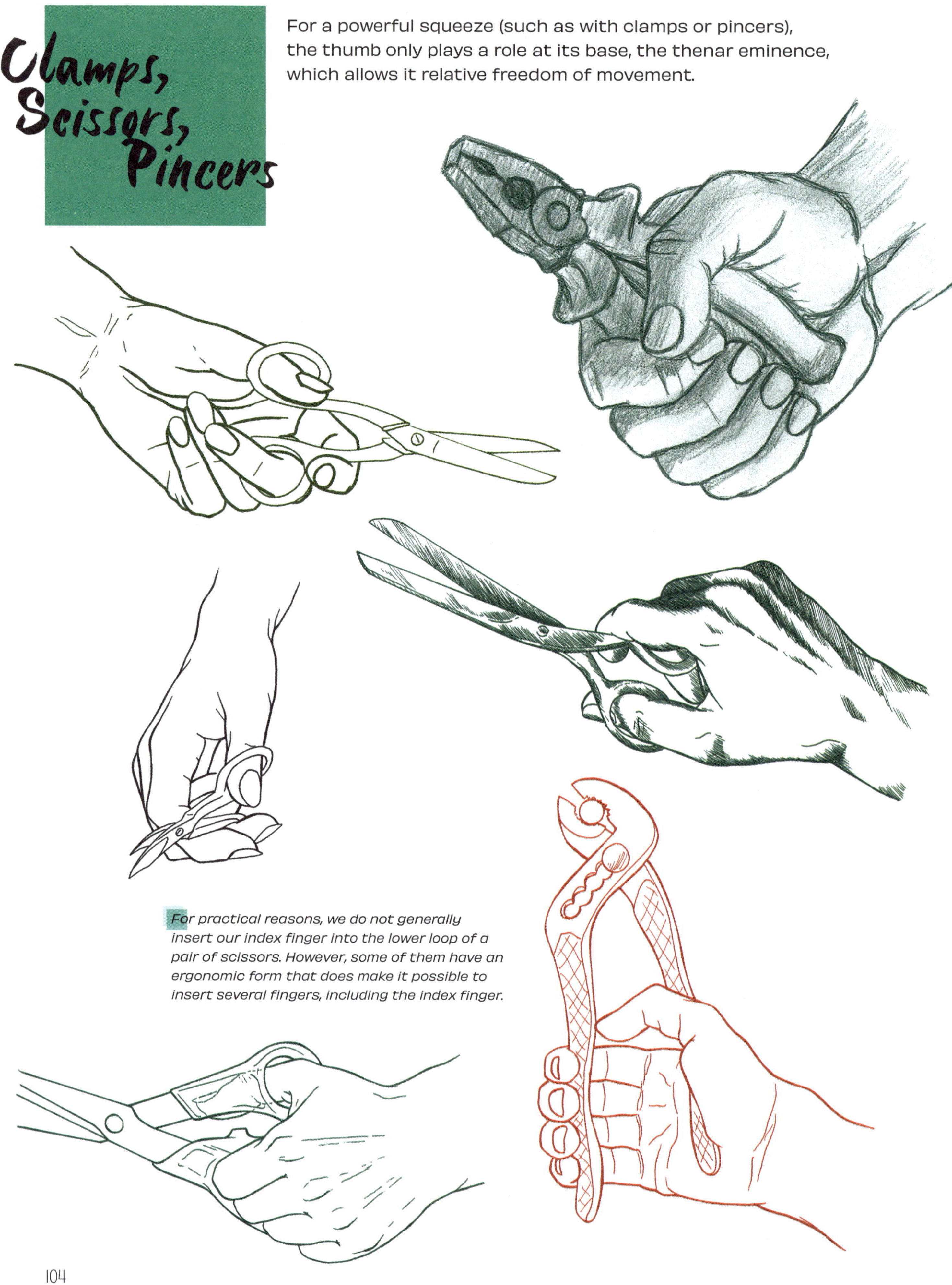

Clamps, Scissors, Pincers

For a powerful squeeze (such as with clamps or pincers), the thumb only plays a role at its base, the thenar eminence, which allows it relative freedom of movement.

For practical reasons, we do not generally insert our index finger into the lower loop of a pair of scissors. However, some of them have an ergonomic form that does make it possible to insert several fingers, including the index finger.

Spraying

Position of the Middle Finger

If the body of the spray can is too large for the hand that is holding it, the middle finger will be partially placed across the top of the receptacle.

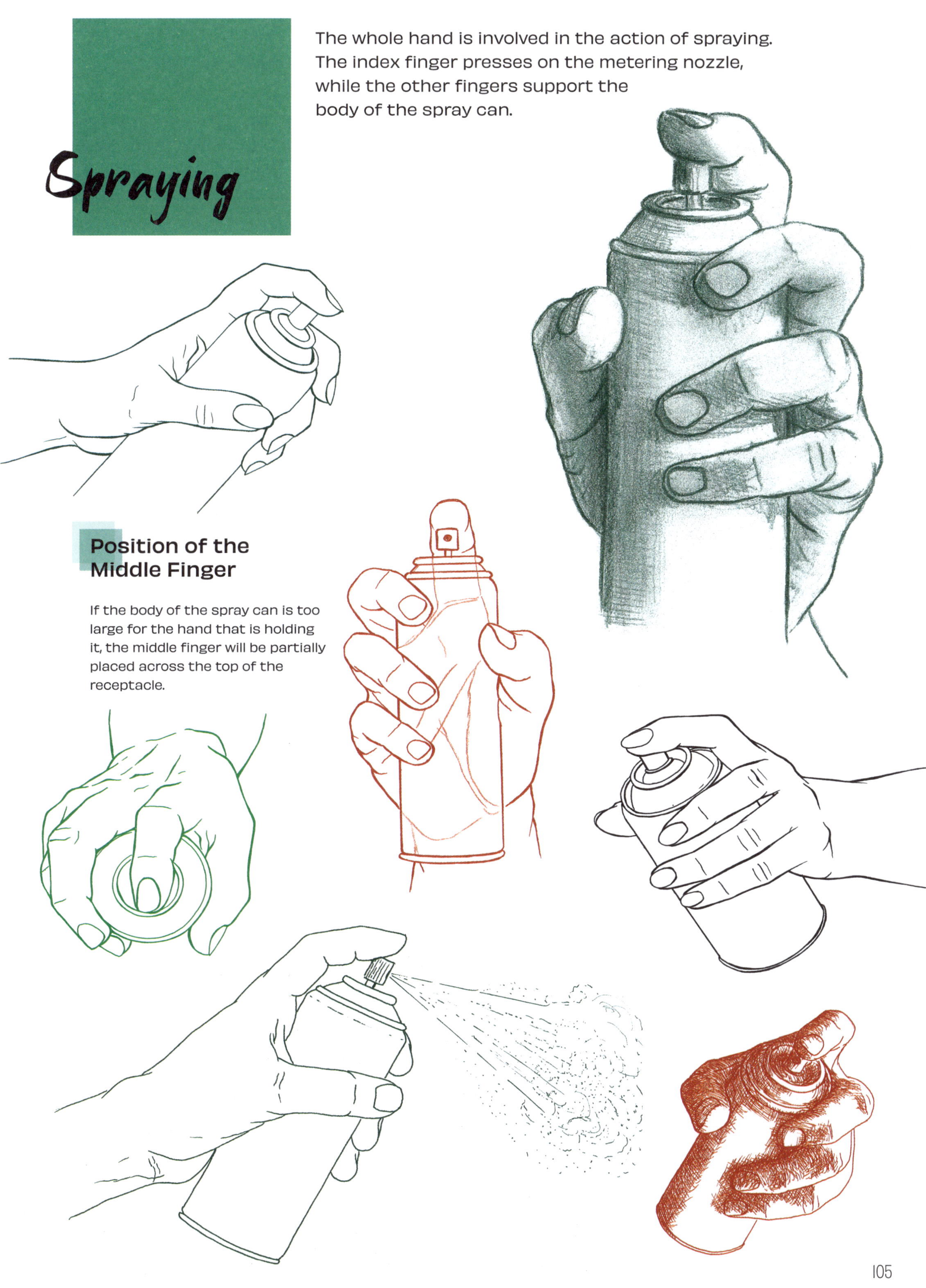

Knife, revolver, flashlight...
To finish up, here are a few objects
that partake of the ambiance of
a thriller.

Noir Series

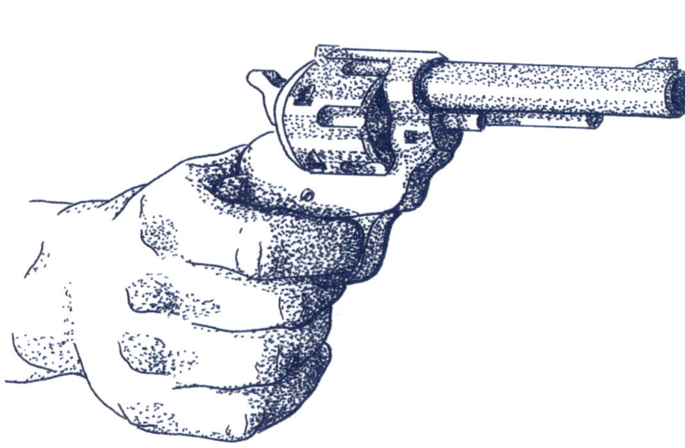

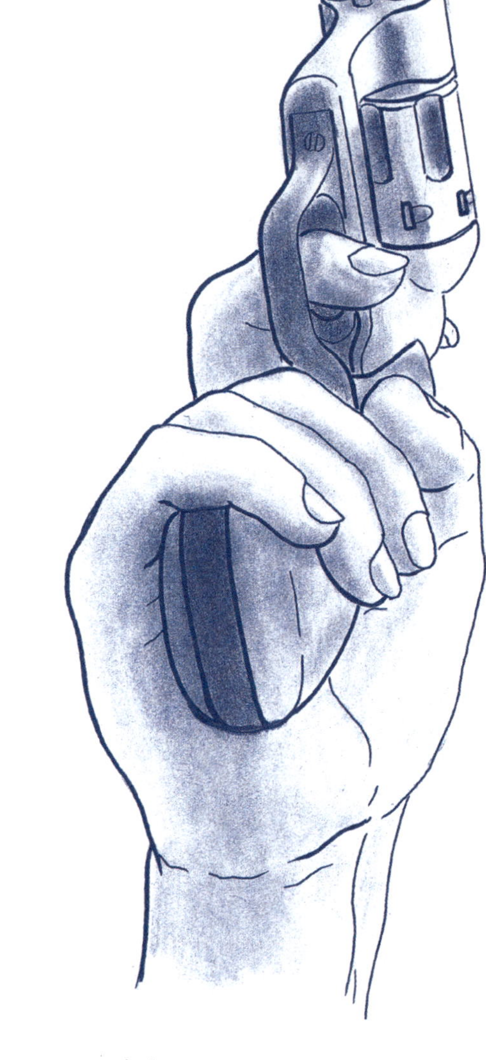

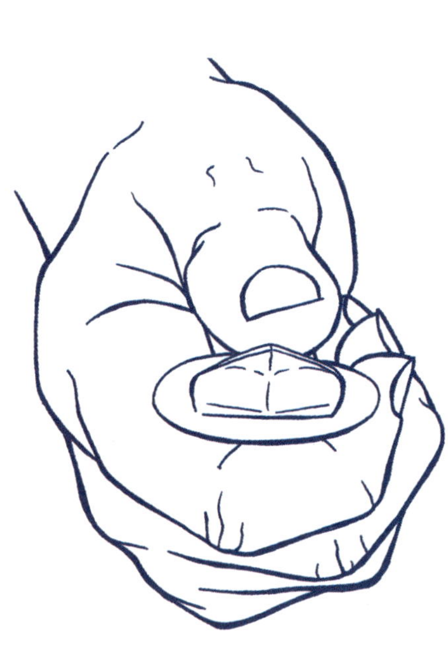

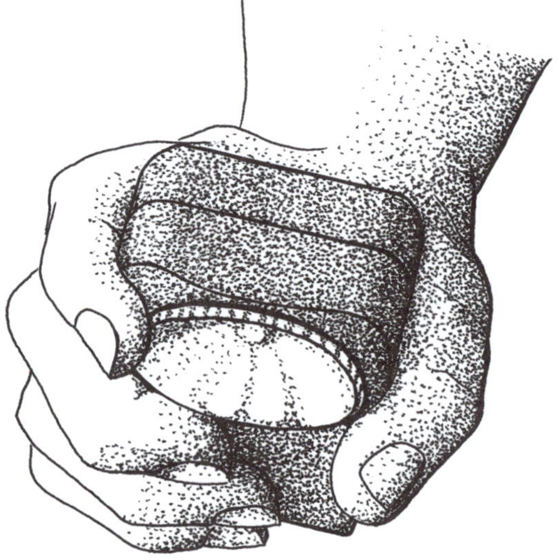

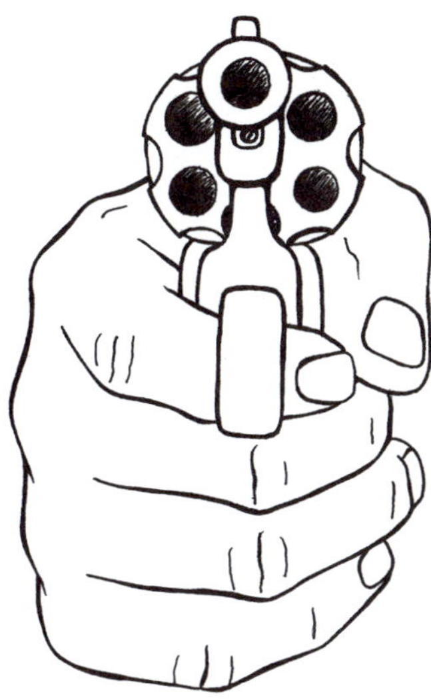

The position of the fingers on the handle of the revolver and the orientation of the barrel reveal a certain nonchalance. There is no tension in this gesture.

Seen from the front, the hand that holds the revolver looks more threatening: the eye is guided vertically from the barrel of the gun to the index finger that is resting on the trigger; the imminence of the movement is thereby dramatically highlighted.

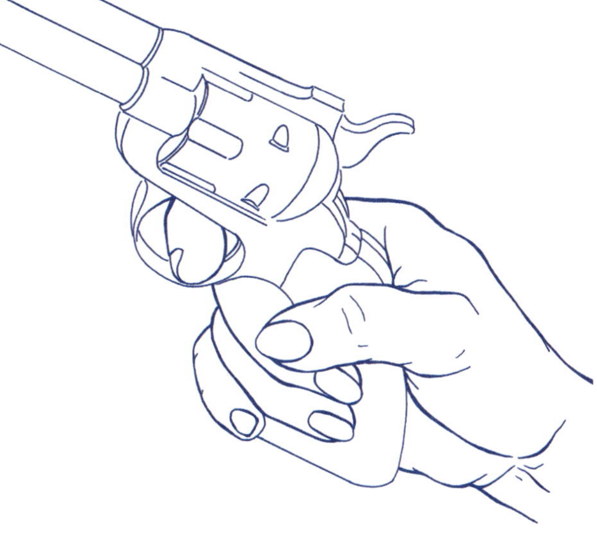

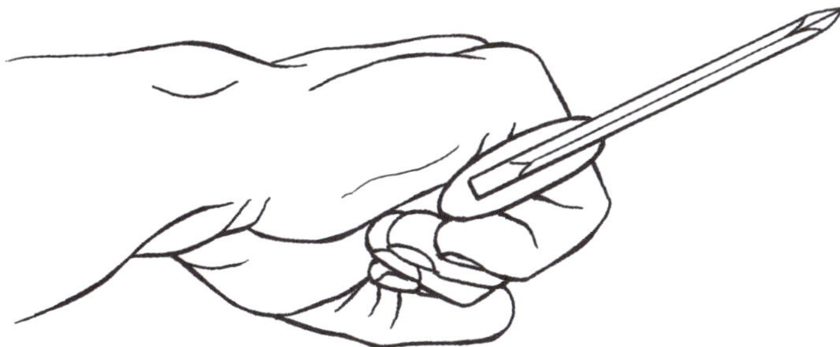

This viewing angle immediately gives the illusion of movement. The fatal blow is about to be struck..

A transparent thumb is shown here behind the sword to indicate its correct placement, on a slight diagonal.

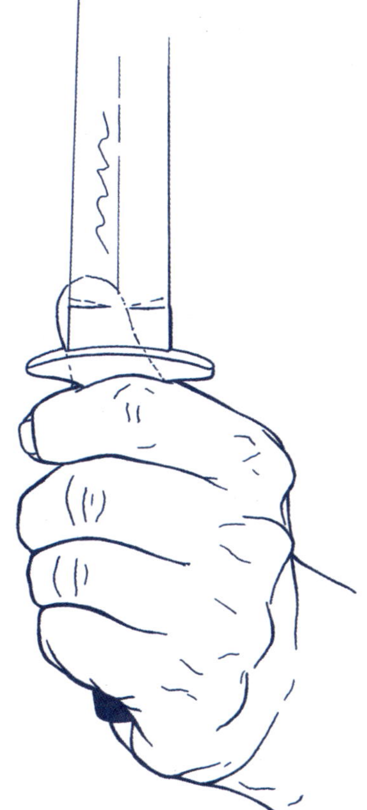

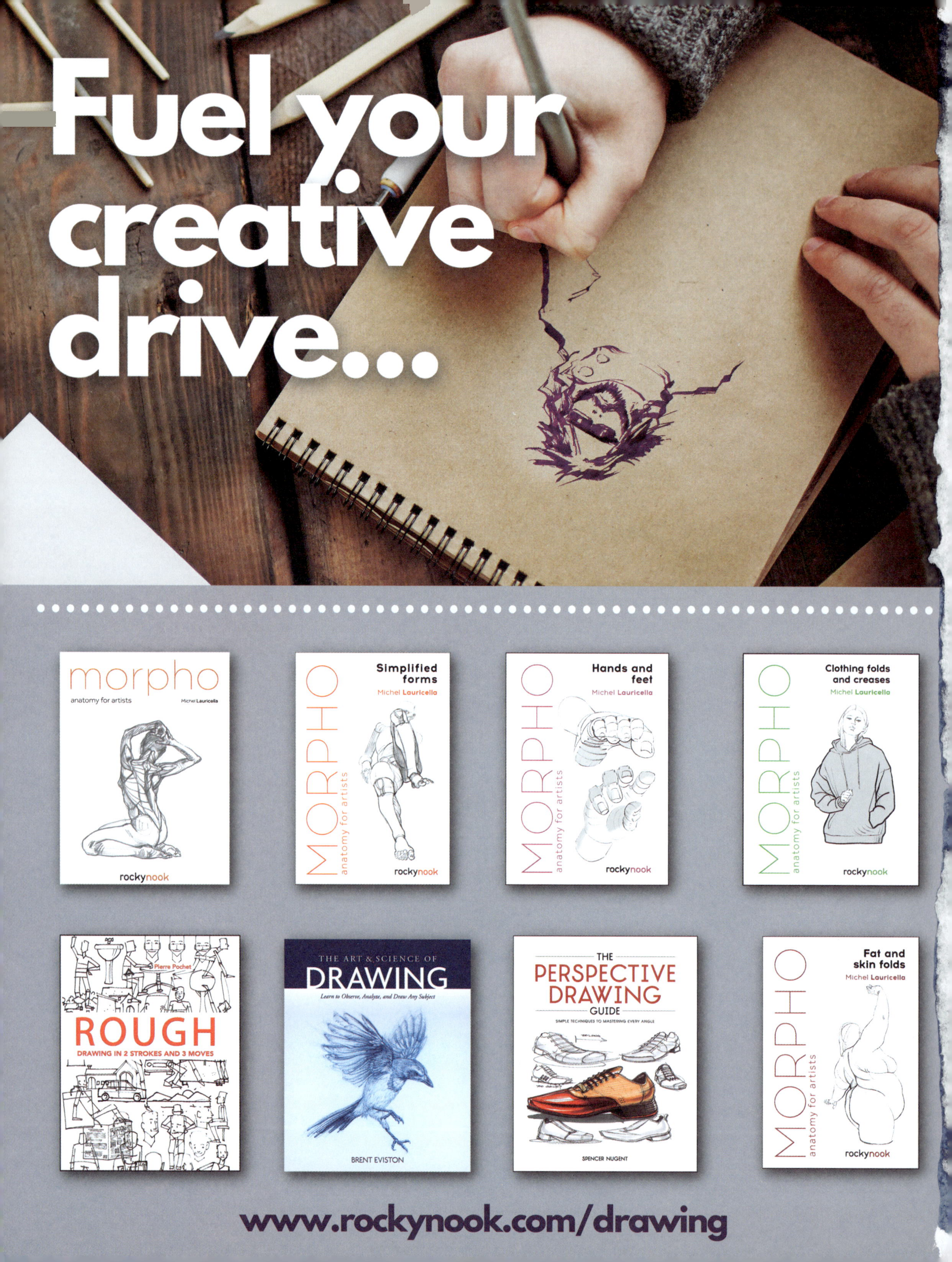

Fuel your creative drive...

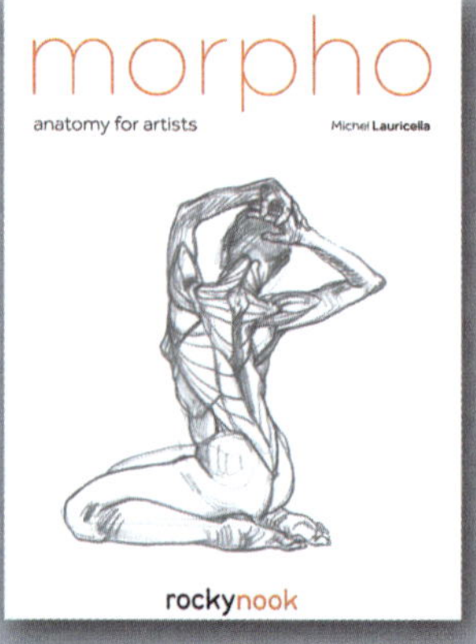

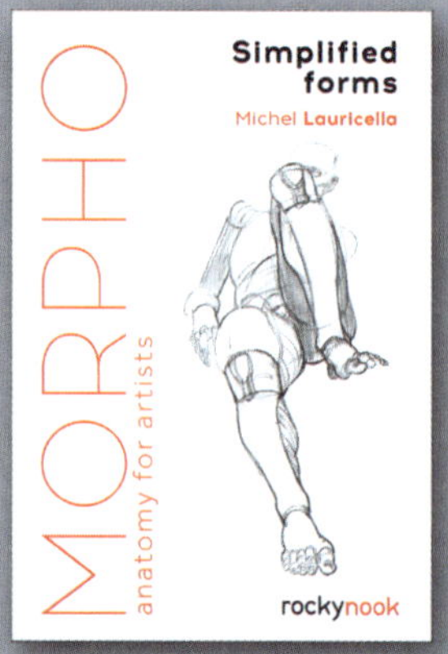

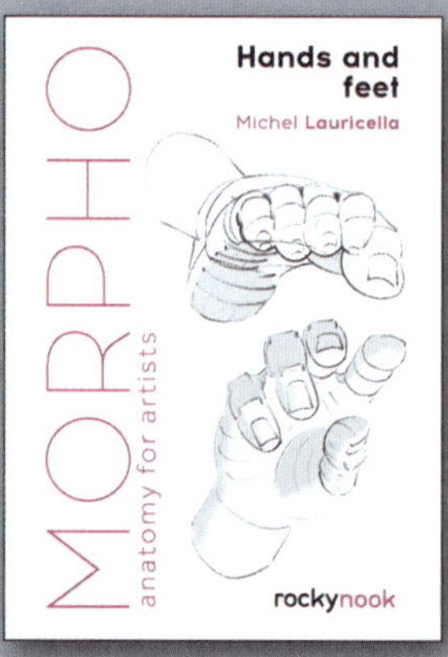

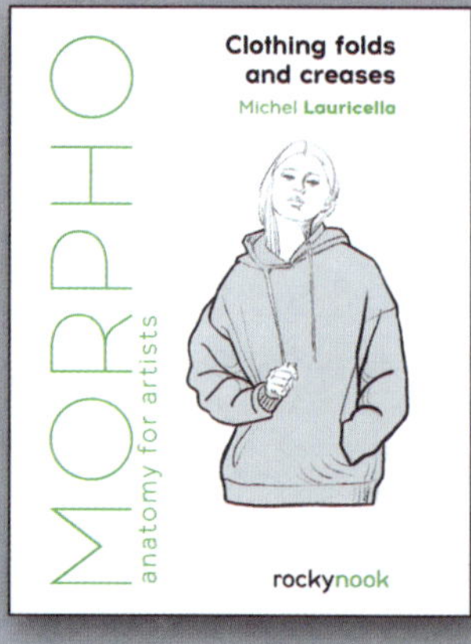

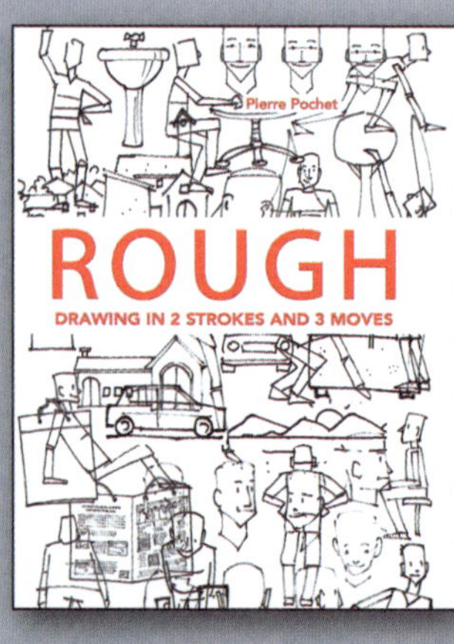

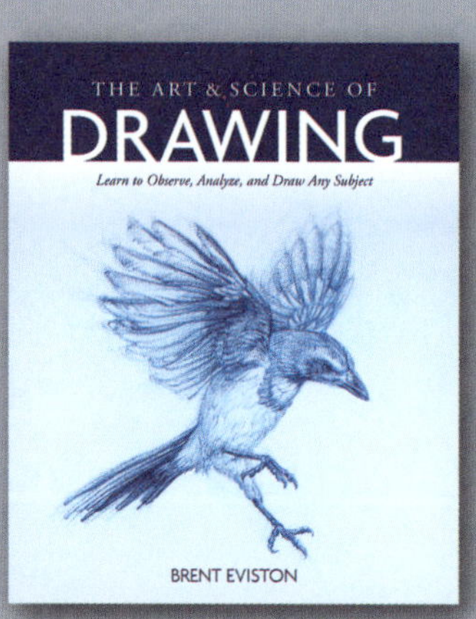

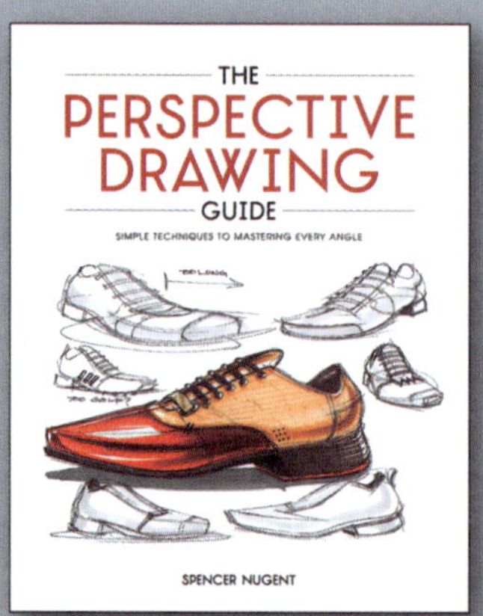

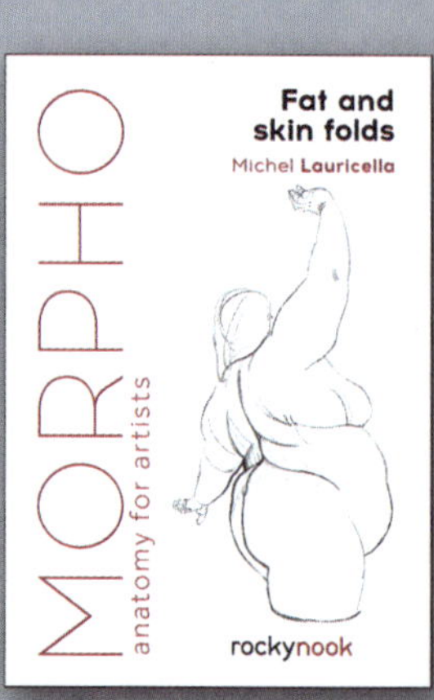

www.rockynook.com/drawing